Work Hard. Be Nice.

How Two Inspired Teachers Created
the Most Promising Schools in America

Jay Mathews

ALGONQUIN BOOKS OF CHAPEL HILL 2009

Published by
ALGONQUIN BOOKS OF CHAPEL HILL
Post Office Box 2225
Chapel Hill, North Carolina 27515-2225

a division of
WORKMAN PUBLISHING
225 Varick Street
New York, New York 10014

Library of Congress Cataloging-in-Publication Data
Mathews, Jay, [date]
    Work hard. Be nice. : how two inspired teachers created the most promising
schools in America / Jay Mathews. — 1st. ed.
        p. cm.
    ISBN-13: 978-1-56512-516-2
    1. Children with social disabilities — Education — United States.
2. Poor children — Education — United States.   3. Educational
innovations — United States.   4. Feinberg, Michael.   5. Levin, Dave.
I. Title.
LC4091.M327 2009
370 — dc22   2008033090

10 9 8 7 6 5 4 3 2 1
First Edition

Contents

THIRD PERIOD: Starting Two Schools

FOURTH PERIOD: Starting Many Schools

To Linda

ORIENTATION

Many people in the United States believe that low-income children can no more be expected to do well in school than ballerinas can be counted on to excel in football. Inner-city and rural children raised by parents who themselves struggled in school are thought to be largely doomed to low grades, poor test scores, menial jobs, and hard lives. These assumptions explain in part why public schools in impoverished neighborhoods rarely provide the skilled teachers, extra learning time, and encouragement given to children in the wealthiest suburbs. Educators who do not think their students are very capable are less likely to arrange challenging lessons and longer school days.

That is the great shock of the story of Mike Feinberg and Dave Levin. Before either had reached his twenty-sixth birthday, their Knowledge Is Power Program revealed that many of these low-income students could achieve just as much as affluent suburban kids if given enthusiastic and focused teachers who believed in them and had enough time to teach them. They recruited and trained young principals like themselves who proved the skeptics wrong in cities and towns across the country.

About 80 percent of KIPP students are from low-income families. About 95 percent are black or Hispanic. The fourteen hundred students at twenty-eight KIPP schools in twenty-two cities who have completed three years of KIPP's four-year middle school program have gone on average from the 34th percentile at the beginning of fifth grade to the 58th percentile at the end of seventh grade in reading and from the 44th percentile to the 83rd percentile in math. Gains that great for that many low-income children in one program have never happened before.

Feinberg and Levin and the hundreds of educators they have enlisted in this effort still have to demonstrate that their progress can be sustained. But no other inner-city educational initiative has gotten this far. KIPP now has sixty-six schools in nineteen states and the District of Columbia, including schools in nine of the ten largest U.S. cities. It plans to serve twenty-four thousand students in one hundred schools by 2011. KIPP teachers are paid extra for the more-than-nine-hour school days, the required four-hour every-other-Saturday sessions, and the three-week summer schools, but they know how much easier their working lives would be if they chose jobs in regular schools. Their enthusiasm for hard work in the classroom springs from the impact they are having, like nothing they have seen in any regular urban or rural public schools.

Some of these teachers joke that KIPP has all the best qualities of a cult, without the dues or the weird robes. They wonder among themselves how long they will stay and what direction KIPP's growth will take. No other program has sparked so much debate over what ought to and can be done for children stuck at the bottom of our public education system, the prime civil rights issue of this era, and this debate has for the first time become a positive discussion. How much further can these kids go?

Levin and Feinberg learned to teach from two classroom veterans whose unusual techniques and high standards led some colleagues to resent them, but who seemed to their two apprentices to be the answer to their prayers. The two veterans, Harriett Ball and Rafe Esquith, wondered if Feinberg and Levin could survive the pounding that was in store for them. They warned the young teachers that they were going to encounter many reversals and much discouragement. Levin and Feinberg proved to be just as aggressive and annoying as Ball and Esquith had hoped, sparking several clashes with educational authorities and cementing their reputations both as troublemakers and as educators whom parents and students could trust.

KIPP teachers these days live by results; they are devoted to seeing what helps disadvantaged children achieve and to passing on to other teachers what they have discovered. Like their heroes Levin and Feinberg, they have found that through hard work, fun, and teamwork, their students can earn for themselves choices in life that many people thought they would never have. But in the beginning, few people had great hopes for those children. Or their two young teachers.

Starting Out, or A Tale of Two Teachers

1.

Learning to Push

AT AGE TWENTY-SIX, Mike Feinberg was supervising seventy low-income, mostly Hispanic fifth graders at Askew Elementary School in west Houston. It was 1995. They were the latest recruits for the Knowledge Is Power Program, or KIPP, which rhymes with *trip*. It was a new but imperiled middle school program Feinberg and his friend Dave Levin, twenty-five, had started the year before.

That first year, they had run the program together in one crowded classroom at Garcia Elementary School in north Houston and they had doubled the number of students passing the state tests in that group. They wanted to create full-size fifth-through-eighth-grade middle schools, and they were going to do it in two separate cities. Levin had decided to move back to his hometown, New York City, to start a KIPP fifth grade in the South Bronx. Feinberg stayed in Houston to start a new KIPP fifth grade at a different school, Askew Elementary, since there was no room for his expansion plan at Garcia. Few of the people they knew thought KIPP would last very long in either Houston or New York. It was too stressful an approach, with long school days and very intense lessons. And Feinberg and Levin? They were too young and inexperienced to pull it off.

Feinberg had only one important ally, the Houston Independent School District's west district superintendent, Anne Patterson, and he had already tested her patience far beyond the point most school administrators would tolerate. He was hard to ignore, six foot three and very talkative, with a very short haircut as accommodation to his premature baldness. He was full of creative ideas but also had many demands and complaints. He was developing a reputation for being an unholy nuisance.

Patterson, a stylish dresser with a crown of thick red hair, often ended her day in tense meetings with Feinberg. She leaned forward on her desk. She kneaded her forehead with her fingers. She tried to figure out a way to get this effusive, overgrown adolescent to accept her view of the latest crisis so that she could go home.

At this particular moment in Feinberg's first year running KIPP Academy Houston by himself, he was near the breaking point. Space had to be found somewhere the following year for Feinberg to add a sixth grade on his way to a fifth-through-eighth-grade program. Patterson needed a building principal who could stomach Feinberg, and whom Feinberg, one of the least collegial educators she had ever met, would be capable of sharing a building with.

"I can be quiet and accommodating," Feinberg told her, "until I perceive in any way, shape, or form that someone is doing anything directly or indirectly to fuck with my babies, and then I become Mama Bear." Patterson already knew this. Patterson had promised to tell Feinberg by the Christmas holiday what space she had found for his expanded school, but it was January and she had no information for him. He kept calling her and showing up at her office. "Mike, you've got to be patient," she said.

Feinberg felt the Houston Independent School District was like an ocean liner: it took forever to make even the smallest turn. He would have preferred to be paddling a canoe — small, light, versatile, ready to careen down any rapids in its way. It occurred to him, not for the first time, that he would not be having this trouble if he were teaching the children of affluent Anglo parents in the River Oaks neighborhood. His students lived in Gulfton, a sprawling collection of apartment complexes full of Central American immigrants. If KIPP had been in River Oaks, getting reviews from parents as favorable as Feinberg was getting in Gulfton, and if that mythical River Oaks KIPP had not been able to find space for the following year, those rich parents would have been screaming and yelling and the school district would quickly have found a way to give him everything he wanted.

Perhaps he should start screaming and yelling. Perhaps not. It often seemed to do more harm than good. But what if it were not him but his students who made the noise? With that thought began the KIPP Academy's first advocacy-in-democracy lesson. One of the advantages of the long KIPP day, from 7:30 a.m. to 5:00 p.m., was that there was time for creative diversions. He explained to the children that American citizens participated in their government not only by voting but also by exercising their right to file grievances with whoever was in charge. This included the people who ran schools, motor vehicle departments, housing agencies, public hospitals, tax assessment bureaus, and garbage collection companies. Some people petitioning for redress wrote letters. Some used the telephone. The point was never to accept bad service or bad products without a protest.

Feinberg had his fifth graders practice proper manners when complaining to officialdom. It was important to be persistent, but also polite. They had to act like serious adults. "Look, the minute you call up and start giggling on the phone, this is all ruined," he said. He waved his arms as he stood in front of a blackboard full of key words and phrases. "These are not crank calls. You are not Bart Simpson, calling Moe's Tavern and seeing if you can get the bartender to say something nasty."

He gave them a script to practice with: "Hello, my name is Armando Ruiz. I am an extremely hardworking student. I am part of the KIPP Academy and we were supposed to know where we were going to be next year, which school building we would be moving to, but we don't know yet. I wonder if you have any information to give me about where our new school is going to be. My family and I are very worried about where we're going to be next year because we want to make sure we continue to get a great education."

The next day would be a good time for them to make the calls, Feinberg told them, since they would be at home. It was a professional development day. Only teachers would be in school. He handed each child a list of the telephone numbers of twenty administrators, including the Houston Independent School District superintendent, the deputy superintendent, the director of facilities, the director of transportation, members of the school board, and Patterson herself.

About 9:30 a.m. the next day, he got a message that he had an urgent telephone call. There was no phone in the KIPP trailers. He had to walk to the Askew main office. The call was from Patterson.

"Mike! Make them stop! Make them stop now!"

"Anne? What are you talking about?"

"You know damn well what I'm talking about. They are calling me. They are calling the district. I am starting to get people in the district calling me and yelling at me. Make them stop now."

"Anne, I can't," he said. "They're at home."

"What do you mean, they're at home?"

"This is our professional development day. They are at home."

"How are they calling, then?"

"I gave them all the numbers."

"You *whaattt*? You gave them all these numbers? The switchboard is ringing off the hook. They're all calling."

"What are they saying?" he asked. He was interested in how well his students had carried out their assignment.

"They want to know where they're going to be next year."

"And what's wrong with *that*?" Feinberg said. It was best to keep Patterson on the defensive. "Like, *you* don't tell me where we are going to be next year, so I am having the kids ask."

Patterson ended the conversation quickly. Feinberg, as she expected, was going to be no help. She would have to explain to her bosses what had happened. As was standard operating procedure for administrators dealing with mischievous underlings, she would tell everyone she was going to put a stop to this.

But that was a lie. There was something about Mike, and his friend Dave, that she thought deserved both protection and encouragement, even if they were two of the most exasperating teachers she had ever met.

LEVIN WAS HAVING similar trouble in New York City. Now fourteen hundred miles apart, he and Feinberg still spoke to each other by telephone nearly every day. Levin envied Feinberg's chutzpah in unleashing his advocacy-loving students on the Houston school bureaucracy. He was sure the Houston officials would bend. He wished New York were as easy.

Like Feinberg, Levin was hard to miss. He was the same height, six foot three, although a bit leaner. While teaching a lesson, he was always moving, talking, asking questions, keeping everyone on top of what was going on. Levin was making some progress in the classroom. He was turning into an exceptional teacher, but it was clear to him that he was not good enough.

Twelve of the forty-seven students Levin recruited his first year in the South Bronx had quit by the time he started his second year. The woman he had hired to serve as an administrative director had developed a philosophical dislike of his methods and had left. Frank Corcoran, the sweet-tempered teacher who had come from Houston to help him, was having trouble maintaining discipline in his classes. The Porch, a way of disciplining children by isolating them in the classroom, had worked in Houston but not in the Bronx, and Levin stopped using it. His students were used to punishment and hard times. They didn't see being forced to sit in the corner and not to talk to classmates as any great penalty. Levin looked for ways to raise his students' morale and his own. He asked his barber to shorten his big mop of curly hair, hoping it would make him feel sharper. But it still wasn't enough.

Levin was not sure where to turn. Marina Bernard, a young teacher he hired after he fired his school director, had a suggestion. She had taught at Intermediate School 166, a public school for sixth-through-eighth graders, also in the Bronx. It was full of kids with the same troublesome attitudes the KIPP students had.

"I know what you need," she said to Levin. "You need to go over to 166. *He's* there. You just got to learn how to control him."

She was speaking of a Bronx public school legend, Charlie Randall.

He was a forty-nine-year-old music teacher who had grown up virtually parentless in the poorest neighborhoods of Orlando, Florida. He was a talented teacher, famous for producing terrific bands and orchestras with children who had never played instruments before. But he was also, everyone said, quite volatile. There were stories of his violent temper. On at least two occasions, they said, he had done serious harm to school staffers who had wounded him in ways he could not forgive.

Randall's first look at Levin confirmed his assumption: another crazy white boy. The kid was arrogant too. Who the hell did he think he was to come into Randall's neighborhood and act as if he was going to rescue Randall's kids? The veteran teacher already knew how to help disheartened and confused students find a way in life. He had grown up like that himself. He knew how to reach them. Could this Yale man ever understand such children?

Randall was polite, but he told Levin he was going to stay where he was. Levin kept calling. He knew as well as Feinberg the power of the personal approach, of advocacy that politely and persistently made the points that had to be made, over and over. He called Randall nearly every day. "How you doin', Charlie? How are things going?" he said. Did Randall have some advice for Levin on adding a music program? Could he come over on Thursday afternoons to teach music to a few KIPP kids?

The last request was a way to earn extra money, so Randall agreed. He brought with him the battered instruments he always kept in the trunk of his car: an old keyboard held together with duct tape, a beat-up violin, a couple of drums, and a few bells. When he got to KIPP, he was surprised. There was a warmth that he did not usually find in schools in the Bronx. The bulletin boards were colorful and welcoming. The kids were absorbed in what they were doing.

Levin kept coming at him. But the young teacher had no master plan. If he had envisioned what would happen — that Randall would create an orchestra that would include every student in the school and become an East Coast sensation — if he had dared even to suggest such a thing to Randall, he would have been dismissed by the older man as completely insane.

Finally Levin came up with the right argument. During one of their telephone conversations, Randall was explaining for the eighty-ninth time that he was just too old and too set in his ways to change schools. "I'm established. I am a master teacher. I have teacher-of-the-year awards and other stuff like that. I just don't need this."

"Wait," Levin said. "When you retire, what are you going to leave behind?"

Randall thought about it. "Well, nothing," he said. "I have these awards, and some memories. That is all I expect."

"That's a mistake," Levin said. "If you come with us, you will have me, and Marina, and the other staff that will be coming on board. You can leave everything you know with us, and we can carry on your legacy."

Whoa, Randall thought. That was a tough one. It was coming from a smart-ass kid. What did he know about legacies? But Levin wasn't going to give up, as Randall had thought he would. Levin said he wanted to stay in the ghetto, unlike those other Ivy League guys that always left. If he was working that hard to get Randall, maybe he meant it.

2.

Risk Takers at Play

MIKE FEINBERG AND DAVE LEVIN met in Los Angeles in July 1992, at the summer training institute of a new program for recently graduated college students called Teach For America. The idea was to take the brightest products of the nation's finest colleges and sign them up for two-year commitments to teach in the worst classrooms in the largest and poorest cities and most backward rural communities.

The creator of Teach For America, a Princeton graduate named Wendy Kopp, was just a year older than Feinberg and three years older than Levin. She was not naive. She acknowledged that her idea carried some risk. But at the very least, the Teach For America corps members would learn something useful about this part of society. In the future, when they became lawyers and doctors and financiers, she hoped they would remember their Teach For America years and use their money and political influence to ease the poverty they had witnessed firsthand.

Levin and Feinberg agreed with the concept. Like many Teach For America recruits, they couldn't think of anything better to do. They weren't ready for graduate school. They weren't ready for real jobs. This sounded like an adventure. The other corps members were all their age. It was like an extra two years of college — some drudgery during the day but still time for fun at night.

They had both been assigned to teach in Houston, so they bunked in the dormitory at California State University, Northridge that the summer institute organizers dubbed Texas House. They ate dinner together the first night at a barbecue to welcome the new trainees. They noticed the basketball courts nearby before they noticed each other.

The first words Feinberg remembers saying to Levin after being introduced were, "Hey, Dave, do you play basketball?"

"Yeah, I play a little," Levin said. Feinberg soon discovered this was typical Levin understatement, a way to both charm strangers and put them at a disadvantage.

In the summer of 1992, Teach For America was just one of dozens of plans to fix what was proving to be the most intractable and devastating social problem in the country — the stubborn persistence of poverty and ignorance in the country's biggest cities and smallest farm towns. Most American public schools in the suburbs were adequate, and some were quite good. But the 25 percent of schools at the bottom of the academic and social scale were mostly awful and not getting any better. Their students were at a severe disadvantage in making lives for themselves that did not repeat the cycle of poverty from which their parents and grandparents had found no escape.

The National Assessment of Educational Progress, the federal government's sampling test of student achievement, showed almost no progress in reading for nine-year-olds, thirteen-year-olds, and seventeen-year-olds between 1971 and 1992. Math achievement was only a little better, with nine-years-olds improving by ten points, thirteen-years-olds by three points, and seventeen-year-olds by two points during those twenty-one years.

In urban school districts, about 40 percent of fourth graders could not read well enough to study independently. Their progress for the rest of their school days was likely to be slow and to hit a dead end of adult illiteracy and frequent unemployment. After a 1983 national report, *A Nation at Risk,* pointed out how badly many students were doing, several states raised teacher salaries and created new tests to measure both student progress and teacher competence. But millions of low-income children continued to fail to learn to read, write, and do math well enough to go to college or get a good job. Many people accepted this as inevitable. A 2001 Phi Delta Kappa/Gallup Poll found that 46 percent of Americans thought only some students had the ability to reach a high level of learning.

One widely discussed educational remedy was a national program of learning standards that would set a goal for all public schools to make a certain amount of progress each year, particularly with disadvantaged students. Schools would be made accountable, proponents said. State and local governments would provide extra support for those schools that did not make the grade. The federal government would budget extra dollars for the effort.

Shortly before Feinberg and Levin reached Los Angeles, the administration of President George H. W. Bush adopted such a plan, called America 2000, which would evolve into the Goals 2000 program. Several Democratic governors, including Bill Clinton of Arkansas and Richard W. Riley of South Carolina, had supported the idea. They had created similar accountability programs so that multinational companies would no longer be reluctant to build plants and offices in their states for fear that the public schools would not be good enough to provide skilled workers and would not be able to prepare the children of their executives for college.

Some scholars and legislators, many of them politically conservative, supported a different kind of school reform. They argued that the public school system was a monopoly with little incentive to improve because it had no competition. They recommended two changes: a system of tax-funded scholarships, called vouchers, that would allow public school students to attend private schools, and a new category of public school, called a charter school, that would be run by energetic educators with fresh ideas who would not have to follow the usual school district funding, hiring, and curriculum policies. In particular, they said, charter schools would not be beholden to teachers' unions and work rules that sometimes lessened the available time for teaching.

Over the next fifteen years, these two strands of reform — sometimes in opposition, sometimes in an uneasy alliance — would come to dominate educational policy and provide the conditions that allowed Feinberg and Levin's schools to flourish. Each side of the debate would produce one far-reaching change in the way public schools operated. The Goals 2000 program evolved into a bipartisan federal law, the No Child Left Behind Act. It required schools to raise the achievement of black, Hispanic, and low-income children or risk being taken over by outsiders who would pursue those goals. At the same time, the movement to challenge the power of public school bureaucrats would lead to an upsurge of public charter schools, particularly in large cities. This would provide a haven for Levin-Feinberg methods such as longer school days and school years, principals' power to fire poorly performing teachers, and regular visits to students' homes.

Teach For America, in its first year in 1990, sent about five hundred very inexperienced teachers into inner-city and rural classrooms. Thirty percent of them did not fulfill their two-year commitments. Some of the most prominent experts on teacher training in the nation's most highly regarded education schools said Teach For America was a terrible idea: it subjected the low-income students it claimed to help to clumsy, ill-trained, inexperienced teachers who would do much harm.

But most principals who hired the corps members said they appreciated their energy and enthusiasm. The number of school districts in the program grew. Levin and Feinberg were among more than 560 new corps members in 1992. The program would continue to grow so rapidly that by 2007 there would be 3,000 new recruits, for a total Teach For America corps of more than 5,000. Less than 10 percent dropped out after their first year. On many college campuses, Teach For America would become the leading single employer of recent graduates.

FEINBERG'S EXUBERANT SELF-DEPRECATION and gregariousness were what first impressed Levin when they were introduced at the Los Angeles Teach For America barbecue. Feinberg seemed to be one of the nicest, funniest, and most social human beings Levin had ever met. Everyone loved Mike. He became the nucleus of their group, as he had often been with his friends in high school and college. Levin was happy to be in his orbit.

Levin had just turned twenty-two and looked younger. He had dark, curly hair and a wide-eyed smile. He was quieter than Feinberg, but not shy. His self-confidence was particularly evident when he was talking to women. Feinberg would turn twenty-four in October, having completed his undergraduate studies at Penn a year late, after taking time off to earn some money as a bartender. He wore his brown hair long then, often in a ponytail, but in a very few years most of his hair would be gone.

Feinberg and Levin bonded quickly over their mutual fondness for putting themselves into situations for which they were ill prepared. When their group in Texas House ran out of beer one night, they heard one thirsty trainee say she had a car but didn't want to drive to a liquor store that late. Feinberg decided to impress the young woman by chivalrously volunteering to take her keys and do the errand for her. He invited Levin along.

"You know how to drive a stick shift?" Feinberg asked Levin.

"No."

"Well, that's okay. I got it."

In the car, Feinberg turned the key and listened with satisfaction as the engine roared to life. Then he turned to his new friend and said, "You know, I really don't know how to drive a stick either." Levin smiled. This was his kind of guy. They set off anyway, the gears grinding and the engine stalling, grinding and stalling, as they lurched down Reseda Boulevard.

In planning their days at the institute, Levin and Feinberg agreed that the afternoon courses in classroom management and educational theory were mostly a waste of time. They read all the mimeographed materials and completed the projects required. But they almost never went to class. They took their morning student-teaching duties at inner-city Los Angeles schools much more seriously. The bus picked them up at 7:00 a.m. That was much earlier than they were accustomed to rising in college, but they were always on time, properly attired in dress shirts, ties, and khaki pants.

Feinberg was assigned to Latona Avenue Elementary School. On the first day, he observed the class. On the second day, he was supposed to teach a lesson for an hour. But his mentor teacher thought that was baby stuff. "Look, Mike," she said. "This is sink or swim. I'm not going to have you teach for just an hour. You are going to take over the whole class." He taught the class nearly every morning for the next three weeks. It was difficult, and a bit frightening, but his mentor teacher guided him along. He thought he made progress.

Levin's mentor teacher, on the other hand, mostly ignored him. She gave him a small group of students and a list of questions to review with them. She did not offer many suggestions. This part of the day, he thought, was proving as useless as the afternoon methodology classes.

At night the Texas House partying resumed, with food and beer and epic basketball games. They were passing time, waiting to go to Houston.

3.

Road Trip Wisdom

LEVIN'S CAR, WHICH he'd had shipped from New York, arrived just as the summer institute in Los Angeles was ending. Feinberg agreed to help him drive it to Houston. They stocked the backseat of the gray Ford Taurus with Doritos and Cokes to tide them over between stops at McDonald's.

The Texas House gang celebrated the end of their training with a tour of the Sunset Strip's tawdry wonders. Feinberg acquired a tattoo on his left shoulder blade. It was the earth, about half-dollar size. He was told to keep it moist. As he and Levin drove through the Mojave Desert the next day, they pulled over every two hours so that Levin could apply some Neosporin to the spot that his new friend couldn't reach.

The road trip, despite such delays, was a triumph, at least from the point of view of two self-confident men aged twenty-two and twenty-three. They thought they were operating on the highest intellectual and programmatic plane. The car radio played a report on the activities of White House drug czar William Bennett. What if the nation had an education czar, they wondered — not a bureaucrat like the secretary of education but someone with real power to make changes?

By the time they stopped for a Neosporin break in the sunbaked town of Blythe, on the Arizona border, they had completely dismembered and reassembled the public education system. They had figured out how to fix everything. They had detailed plans for better schools. They had ideas for financial incentives for students, families, and teachers so that more students could go to college. They even had a budget, about $150 billion, which they would take from the Defense

Department, since it no longer had to spend all that money on the cold war.

They had a late lunch in Phoenix with a friend of Feinberg's who attended Arizona State University. Then they kept driving. About midnight they passed a sign that said a state park was fifty miles ahead. Levin said he was too tired to keep going. Feinberg insisted they push on until they got to the park. The gate was locked, so they climbed over it and slept on a flat patch of grass in their sleeping bags until dawn.

They arrived in Houston later that day. With a posse of other corps members, they arranged housing at the Creole on Yorktown, an apartment complex near the Galleria mall in west Houston. Feinberg, Levin, and their roommate Tim Dibble, from the University of Arkansas, rented a three-bedroom, second-floor apartment for $750 a month. A game of twenty-one on a nearby basketball court determined who would get the biggest bedroom. As expected, Levin won.

They visited Wild West Outfitters. Feinberg fell in love with both cowboy couture and the very loose alcohol laws. He tried on a hat. A man with an eerie resemblance to Clint Eastwood walked up and said, "If you wear your hat like that, you look like a tourist." The man's name was Sonny. He adjusted the hat for this greenhorn customer. "If you need any help with anything in the store, let me know," he said. "And go ahead and have a beer."

Feinberg's and Levin's eyes widened. Beer in a clothing store? Were they in heaven? They found the keg in a corner. Soon they were happily making several purchases. Levin bought boots, but not a hat, because everyone told him he looked fourteen years old when he put it on. Feinberg got the whole outfit and began wearing it immediately, even to work.

Because of his alleged bilingual abilities, Feinberg already had a teaching assignment at a new school, Garcia Elementary, although the Garcia faculty was using classrooms at Berry Elementary until its building was finished. Feinberg was not sure this was the best assignment for him. His Spanish was not good. In fact, Feinberg had begun his training earlier than most other corps members. He and thirty other recruits had flown to Cuernavaca, Mexico, in June for three weeks of extra practice to hone their Spanish so that they would be ready for jobs as bilingual teachers. He later remembered the Cuernavaca program as a three-week-long social gathering. It did little for his language fluency other than to teach him that two Dos Equis at the local grocery store in Cuernavaca cost one American dollar. The program organizers, realizing how far behind Feinberg and three other recruits were, relegated them to what Feinberg called the dumb class. Much of the time, they played Spanish Scrabble. On his last day in Mexico, he won a game by putting down the word *zorro* and getting a triple-word score.

The Garcia principal, a short, trim, well-dressed woman named Adriana Verdin, shrugged off Feinberg's confession that he wasn't a fully qualified bilingual teacher. She was going to give him one of the older grades, where his Spanish skills would not matter so much. She had no intention of going easy on him in other matters, however. He had to have a semester's worth of lesson plans ready by the end of the week. His class roster had thirty-three names. Twenty-seven of them showed up the first day. They were all fifth graders, but their ages ranged from nine to fourteen. They were all Hispanic. Several knew no English at all. The first day of class, one little girl became upset, talking frantically, tears flowing, mucus coming out of her nose. Feinberg did not understand a word. He panicked. He thought, God, what have I gotten myself into?

It took Levin much longer to get an assignment. Teach For America did not select schools for its corps members. They had to interview with principals. Levin had the impression that the first two principals he spoke to would not hire him because he was white and their schools were nearly 100 percent African American. At a Teach For America luncheon, one of the speakers, Joyce Andrews, principal of Bastian Elementary School, sounded like someone who might be willing to give him a try. Her school was 90 percent African American, but when he told her he was still looking for a job, she seemed receptive to hiring smart young people just out of college, no matter what their ethnicity.

After asking him some questions, however, she said she couldn't take him. Her only opening required a teacher with a certificate in teaching English as a second language. He didn't have that.

A job was available at Patterson Elementary, a more affluent school on the west side that was about one-third white, one-third black, and one-third Hispanic. Levin did not want that. He felt he could give more to a school like Bastian. On the Friday afternoon before the first Monday of school, Levin drove to Bastian and walked into Andrews's office. It was time for extreme measures. He remembered Feinberg's pretense at skill with a manual transmission during their beer run in Los Angeles.

"I got that certificate," Levin said to Andrews.

"You do?"

"Yes."

"You're hired."

He figured, correctly, that she was either too busy or too clever to check his story. But he soon regretted his lie. The first week, his class had just sixteen sixth graders. It looked easy. By the second week, in a typical reshuffling of latecomers, he suddenly had thirty-two. Some of his sixth graders were associated with rival gangs. They ranged widely in age, just as Feinberg's students did. One of the older children walked across the room during class, zipped down his fly, pulled out his penis, and asked a girl for oral sex. Levin sent him to the principal. He was sent back in thirty minutes. Another student threw a book at Levin's head. The office kept him an hour before sending him back, sucking on a Tootsie Pop.

By the end of September, both Levin and Feinberg were wondering if the Teach For America idea had been a mistake. They had not considered, when they worked out their plan for the salvation of public education, that they would be such terrible teachers. It was becoming clear that no one — not even ten-year-olds — would ever listen to a word they said.

At their apartment they worked on their lessons until 11:00 p.m., and sometimes later. They were so exhausted that they fell asleep almost the second they slid into their beds. Their clock radios seemed to buzz them awake a minute or two later, the beginning of another long day.

Neither teacher knew how he was going to survive. They were both ashamed at how awful they were. They began to talk about what they might do, not to get any better, since that was out of the question, but at least to make it to the end of the school year still sane.

Problems in Houston

THE CHAOS IN THEIR CLASSES demolished Levin's and Feinberg's assumptions that their charm, intelligence, and energy would guarantee their success. Anarchy reigned. Children raced up and down the halls. Few of them did their homework. Noise was a constant problem. Students were unimpressed with the new teachers' Ivy League degrees and clever patter.

Quincy, for instance, was in Levin's class at Bastian. He was a sixth grader but didn't look it. Five feet ten inches tall, he was often angry and mean. He teased, taunted, and slapped other children. He ignored teachers who told him to stop. He saw no reason to do anything asked of him by Levin, who had almost no experience disciplining children.

Levin sought advice from his principal and the mentor teacher assigned to him. Much of what they told him was vague or didn't work. The general disorder at the school convinced him that the principal, despite her good heart and sincere desire to make things better, was not going to be much help with Quincy.

It occurred to Levin and Feinberg, in their weary conversations, that they were trying too hard to be what they thought teachers should be, and not trying hard enough to be themselves. They had good instincts in other parts of their life. Why not in their classes? On a particularly tense day, Levin responded disastrously to this insight without considering that it might conflict with rules for teacher behavior, and with the law. As usual, Quincy was wandering around the room, harassing other students. "Sit down, Quincy," Levin said.

Quincy acted as if Levin did not exist.

"Sit down now!"

No response.

Levin walked up to the boy in the middle of the classroom, grabbed him under both armpits, picked him up, and carried him back to his seat. Levin had never lifted a child that heavy. He wondered, in a panic, if he could make it all the way to Quincy's chair without dropping him. His strength gave out just as he got there. Instead of gently lowering the boy into his place, he dropped him into it, with more force than he had intended. Mortified, Levin retreated to his desk and began to wonder exactly when he would be fired.

He had been told, more times than he could count, not to touch kids. It was a huge no-no, an invitation to lawsuits and a cause for dismissal. He worried about his job. He worried about Quincy. What did it say to a child who had probably been mistreated from an early age that a teacher could slam him into his chair?

But Levin noticed that the class quieted noticeably after Quincy had been put in his place. The boy was a bully. Levin wondered if his failure to protect other children from Quincy had contributed to the sour mood that usually enveloped his class.

Levin decided to visit Quincy's parents and apologize, even though home visits were another thing he had been told not to do. The rule was that contact with parents had to be limited to the telephone and their visits to the school. It was made clear that young white teachers should not be wandering into the neighborhoods served by Bastian Elementary.

Levin didn't care. He felt bad about what he had done and could see no alternative to making a personal visit and apology. He found the small wood-frame house where Quincy lived, not far from the school. He knocked. Quincy's mother came to the door. She was heavyset, shorter than her sixth-grade son. She looked weary. "Evening, ma'am," he said. "I am Mr. Levin, Quincy's teacher. May I come in?"

She looked surprised to find him on her doorstep. She seemed apprehensive. Conversations with teachers about her son were rarely pleasant. But she invited him in. Levin sat down on the couch and gave her an honest look of sadness. "Ma'am," he said, "I feel really bad. Something came up today in class. I don't know if you know that your son has been slapping other kids."

"I know my boy," she said in a neutral tone.

"Well, today he wouldn't listen to me, so I had to carry him back to his chair."

She nodded.

"I hope you don't mind me doing that. I hope I don't have to do it again."

"Do whatever you have to do," she said. She saw the relief in his face. "Listen," she said, "you're the first teacher that ever came to the house. Do whatever you have to do to my son. He doesn't listen to me. Do whatever you have to do."

Levin walked out of the house feeling better but puzzled. Why had he been warned not to visit parents? What could be so wrong with it? It had helped in this case. He had met the mom. As far as he could tell, in her eyes he had shown her respect by coming to her home rather than telephoning her or summoning her to the school. Quincy never became a model student, but his behavior improved a bit after that day. Levin began to react to classroom crises with more confidence. Why, he asked himself, couldn't he be more active in handling misbehavior, rather than cower in his corner of the classroom? Why could he not make the same connection with other parents that he had with Quincy's mother?

He made out a schedule of home visits for himself. He tried to call on the parents of at least one student every day, right after school. It didn't matter if the student was doing well or not. He wanted to meet the people who were raising these kids. He needed clues to what might motivate them. More important, he wanted the children to know that he cared enough to spend some of his after-school hours visiting their homes, the center of their lives. Once he met their parents, he thought, he could more easily solicit support if the children were not doing what they ought to be doing.

Feinberg had begun dropping in on parents too. He had an

additional excuse for violating the no-home-visit rule. He needed to improve his Spanish. Only half of his students both understood his English and responded to him in that language. A few more seemed to understand what he was saying but answered only in Spanish. Several were still completely adrift in an English-speaking sea.

Like Levin, Feinberg had been assigned a mentor teacher who was not as much help as he had hoped. The teacher had some good ideas for decorating his room, but when it came to teaching, she had little to say. Eager for help from anyone he could find, Feinberg latched onto another Teach For America corps member, a thin, blond Notre Dame graduate named Frank Corcoran. He had been teaching for a year when Feinberg arrived. Corcoran was artistic and musical. He would eventually become a founding KIPP teacher in New York and a national award winner, but in 1992 he was full of doubts about his abilities. He would answer questions Feinberg had, but he took no initiative in offering advice.

Feinberg's students mostly lived in small wood houses surrounded by low wire fences. They had flowers and dogs, many dogs, of every imaginable breed. When Feinberg knocked, it would often be his student, or a brother or sister, who opened the door. The child would look startled, then slam the door in his face. Feinberg would hear laughter and whispering inside. He would knock again. There would be footsteps, adult footsteps, and the door would open. It would be a parent or grandparent, surprised but impressed. Maestro! Come in, please.

He often sat down in a tiny living room with a kitchen just beyond. Some of the paint was peeling. There were travel posters and pictures of Jesus on the walls. He was offered a drink. He mentioned the letter in Spanish that he had sent home to parents, introducing himself. He reminded them that he had said he was looking forward to teaching their children and planned to visit them at home.

"I am Señor Feinberg," he said again in Spanish, to help them become familiar with his name. "I am very impressed with what I am seeing from your child in my class. I am sorry about my bad Spanish and my Chicago accent. If there is anything I can do to help you or your child, please get in touch with me."

The families were mostly from Mexico, although Feinberg met parents who had come from all parts of Central America. Often, they invited Feinberg to stay for dinner. At first he felt uncomfortable accepting. Many of his students seemed hungry in the morning. He didn't like the idea of eating food their families could not afford. But when he stayed, the evening often went so well that he decided he was foolish to worry. If he wanted to fit into their culture, he should not turn down invitations to share a meal.

He still found it difficult to entice students to focus on his lessons. Every week he tried something different: group learning, learning centers, direct instruction, whole language. He was lost. At one point he had the class of thirty-three students divided into seven reading groups. It was a recipe for chaos. He had low, medium, and high reading groups for English speakers; low, medium, and high reading groups for students who could handle only Spanish; and a seventh group for those he didn't know what to do with. No matter what the group, he did not know how to teach it. He could not communicate his expectations.

But listening to Levin's stories, he was grateful there were no fights, no bullies like Quincy. His students saved that kind of activity for lunch or recess. He saw no outward displays of defiance toward him, but he began to understand that some of the Spanish remarks might have that intent. He kept hearing one word, "chupa," over and over.

"¿Cómo se dice 'chupa' en ingles?" he asked one little girl.

"That means 'suck,'" she informed him solemnly.

"Oh, thank you," he said.

Each night he and Levin tried to figure it out. They liked to get home by 6:00 p.m. so that, before planning the next day's lessons, they could watch *Star Trek: The Next Generation*. It was so full of hope, so different from their daily grind. In the twenty-fifth century, they noted, everyone was literate. All these people of different races walked around with little tricorders, which they operated with great skill. The fifteen-year-old on board the *Enterprise* was doing nuclear fusion.

They would have dinner, usually something they cooked up from the large stock of cheap meat and vegetables they bought at Sam's Club. Whatever it was, the recipe was the same: bake it for thirty minutes, and wolf it down.

Back in class, Feinberg worried about the pace of his lessons. Whatever he wanted to do each day, he often got through only 25 percent of it. He could not manage his time or his class. Something was always slowing him down. His fifth graders were mostly reading at a third-grade level or below. He was tempted to do the reading himself aloud in class, yet that seemed like giving up. He forced his students to read, making the lessons even slower. The students who were reading would stumble. The students who were not reading would be bored.

It helped both Feinberg and Levin to bounce ideas off each other at night. But it was like trying to learn how to pilot the *Enterprise*. Neither of them knew quite what galaxy they were in. They needed help.

5

Meeting Harriett Ball

At Bastian Elementary, a one-story building surrounded by low shrubs, the principal's office was just inside the main entrance, to the right. Thirty steps farther down the hall was Levin's room, on the left. On the right across the corridor from Levin was the room of a tall female teacher he had begun to notice. She seemed to have everything he lacked: creativity, charisma, organization, timing, and the absolute devotion of her students.

Her name, he learned, was Harriett Ball. He peeked into her classroom every chance he got. She was a whirlwind. She laughed and sang, and scolded when necessary, but so quickly and with such rapid changes of tone and mood that he had to listen carefully to catch every word. She played her students like an orchestra. With her nod, the fourth graders would begin a musical chant, something that sounded like the multiplication tables. With her raised hand, they would snap back into silence.

Levin had heard the legends about Ball. The other teachers had voted her teacher of the year twice. She was African American, stood six feet one inch tall, and wore her hair down to her shoulders. Her voice was a deep, vibrant alto. She had a lively sense of humor and a foul mouth when crossed. She was seriously addicted to tobacco. She would dress soberly one day, dark solid colors, then appear in her favorite leopard print the next day. At age forty-six, she was a strikingly charismatic figure: Parents wanted their children in her class. Kids loved her. She was always bending, leaning, exerting herself to gain students' attention. Some of her classroom exercises were noisy and bothered teachers in nearby classrooms. But her splendid test results indicated that all that movement helped children learn, particularly the restless boys. It was further proof to Levin that skepticism about low-income students' abilities was misplaced.

One morning while Ball had her class working on their warm-up lessons, Levin stepped hesitantly into her room and walked over to speak to her. Ball saw a tall young man with a slight slouch. He seemed to have rehearsed what he wanted to say. "Ms. Ball?" he said. "Excuse me. I'm Dave Levin. I have the class across the hall. I've been noticing your class and I have never seen a teacher like you before in my life. It is amazing every time I pass by your kids. Do you mind if I sit in your room during my breaks and just watch what you do?"

Ball was happy that he was interested in improving as a teacher. She had grown accustomed to sloth and stagnation among some of her colleagues. Even if they heard something useful at a professional development session, they would often return to their classrooms, close their doors, and resume their old habits. Ball called that "going status quo."

She told Levin he was welcome to watch her and then got back to her class. She was bothered during one of his visits when he propped both feet on her desk. She did not say anything at first, since the children were present, but she eventually broke him of that bad habit. He was ready to do anything she told him.

Each evening, back at their apartment, Levin would tell Feinberg what he had seen Ball do that day. Feinberg arranged to take a half day off so he could visit Bastian. He had to see firsthand what his friend was so excited about. At first, Feinberg found it hard to understand what Ball was doing. He could not catch all of the words and gestures. She moved too quickly for him to absorb it all. As he listened to one chant after another, he began to comprehend the calls and responses. A series of very simple chants had the multiples of each number from two to twelve embedded in the song. Ball started with a marching beat. The students shouted out the numbers in tight groups: "Seven, fourteen, twenty-one! Twenty-eight, thirty-five, forty-two! Fortyniiiiiiiiiiine, fifty-six, sixty-threeeeeeeeee, seventy, seventy-seven, eighty-four! Whoomp, there it is!" Ball referred to them as "finger rolls," which KIPP would later come to call "rolling the numbers."

Ball drilled her students on their times tables as well as verb conjugations and place-names. But it wasn't all chants. Feinberg watched Ball conduct a reading class. He was intrigued at how different her approach was from his own. Her students read out loud as his did, but the pace was faster and the conversation more detailed and more engaging. She interrupted, asked questions, made comments.

Feinberg was transfixed. He stayed there for two hours. Then he, Levin, and Ball had lunch. It was the beginning of the Ball tutorial, one master teacher and two rookies meeting for the next two years. They watched her in class. They asked her questions over drinks at King Leo's and the other Houston clubs she favored. They invited themselves to her home on weekends for more instruction. She warned them that if they just copied her routine, they would not be doing their students much good. They had to incorporate their own personalities into their lessons. Trying to turn themselves, two clumsy white boys, into one-of-a-kind classroom diva Harriett Ball would not work. The point was to make the classroom vibrant, fun, and interesting for their students and for them. A teacher who did not enjoy teaching was going to make a mess of it.

Ball had one concept that took some time for them to grasp but eventually proved vital. She called it "disposable crutches." Her lively mind produced a stream of mnemonic chants that attached essential rules of grammar and mathematics firmly to the brains of her nine-year-olds. The children learned the words as easily and eagerly as rap lyrics, which was not surprising, since Ball had some of the same musical gifts as the new urban singers and composers. The finger rolls and other chants were short, funny, often nonsensical songs that had the advantage of being hypnotically rhythmic and allowing fourth graders to shout the words as if they were praising God at church. Which was appropriate, since Ball felt it was the Creator who had revealed to her this inspired way of teaching. He'd spoken to her when she moved from Austin to Houston with her four children right after her divorce, another decision she'd made with God's help.

Ball explained finger rolls to Levin and Feinberg very carefully. The device was only a temporary means to an end, she said. It was a crutch, one to be disposed of eventually. They should not want their students to feel they had to recite the entire rhyme whenever they had to multiply. The chant was an entertainment, a bit of fun that created a team spirit and gave the students an excuse to repeat the algorithms again and again. The more they rolled their numbers, the more the multiplication tables would become second nature. Nine times 8 would be 72, and 11 times 12 would be 132, just like that.

There was an even more important dimension to the repetition. She made the point several times: success in increasingly complex arithmetic carried with it a feeling of accomplishment that thrilled inner-city children. If Levin and Feinberg succeeded in adopting her methods, their students would soon be doing difficult problems quickly and correctly, which would surprise and impress their parents and older siblings. They were crossing a bridge from today, where school was an annoyance, to tomorrow, where they understood tricky concepts and wanted to learn more.

Ball had a slogan, a bumper sticker taunt whose origins were obscure: "If you can't run with the big dogs, stay on the porch." Feinberg and Levin were her playful big dogs. She liked their sense of humor. She was full of jokes herself. But she told them they had to work hard at being teachers.

It took Levin and Feinberg many weeks to get the rhythm, but gradually they felt their classes coming together. The students seemed to appreciate how hard they were working. Feinberg discovered he was able to win over difficult but influential students like Rosalinda. Already thirteen, she had dyed her hair blue. She was street smart and the obvious class leader. Once she developed a fondness for Feinberg, she cracked her whip on his behalf. "We all need to behave and listen to Mr. Feinberg," she said. She became Feinberg's principal Spanish interpreter. She adopted new kids, the frightened children who knew little English, and introduced them to the big, goofy gringo. She was a mother by instinct, which at first delighted Feinberg but would eventually make him sad: two years later, as a seventh grader, she became pregnant and dropped out of school.

In November, when Feinberg and his students finally moved from Berry Elementary, their temporary quarters, to the newly constructed Garcia Elementary School, he had enough confidence to begin sticking his neck out. He put a sign up in big block letters above the door of his new classroom: WELCOME TO MR. FEINBERG'S FABULOUS, FANTASTIC FIFTH-GRADE CLASS. The letters were several different colors. His was the only class to have such a sign. Some teachers thought that was pushy, but he didn't care. He thought the sign gave his students a feeling that the move to the new school was a great adventure. He was still an awkward teacher, but he was beginning to see how he and Levin could improve.

Adriana Verdin, the Garcia principal, noticed the sign at once. She pointed out that Feinberg had not gotten permission to affix it to the wall with the blue stickum that had become his adhesive of choice. In the future, she said, he would have to get official approval for anything that might mark the walls. "Yes, ma'am," he said.

His increasing use of the Ball chants drew attention. Other students would peer in as they passed Mr. Feinberg's fabulous, fantastic fifth grade. His class wrote their own Christmas minimusical. His students seemed happier and calmer and were paying closer attention.

Levin found his class improving in the same way. At the beginning of the school year, both he and Feinberg had taught the standard rules of discipline: respect one another, keep your hands to yourself, raise your hand before speaking. By December, having had several meetings with Ball, they began to focus just on what worked — quick attention to misbehavior, regular rewards for good effort, lots of choreographed movement, rhymes, songs, and energy from the teacher. They learned to apply what they knew about each student, particularly the connections created by their home visits, and to use a bit of humor when they could, but never to let their standards slip.

They decided to motivate their classes with the promise of a trip to the Houston theme park AstroWorld if the class continued to improve. End-of-the-year field trips — Levin and Feinberg would call them field lessons — eventually became an essential part of the KIPP method. But their first attempt was an embarrassment.

During the year, they had spent some of their own money on little excursions, such as miniature golf on Saturdays. But AstroWorld tickets for the thirty students in Feinberg's class and the twenty-five students in Levin's class would cost more than one thousand dollars. That was a lot of money. Despite their comfortable upbringings, Feinberg and Levin were proud and frugal young men who had gotten jobs in college so that they wouldn't have to ask their parents for living expenses. They were determined to live on their teaching salaries. After Feinberg paid the five hundred dollars for his kids' tickets, he didn't think he had enough left in his bank account to rent a bus to get them to the park. Levin's Bastian families lived closer to AstroWorld and had enough cars to get there on their own. Feinberg didn't want to force his families to scramble for transportation. He decided to rent a U-Haul van instead.

Feinberg thought this was a brilliant solution. None of his students or their parents complained about his choice of transportation. But in the years after, as Feinberg became more familiar with the power of certain images in the Houston barrios, he was ashamed that he had been responsible for pulling a U-Haul van into the parking lot at Garcia and, as parents watched, putting thirty Hispanic children in the back. To Feinberg's mind, the only consolation was that he had another teacher drive the van while he stayed in the back with his students, soaking up their excitement as they rode together toward AstroWorld.

6

Staying Late after Class

BALL REFERRED TO HERSELF, Levin, and Feinberg as the three musketeers. But they more resembled Gladys Knight and the Pips. It was clear who was the lead singer and who were the backups.

Their chats at King Leo's were playful tussles between Ball, who wanted some after-school relaxation, and her puppy-dog novices, full of questions.

"Can you tell me how you pace that reading lesson so quickly?" Feinberg asked, the minute they sat down for a drink.

"Wait a minute," she said. "I just got off work."

"I know," Feinberg said, "but I just want to know about this one thing."

Her relationship with Levin was easier and deeper. They worked across the hall from each other. He would watch her, listen to her, and adopt some of her sharpest opinions. One popular slogan irritated her: "All children can learn." That was not the right message, she thought. It ought to be "All children *will* learn." The word "can" was too passive. It meant the child was capable. That was not enough. There was a big difference between capability and achievement. Many educators thought it was up to their students and their parents to summon the motivation to use their God-given talents. Ball took her responsibilities more seriously. She brought this up every time she saw the slogan: "Uh-uh, I don't want no 'can,'" she said. "All of us *will* learn. I *will* learn from the kids. They *will* learn from me. Ain't no 'can.' We *will* all learn."

When Levin and Feinberg came over to her house on weekends, she demonstrated the finer points of classroom management. She did not like, for instance, the way Levin drew the signs for his walls. "Dave," she said, "you write like a drunk chicken." His letters were thin scratches that wandered all over the paper. She cleared off her dining room table and spread out a sheet of butcher paper. Following her instructions, Levin and Feinberg cut the paper into pieces shaped like the word clouds hanging in her classroom. Each cloud had a word she hoped students would learn. She showed Levin how to make his letters in each of the clouds straighter, thicker, and clearer.

Watching Ball teach, Levin and Feinberg took careful note whenever she dealt with inattention or mischief. One of the mysteries of her classroom was how well-behaved and yet happy the children were. Hers was not a prison camp operated by an ogre with a teacher's license, something they had observed in other classrooms. Her children seemed lively and free. Yet her class ran smoothly.

One day, Levin watched Ball approach a fourth grader who was daydreaming and hadn't done any of his work. "*What?*" she said, leaning over and putting her nose close to the child's face. She would often switch to street talk on such occasions. "You're not doing the work? You got three choices." She spoke very slowly and distinctly. "You . . . can . . . change . . . rooms." She took a breath. "You . . . can . . . change . . . schools." The next sentence she delivered in one quick breath: "But don't nobody else want you but me."

"Or . . . you . . . can . . . . *change your attitude and actions* . . . because I'm not changing."

The child listened gravely. It was impossible to ignore Ms. Ball when she spoke to you. "Now, which one do you want?" she asked. She adopted the tone of an impatient waitress who had other customers. "Pick a letter, pick a letter, A, B, C . . ."

"I don't want any of those, Ms. Ball."

"You gonna pick one," she insisted. "This ain't Burger King. You don't 'have it your way.' Change rooms, change schools, or *you* change."

The child looked bewildered. Ball repeated the three-part question in a gentler tone. The student gathered himself together and made a choice — the third option. She said she would give him another chance. She reminded him that his being assigned to Ms. Ball's class was a fortunate chance, and his permanent place in her world had to be earned. There were always those other classes, other schools, other universes she could send him to. The child heard the love and concern in her voice. He felt better. He had lost the need, at least at that moment, to express his rage at whatever was bothering him — what his brother had said to him or what his stomach felt like or how uncertain he was of what was to become of his life.

Levin and Feinberg were near the age of Ball's oldest child. She acted like their cool mom. With Levin in particular, there was a lot of teasing. If someone asked Ball where she'd met the young teacher from New York, she would look startled and say, "Why, I am his mother. Where do you think he got that frizzy hair from?" If Ball and Levin felt particularly daring, they would suggest a romantic attachment. "This is my wife," Levin said to one friend as he introduced Ball. "I love older women." Ball kissed Levin on the cheek. "You know what they say," she said. "Once you go black, you can't go back" — a statement made in fun that eventually turned out to be more or less true for Levin.

BASTIAN ELEMENTARY WAS still a frequently chaotic school. Just before Christmas the principal announced a reorganization. Ball became the Title I teacher. She would be paid by that federal program to roam from classroom to classroom, helping everyone. She insisted that Levin take over her fourth-grade class. Another teacher took Levin's sixth graders.

Levin regretted leaving his class. He thought he was making progress with them. But he was in no position to argue, having been a teacher for only four months. He was still in over his head. The change meant he could get more frequent instruction from Ball. She watched his classroom management techniques and his struggle to keep every child engaged. She was authorized to pull some of the most difficult students out of class for special attention, but Levin asked that she not do that in his case. He wanted to learn how to handle them on his own. She decided they would do some team teaching. Sometimes she would teach the class and he would watch. Other times he would teach and she would watch. Sometimes they would do it together. Levin began to see how two teachers in the same room could augment each other's work. He discussed this often with Feinberg.

Years later, after Levin had become a nationally renowned expert on effective teaching, he would remember those first months with Ball as a perfect example of what teacher training should be. It was, he knew, hard for some young teachers to watch someone else run their class. But he was so convinced of Ball's talent that he could suppress his considerable ego and take whatever she was giving him as a gift. He had to be extremely alert to what she was doing because she could not spend all her time with him. She would often stop in the middle of a lesson and say, "Now, Dave, you pick up." After a while the students became accustomed to these handoffs.

Someone later asked if it had slowed his progress to take over Ball's class, already housebroken by the master teacher. He smiled and explained that no class is trained for another teacher. He knew Ball well, and her students had seen him there often, but they treated him like any new teacher. Worse, they treated him like a substitute. He was an interloper, a worthy victim of their favorite fourth-grade tortures. He had to work even harder than he had in his old class to win their cooperation.

He was replacing someone who, it would become clear, was one of the best teachers in the country. Her students' expectations of him were much higher than they would have been for someone replacing an average instructor. Levin had to hit those high marks or he was going to be a tall, curly-haired piece of roadkill. He worried that he could ruin what she had accomplished. It was like being asked to fill in for Hakeem Olajuwon as the Houston Rockets headed into game seven of the NBA Finals.

Levin noticed the way she talked to kids. Communication had to be positive. She would raise her voice, but with the proper tone. He practiced that voice, the combination of distress and love. His students needed to understand where he was coming from. He thought he had taken a possibly fatal risk when he picked Quincy up and dropped him in his seat, but Ball told him his instinct was right. The boy was harassing other children. That could not be tolerated. "If you don't protect your kids, they won't respect you," she told him. "So you can't walk by a fight." There would henceforth be, in both Levin's and Feinberg's classrooms, no greater sin than hurting or even teasing another student. Both would be on top of the aggressor Ball-style, as fast as a grizzly bear mother seeing a wolf near her cub.

What their students needed most in their lives, Feinberg and Levin thought, was love. What they needed most in the classroom was help with reading. Their weak grasp of the language was the handicap that slowed what they did in math, social studies, science, and writing. There were some helpful Ball chants for reading, language mechanics, science, and social studies, but Levin and Feinberg found themselves making up most of what they were doing as they went along. They had the standard basal readers, full of simple stories that they could dissect with their classes. They would read, sometimes as a group and sometimes with one child doing the duty. Then they would ask questions, taking unusual care to make sure each student comprehended what he or she had read. They had games like vocabulary hopscotch: cards with words would be placed on the hopscotch squares, and students would hop and reach down to retrieve them from the classroom floor.

School ended at 3:00 p.m., but both Levin and Feinberg stayed late. Some students needed extra work. They found different ways to persuade children, particularly those who were far below grade level, to delay their walks home. Some, they just had to ask. Others, they bargained with. They always made sure they had parental permission to keep kids late. The parents seemed pleased, or at least unconcerned, that Mr. Levin and Mr. Feinberg were spending so much time with their children. Each of them would have about a dozen students after school, although often not the same dozen. It depended on who needed help with what. They would focus on the homework, sometimes guiding the students through it as a group and sometimes working with them individually.

Both teachers felt they were no longer so awful. The year had been horribly disorganized, with their bad starts, switching classes, switching schools. But they thought they were getting their classes under control, and they could not wait for their second year to begin.

7

Michael's Smoke Signal

FROM AN EARLY AGE, Michael Harris Feinberg was everyone's favorite kid. Teachers in his suburban Chicago school loved him for his hard work. Other students liked his kindness, his sense of humor, and the way he included everyone in his social life. There were very few other Jewish children in what was a predominantly Irish and Italian Catholic neighborhood, but that did not bother him. His father, Fred, who worked in the family pipe-fabrication business, shared his love of math. Michael enjoyed basketball, his favorite sport, as well as anything that interested his friends. They put the well-endowed parks of River Forest, Illinois, to good use.

Still, his mother, Alix, worried about him at the beginning. She had stuttered since she was a child, as had others in her family. When Michael, as she called him, was two and a half, she began to see evidence of the speaking blocks that plagued her. She had seen research suggesting that stuttering had an emotional or psychological basis. One day, when he has having a bad block, she sat him down. "You know, Michael," she said, "what you are doing is called stuttering, and some days it's going to be like that. You should think of it as a smoke signal, a sign that you are trying to tell me something that is very important to you." She told him not to hold back anything vital.

"Come here, Mom," he said. He wanted to play tag with her, something active. She thought what he needed was more of her time, a chance to talk and play and be with her. She changed her schedule to allow that. Michael became the model for her own approach to stuttering, which turned into a specialty after she went back to school in psychology and developed her own practice. Later, when her son became a teacher, she saw some of that in the way he expanded the amount of time he spent with his students, even visiting their homes. That personal connection was important. Time was precious.

When Michael was four, he began regular tutoring with a speech therapist, and gradually his stuttering receded. By second grade, it was gone. He attended Sunday school at his Reform Jewish temple through eighth grade and was bar mitzvahed at age thirteen. At the huge Oak Park and River Forest High School — there were more than nine hundred students in his graduating class — he had a difficult adjustment at first, but he was soon leading his entourage on various adventures, as he had done all through elementary school. They called him Feiny, Feiny the Nice Guy. He took care of everything. It was hard to reach other members of his family — his sister, Jessie, was two years younger — at their big beige brick house on William Street because he was always on the phone, arranging everyone's social schedule and giving advice on homework. He enjoyed the more raucous side of the parties he organized, making a special effort to learn to drink with aplomb. By the end of high school, he was tall and slender and an avid member of the golf team, good with his woods, erratic with his short irons. He covered sports for the school newspaper and was elected senior class vice president. Despite some difficulty with science courses, he was sixth in his class.

At the University of Pennsylvania, Feinberg's social and political skills expanded. He joined a fraternity, Sigma Alpha Epsilon, eventually becoming social chair and then president of the chapter. In student politics, he was elected to the undergraduate assembly and later became vice chair. Junior year he took a job as a bouncer — he wasn't mean, but he was tall — and a bartender at the Chestnut Cabaret, a concert hall that welcomed alternative rock groups. These were good jobs, allowing him to pay his living expenses, something he wanted to do to thank his father for all the years of support.

He liked the bartending job so much that he cut back on classes and worked full-time, eventually graduating six months late with a degree in international relations. He had successfully avoided most of the theory courses. He only wanted to deal with the real world. His senior thesis was on the Middle East peace process. After receiving his degree in December 1991, he interned in Illinois senator Paul Simon's office during the first few months of 1992. His family detected political ambitions. His supervisor in Simon's office, Alice Johnson Cain, said years later that he was "one of the most exceptional interns" she had ever worked with. But he found the real world of government dispiriting. He decided he had been happier the previous summer, in 1991, during a six-week program in Israel. There he had worked with the children of Ethiopian Jews who had escaped their war-torn country.

He loved the Ethiopian kids. His Hebrew was rudimentary and they spoke little English, but the big guy from Chicago and the slender, big-eyed children from eastern Africa enjoyed one another's company. When he returned to the States, they sent him letters and photographs. He figured that Teach For America might like someone with his gift for making friends, so in 1992 he headed for the summer institute in Los Angeles.

8.

Feeling Like a Lesser Levin

DAVID JOHN LEVIN was a happy and athletic child, the youngest of four children who would all attend Yale or Harvard. They lived in a tenth-floor six-bedroom apartment near the corner of Eighty-first Street and Park Avenue on Manhattan's East Side.

The only significant problem in his otherwise blessed childhood was a learning disability his mother discovered when he was in the fourth grade. He was at the Collegiate School, a prestigious Manhattan institution, and spending more time on his homework than Betty Levin thought was right. She asked some questions that led the school's staff to give him a closer look. A counselor at Collegiate put him in a program to strengthen his grasp of phonics, but it didn't help much.

Like many high-achieving families, the Levins were a competitive bunch. John Levin, David's father, was a lawyer who became a successful money manager, as David's maternal grandfather had been. The year David was recommended for special education was the same year his brother Henry was accepted at Yale. The nine-year-old wondered if he was the only dumb one in the group. Betty Levin, like Alix Feinberg, was not going to let some annoying disability get in the way of her son's future. She contacted Jeannette Jansky, a well-known reading specialist, and set up a regular schedule of appointments for David. Jansky discovered that phonics instruction would not work for David because he could not hear the difference between many of the sounds. She taught him a method called structural analysis. He memorized the parts of words, making it easier for him to recognize them whenever and wherever they appeared. It was slow at first, but soon he got into the rhythm.

His afternoons with Jansky would be a pivotal time in his life, not only because his schoolwork improved but because he learned what it felt like to be what some unkind children might call the stupid kid. He became attuned to the insecurities of students struggling with their lessons. When he became a teacher, he was quick to stifle student attempts to ridicule a classmate because of some personal flaw. Feinberg had the same instinct, probably for the same reason, but with typical male reluctance to get into such issues, he and Levin rarely talked about the similarity of their childhood struggles with disability. It seems likely, however, that they had both chosen teaching in part because they remembered how much well-trained and caring adults had done for them when they were very young.

David's mother shared his distaste for unfair comparisons. All the time he was at Collegiate, she was on the lookout for any teachers trying to compare him to his brother Henry, who had graduated from the same school. When David was in eighth grade, Betty Levin heard a chance remark about Henry and David that most mothers would have shrugged off, but she decided that was it. She transferred David to the Riverdale Country School, a similarly prestigious private school in the upper Bronx. David did not mind. He had been bar mitzvahed, so he was now a man. He liked the fact that Riverdale, unlike Collegiate, had girls.

There were other issues weighing on his mind. He was developing an array of basketball skills and would eventually top six feet, but as a new Riverdale ninth grader, he was only five foot two, and rail thin. Establishing his athletic credentials was going to be a problem, as were the academic demands of high school. He did not enjoy feeling like the dumb kid. He did not like the pressure to excel in a public way, to be called onstage to receive awards like his brother and sisters.

So at age fifteen he resolved to be just as strong a student as his siblings were, and as great an athlete as he thought he could be, but not to talk about it. He was not a nerd. He was not a jock. He would never wave those flags of intellectual or physical supremacy. He was going to define his life his way and make an effort to be casual about the challenges he faced and any success he achieved. Riverdale was rife with cliques. He did his best to adjust, but he did not try to fit in with any one group. He refused to be labeled.

By his junior year in high school, he was frequently taking the subway to Harlem and other parts of the city where spur-of-the-moment basketball games on the public courts were often at a higher level than the scheduled games his Riverdale team played with other private schools in the Ivy Prep School League. He thought the games were terrific, and he began to develop an appreciation for the very different cultures he encountered.

By senior year he had the highest grades in his class and would have been announced as the valedictorian, except that he persuaded the school administrators, who adored him, not to release that information. He did not even tell his family he had graduated first in his class. When he was asked to speak at graduation, he refused that honor too. If he spoke, he was sure he could not resist making bitter remarks about the school's tolerance of stereotypes, and that would have hurt the feelings of teachers and administrators he liked.

When it was time to apply to college, Levin had no doubts. He wanted to go to Yale. His father had gone there, as had his brother and his sister Jennifer. (His other sister, Jessica, settled for Harvard.) Yale took him. He had his parents drop him off in New Haven two days early so that he could acclimate himself. When his roommates arrived, their room was already littered with beer cans, thanks to their new roommate from Manhattan. There were also three or four young women, the usual Levin retinue.

From the beginning, he felt at home in New Haven. College, unlike high school, was fun. His grades did not matter so much. He could do what he enjoyed rather than what would prove to the world that he was as smart as his brother. He began to take philosophy and economics courses and found his intellectual interests deepening.

He had to take Spanish to meet a graduation requirement. At Riverdale he had been advised to avoid foreign languages because of his learning disability, but he felt ready for *español*. The problem was that first-year Spanish met at 8:30 a.m., too early for Levin's active social calendar. He regularly skipped the class, yet found a way to secure a decent grade. He began dating the graduate student who taught the class and made a deal with her. She agreed to overlook all the missed classes if he would study the textbook, learn the vocabulary, and do a puppet show in Spanish for a community group that worked with children in low-income New Haven neighborhoods.

By the end of freshmen year, his affections had transferred to a sophomore, Chris Lin from Scarsdale, New York. She was the first person to talk him into teaching inner-city children, as a tutor for two brothers, ten-year-old Tyrone and nine-year-old John, who were struggling in a New Haven public school. He visited them once a week for two hours. He had little training and made mistakes but found he enjoyed teaching.

Casual acquaintances thought Levin spent all his time playing games and drinking beer. They were wrong, deceived by study habits in line with his practice of keeping his academic ambitions under wraps. After dinner he would excuse himself from the usual dorm debates over sports, sex, politics, and the presidency of Yale alum George H. W. Bush and head for his room. He studied every Monday, Tuesday, and Wednesday night for three hours, from 7:00 to 10:00 p.m. That was enough to keep up.

The rest of the time, he ruled the Yale social scene. Without telling his parents, he took a job in a New Haven liquor store, the Quality Wine Shop. He no longer had to ask his family for spending money. He established a campuswide persona as Dave the Liquor Store Guy, who always knew when and where the parties were. Word of his new image reached his parents, who accused him of neglecting his studies. In the ensuing argument, he was forced to reveal to them that not only was his grade point average a 3.7 but he had been the valedictorian at Riverdale.

Just what Levin would do after four years of overt socializing and covert studying was unclear. Tutoring Tyrone and John had intrigued him. He had decided to major in the history of education. He read Lawrence Cremin's masterwork on that subject, all three volumes. He was influenced by the University of Illinois scholar James Anderson's *The Education of Blacks in the South, 1860-1935,* which argued that American schools had been explicitly designed to oppress black people. That became the subject of his senior thesis.

His academic adviser, Edie MacMullen, was also director of teacher preparation at Yale. Levin did not want to take any teacher-training classes. He thought the methodology units would be deadly. But his fascination with the education of low-income minority children persisted. He read widely on the subject, even as he maintained his image as a partying jock.

Throughout college, he had an assortment of summer jobs. One year he collected petition signatures for New York mayoral candidate Richard Ravitch. Another summer, he worked for his congressman, Charles Rangel, running errands for the Select Committee on Narcotics Abuse. That earned him a signed photograph of himself with Rangel that said, "To Jason: Thanks for all the help." The summer after his junior year, his father found him a job with the Solomon Brothers office in Tokyo. That convinced him that he had no interest in following his grandfather, father, and brother into the investment business.

Levin decided to try a public-service job after graduation. He applied to Teach For America, the National Urban Fellows, and the Coro Foundation. Two Yale friends had joined Teach For America the year before and told him they liked it. But there was more competition for the National Urban Fellows and the Coro Foundation jobs, so being a Levin, he focused on them.

Both programs would keep him in New York. He submitted the same proposal for each, his plan for a comprehensive, community-centered middle school that would have job training and English instruction for parents, prenatal care for pregnant women, day care for preschoolers, welfare counseling, art workshops, the works. He reached the finals in both competitions but was told his project was too unrealistic. MacMullen said she was glad he wasn't selected. "You don't know enough to become a big policy planner," she said. "Go teach."

To apply for Teach For America, he only had to write two pages on why he wanted to be a teacher. He described his feeling of inadequacy when his brother was accepted at Yale and he was sent to a reading specialist. He wrote about Jansky and a few other teachers who helped him out of that unhappy spot. Their work, he said, showed him how an educator could change lives.

9.

Second-Year Teachers

LEVIN HOPED THE EDUCATION courses he took in the summer of 1993 in Houston, as part of the Teach For America teacher certification plan, would give him some ideas for his second year of teaching. Feinberg went to Los Angeles to work at the Teach For America summer institute. Teach For America officials had been receiving good reports on both of them. The organization was happy to tap into the classroom experience of corps members such as Feinberg and Levin, even if they had only been in the classroom for a year.

Feinberg drove the red Cherokee he had acquired to the institute site at the University of California at Los Angeles. He carried his teaching materials in milk crates and taught a course on all the mistakes he and Levin had made their first year. He and Levin had skipped similar classes when they were at the institute the summer before at Cal State Northridge, but Feinberg was determined to be indispensable. He offered himself, aged twenty-four, as the voice of experience. He taught the Ball chants. He supervised a small group of recruits, called a learning team, as they did their student teaching. "If you focus on finding the balance between having fun and keeping the focus on learning, that should take you very far," he told them.

Returning to Houston, Feinberg discovered that Verdin was adding to his responsibilities. On his recommendation she had hired one of his UCLA learning-team members, Andrea Coleman, to be a bilingual teacher in the fifth grade. Feinberg became the fifth-grade-level chair.

His Spanish was improving. He could say anything he wanted to say, although he still had to work on understanding what was said to him. His new fifth-grade class was more diverse than the previous year's class. Most of the children were Hispanic, as before, but the students who had almost no English had been given to Coleman. Feinberg had the most unruly students from the previous year's fourth grade.

He and Coleman decided to share their classes and teach by subject matter. She had good Spanish and a literary bent, so she did reading and writing. He took math and history. It seemed to work and ultimately influenced Feinberg and Levin's decision to departmentalize their first KIPP fifth grades in the same way.

Ball had convinced Levin and Feinberg that learning could only occur in a well-run classroom, and that no classroom ran smoothly unless the teacher was firm. They were both young men of great charm. Most people considered them nice guys, at least before they started making pests of themselves in advocating for KIPP and their kids. But they felt they had to be strict with their students or the behavioral distractions would overwhelm the class. It was difficult for them to be so tough with children who were, with few exceptions, enormously lovable. But they had seen what happened to classes whose teachers had given in to their softer sides. Both became quite strict, rarely giving an inch when tempted to let a child whisper in the back of the room or skip a homework assignment or tease a classmate. Their toughness became a part of their reputations, sometimes leading other educators and some parents to say they were too harsh, even abusive.

Over time, they cut back on yelling — a harsh but sometimes effective tactic — and switched to quieter, if still intense, conversations. But they ignored advice to become more accommodating of childish weaknesses. They told themselves the children had a choice: they could learn because they liked it, or they could learn even though they didn't like it. They took their cues from Ball's insistence that all children *will* learn.

One of Feinberg's new students, Elbert, reminded him of Levin's Quincy. The year before, Feinberg had seen the boy punching another child in the face. The boy's teacher had done nothing about it. Elbert was five foot nine, but Feinberg was a half foot taller, and he used that. Whenever Elbert began to bother other students, Feinberg leaned over and got in his face. If Elbert looked away or rolled his eyes, Feinberg put his finger under the boy's chin and forced him to make eye contact. Every Elbert misstep brought a quick Feinberg response. The boy disliked the teacher's getting so close. But he seemed to appreciate the attention, the message that he was worth all this trouble. He began to calm down.

When Elbert had excuses for not paying attention and not doing his work, Feinberg tried to address each one. After a fight on the playground, he told Feinberg he was angry because he had found a dog in the street and his mother would not let him keep it. Feinberg took the boy home that day and made a deal with the mother. They took the dog to a veterinarian, where Feinberg paid for a checkup. He explained to Elbert what he had to do to keep the dog and convince his mother that he had earned the privilege. Henceforth, whenever Elbert misbehaved, Feinberg would say, "You know, I helped with your dog. What are you going to do for me?"

Students stayed after school to work on projects or go over their homework, and sometimes Feinberg and Levin took them to the Boys and Girls Club for basketball and other games, if they had done their work. When they kept them late, they took them home in their cars. Levin still had the Taurus, but Feinberg had replaced his Cherokee with a white extended-cab Chevy truck that he thought went well with his cowboy hat and boots. When they dropped children off at home, they would often go in and chat with the parents. The students' families had already given them permission to keep the children after school, but it never hurt to say hi. The personal contact made it possible to negotiate disagreements over how parents were disciplining their students. When the father of the lead in the school musical pulled his daughter out the day before the performance for talking back to him about doing the dishes, Feinberg pleaded with him to punish her with some lost privilege at home, not at school. The father finally agreed to let her perform, in exchange for tickets to a Houston Rockets basketball game.

A good relationship with parents was particularly useful with students like Manuel, who took over the role of Feinberg's most disruptive student after Elbert began to improve. Feinberg dropped by Manuel's house and told his mother that he thought Manuel had great potential, but that unfortunately he had come to bring her another story of misbehavior. "Manuel, have you heard what we expect you to do?" she said to the boy. "I am not taking you to soccer practice this weekend." Manuel was ten. Soccer was the joy of his life. He would sometimes cry at that, but the conversation would continue. "I am sorry you feel that way," the mother said. "But you shouldn't make Mr. Feinberg spend time at night coming here and talking to us. I am embarrassed. You have to change."

Levin and Feinberg found that the home visits were important, not only because they taught students they could not misbehave without consequences but because they made allies of the parents. Even the parents of some of their better-behaved students began to call and ask Feinberg or Levin to stop by at night. "I need you to talk to my kid," they said.

10.

Meeting Rafe Esquith

THE FIFTH GRADERS who graduated from Garcia in the spring of 1993 gave an award of appreciation to Feinberg. At first he was proud of the honor. By fall he had changed his mind. He began to hear what was happening to those Garcia graduates as they became middle school sixth graders. What he heard made him think he did not deserve the award. He had not done enough to prepare them for what came next.

Feinberg's and Levin's previous students, most of whom had the telephone number of the men's apartment, called frequently. The two teachers hoped to hear inspiring stories of challenging middle school math, improved thinking skills, new books. Instead they learned which boys had been beaten up outside the school cafeteria and which girls had started dating and which students were not coming to school at all.

Levin and Feinberg felt helpless but tried to be encouraging. "Hang in there," Feinberg said to one boy. "Remember, we know you can do it. Remember how far you came with me, and how much you learned. If your teacher is not explaining the lesson well, remember what you did with me. Put your hand in the air and ask for help."

"Mr. Feinberg, these teachers aren't like you."

"You have to take charge of your own education," he said. This was ridiculous advice for a child in that situation, and he knew it, but he had to say something. "Force them to be like me," Feinberg said. How lame, he thought. He was putting an impossible burden on a sixth grader.

Feinberg and Levin visited some of the middle schools. They talked to their students' new teachers, but the conversations were awkward. The middle school instructors gave them odd looks. What were these guys doing at their school?

Feinberg tried something he called reverse engineering. He studied what was taught at the middle schools. With that information, he hoped to better prepare his students and maybe increase their chances of impressing their sixth-grade teachers and getting enriched instruction. But the more he saw of the middle schools, the less he believed that could work.

One morning while he was visiting Hartman Middle School, a man he did not know stepped out of a classroom doorway. "Hey, are you a teacher?" the man said.

"Yeah."

"Come in my class for a minute, would you?"

Feinberg stepped inside. When he turned back to ask what the man wanted, he was gone. Feinberg assumed he was a teacher with some urgent business and no time to explain. Feinberg looked around the room. He thought he had wandered into a bad movie, one of those *Blackboard Jungle* dramas. It was an English class, but no one was reading or writing. A knot of boys in the back of the room rolled dice. Several girls had their makeup kits out. They were applying lipstick and chatting about whom they planned to see that night. He had no doubt they had been engaged in these activities even before their teacher left.

This would become a galvanizing moment for Feinberg, his personal vision of hell. Whenever he told the story to his students, he sounded like a preacher warning of Sodom and Gomorrah. "I hope you will never be in a class like that, but if you are, it will give you a great excuse," he said. "If you find yourself begging for quarters at the Stop-N-Go and somebody asks you why, you can blame it on your crappy middle school English teacher."

That day at Hartman, Feinberg went around the room asking

students if they had lessons they should be preparing. Each said no. Fifteen minutes later, their teacher finally returned. "Thanks," the man said. "I had to make a phone call."

Feinberg and Levin realized that all their labor with their elementary school students was like building a sand castle on a Coney Island beach: rowdy beachgoers or the tide or something would soon wipe out what they had done. When they asked the teachers at the middle schools how their kids were doing, they received bland responses: "Okay, they're doing okay." The middle schools themselves were anything but okay.

Levin and Feinberg reacted angrily. Middle schools suck, they told each other. The system sucks. As their second year in Houston began, they fought to keep their standards high. They had both been given some of the most difficult children in their schools. That was a compliment, in a way, but still an additional burden. As they struggled to teach at the high level they and Ball felt was important, they began to wonder if there was any point to remaining in teaching.

In late October, Joe Sawyer, a Teach For America corps member at Garcia, told Feinberg about an interesting speaker who was coming to Houston. His name was Rafe Esquith. He was an elementary school teacher in Los Angeles. He had been invited to speak at the Houston Seminar, a lecture series on social topics sponsored in part by a socially prominent woman Sawyer knew. The night before the speech, Sawyer attended a dinner for Esquith arranged by his friend and other sponsors. He came back to school the next day bubbling with excitement, insisting that Feinberg attend the speech and get a dose of Esquith's unique approach to teaching.

Feinberg was in a funk, laid low by his middle school visits. He asked why he should bother listening to a teacher he had never heard of. "Because you are doing a lot of the same type of stuff that he's doing," Sawyer said. "He's speaking tonight at Lee High School. You should go."

Feinberg went home and told Levin about the speech. They were in a listless mood. Feinberg was thinking about law school. Levin wanted to go back to New York. But they had nothing better to do that night, so they went to see Esquith. They sat near a middle aisle in the high school auditorium. A round-faced man, about six feet tall, with a brown mustache, wearing a dress shirt and tie, a sport coat, slacks, and tennis shoes, walked to the front of the audience of about two hundred people. "Thanks very much for having me here," Esquith said. "I brought some of my kids along. They have a whole bunch of experiences they would like to share with you. It is an honor to be chosen Disney Teacher of the Year, but I don't think I am a better teacher than anyone else. I just work really hard at it."

He gestured toward two girls sitting behind him on the stage. One appeared to be Asian; the other, Hispanic. "We believe there are no shortcuts," Esquith said in his high-pitched voice. "That's why my kids come to school from seven o'clock to five o'clock fifty weeks a year. And even after they have gone on to middle school and high school, they come back to see me on Saturdays for SAT training. I work hard with kids to get them into college, because college is where they need to go if they want to have opportunities to do what they need to do."

For the next ninety minutes, Feinberg and Levin felt as if they were in the *Star Trek* simulator, suspended in time. They could not remember ever concentrating so hard on what a speaker was saying. The man was answering so many of their questions. He was addressing all the unresolved doubts that had been pushing them away from teaching. He had solutions for their bitterness and hopelessness. Occasionally they looked at each other with raised eyebrows, or whispered exclamations under their breath. Whoa. Holy shit.

As they felt the thrill of Esquith's triumphs over ignorance and poverty and cant and bureaucracy, they tried to size him up. He was older than they were, but not as old as their parents. He seemed like a regular guy, though very smart and very confident, to the point of being cocky. He was speaking from his heart. Everything he said seemed rooted in common sense.

He introduced his two students to the audience. One was a fifth grader and one a sixth grader. Levin and Feinberg knew what to expect from low-income minority children in this age group. How would Esquith's students be different? Esquith gave them word problems in math: "Okay. Four waitresses work in a restaurant. At the end of their shift one night, they split their pot of tips. There is a hundred and twenty dollars in the pot. The first waitress takes one-third, the second waitress takes two-thirds of what remains, the third waitress takes three-quarters of what remains, and the fourth waitress takes five-sixths of what remains. How much is left in the pot?"

The two students handled it with ease, doing all the work in their heads, without pencil or paper. When they had the answer, they spoke up loudly and clearly, something that Levin's and Feinberg's students rarely did. They did not appear to have memorized any script. They spoke naturally, using their own words. They guided the audience through the problem, describing how they did each step. Levin and Feinberg looked at each other.

The moment that burned deepest into their memories was the Shakespeare skit, vignettes from the Bard. "I am very passionate about Shakespeare, and I've got my kids to be very passionate about Shakespeare," Esquith said. "Every year we pick a play. We read it, we learn it, and then we perform it. Shakespeare is so cool to learn, and we would like to share something with you now."

Levin and Feinberg had high expectations for their students, but they had never thought of teaching sixteenth-century Elizabethan drama to children who loved rap and MTV. They could not deny what they were seeing — two girls doing a twenty-minute skit full of quotes and scenes from Shakespeare, with some modern social commentary thrown in for humor. They had the literary rhythms right. They seemed to understand the context. They were enjoying themselves. How had this teacher done that?

The presentation began at 7:00 p.m. After many questions, Esquith thanked the audience and sent them home at 8:30 p.m. To Feinberg and Levin, it seemed as if no time had passed at all. They thought about introducing themselves to Esquith and his kids, but a knot of people already surrounded the teacher. They felt shy and exhausted. They were going to need several days to absorb what they had seen and heard.

During the drive home, they could not stop replaying the night. After all their frustration and failure, the bitter residue of their visits to the middle schools, Esquith had triggered a different mood. They didn't see problems anymore, only opportunities. Their first thought was, We could do that. It was amazing what Esquith had accomplished, but he had given them enough information to accept what he had said at the very beginning of his speech — it wasn't magic. They could not think of anything but what they had to do to get themselves to where Esquith was.

When they got home, as exhausted as they were, they did not want to sleep. They booted up Feinberg's Macintosh Classic, put U2's *Achtung Baby* on the stereo repeat-play, and began typing up their new plan. They thought it was much better than the nonsense they had conceived on their drive through the Mojave Desert the year before. It was a program that would do all the things Esquith had inspired them to believe they could do.

What should they call it? Names, they thought, were important. If they had a name, they could put it over the classroom door. They could put it on T-shirts. They could use it as the title of the proposal they would present to the principal, so that she could see how brilliant they were and give them all the support they needed.

When asked about it years later, neither Levin nor Feinberg could remember which of them first suggested the name. For all they knew, it might have occurred to both of them simultaneously. They thought it was so perfect it didn't matter which of them came up with it. Their plan would be known as the Knowledge Is Power Program — KIPP for short — after one of their favorite Ball chants.

The words were from "Read, Baby, Read." Their students loved it. Its passion, optimism, and worldliness were infectious.

You gotta read, baby, read.
You gotta read, baby, read.
The more you read, the more you know,
'Cause knowledge is power,
Power is money, and
I want it.

KIPP Today: Jaquan Begins

Sharron Hall of Washington, D.C., was among the thousands of inner-city parents who gravitated to KIPP in the years after Levin and Feinberg got their start. Hall had dropped out of high school when she was sixteen, and although articulate and hardworking, with a job as an assistant teacher at a Baptist school, in the spring of 2006 she found herself very troubled about the education of her daughter and three sons.

She had seen a newspaper article about a woman named Susan Schaeffler who had started in an Anacostia church basement what had become the city's highest-achieving public middle school. It was called the KIPP DC: KEY Academy. The article said Schaeffler's first class of students had all been African American, as Hall's children were. Eighty-four percent of the KIPP students had family incomes low enough to qualify for federal lunch subsidies, just as Hall's children did. The article said Schaeffler's students entered the school in 2001 with average math scores at the 34th percentile, but by 2005 those students who were still in that original class and graduating from eighth grade had average math scores at the 92nd percentile.

The KEY Academy was a charter school, a tax-supported independent public school. Hall was not sure she liked charter schools. That year there were nearly three thousand of them in the United States, including more than fifty KIPP schools in sixteen states and D.C. The article said the KIPP founders were two former Houston elementary school teachers, Dave Levin and Mike Feinberg. Hall thought the KIPP results were impressive. But four years earlier, she had put her daughter in a D.C. charter school fourth grade, and it had not worked out well.

Toward the end of the year in that school, Hall had asked the girl, "What is fifty-eight take away thirty-two?" The child looked puzzled. "Fifty-five?" she said. Hall asked the charter school to make her repeat fourth grade. A supervisor said they didn't think that was necessary. Now Hall's youngest child, Jaquan, a smiling and loving little boy, was a fourth grader also not learning very much. Hall wondered if she would have the same difficulty convincing his teachers that he needed more than they were giving him.

All four of her children were back in regular D.C. public schools. Hall asked Jaquan's fourth-grade teacher what she thought of KIPP. The woman looked it up on the Internet and told Hall she liked what she saw. She thought the KEY Academy would be a good school for Jaquan. Hall discovered that KEY had moved from the church basement to a bright blue building in a commercial section of M Street SE, near the Marine Barracks. She visited, picked up an enrollment package, and looked around. Students the same age as her children walked from one class to another in a straight line. They were quiet and alert. Their shirts were tucked in. This was unlike the D.C. public schools she knew.

Two KIPP teachers visited her apartment. It was just off Martin Luther King Jr. Boulevard in Anacostia. Julia Buergler, the fifth-grade writing teacher, and Casey Fullerton, the sixth-grade reading teacher, sat down in her living room on a Saturday morning and explained KIPP — long school days, required summer school, every-other-week Saturday classes, two hours of homework a night, and frequent contact with teachers, who gave students their cell phone numbers.

They asked Hall and Jaquan to read their Commitment to Excellence contracts. Jaquan read his aloud, his first KIPP reading test. They asked to see proof of residence. The favorable publicity had led some families who did not live in D.C. to try to sneak their children into KEY.

After the teachers left, Hall talked to Jaquan about going to the new school. He was reluctant. He had made friends where he was. But after she explained how important this was to her, and to him, he said he would try.

Jaquan Hall entered the KIPP DC: KEY Academy class of 2014, named for the year those children would go to college. The five fifth-grade teachers loved Jaquan's spirit. He was a joyful, friendly, enthusiastic child. He insisted on hugging his favorite teacher, Mekia Love, the reading specialist and fifth-grade team leader, rather than accept the handshake she offered each student each morning.

He had a great deal of catching up to do. The Stanford Achievement Test 10 that he took when he arrived indicated he was at least a grade and a half behind in reading. His math skills were also poor. He was the kind of child the KIPP teachers thought they could help, even though he had trouble concentrating. On his first day of school on July 10, 2006, Jaquan looked small and thin in his white shirt and beige shorts. He sat on the floor of the small school gym with three hundred other students. It was a Monday, the first day of KIPP summer school.

The school had begun in 2001, shortly after Schaeffler, one of Feinberg and Levin's first principal recruits, turned thirty-one. Over the next six years, while giving birth to three children, Schaeffler would open three more KIPP schools — the AIM, WILL, and LEAP academies — and plan for two more. Across the country, each KIPP school had its own name, hired its own staff, and set its own rules. In 2005, Schaeffler became executive director of the KIPP DC schools and turned KEY over to Sarah Hayes, one of the first teachers Schaeffler had hired in 2001.

On the day Hayes first greeted Jaquan and the other KEY students, she was twenty-nine years old. She wore a brown suit. Her blond hair was in a pageboy cut. She welcomed each grade and then dismissed them to their classrooms. Only Jaquan and the other fifth graders — what she called the freshmen — remained in the gym, with their teachers standing against the wall.

One of the summer school's most important functions was to

accustom the new students to KIPP's rules, KIPP's teaching style, KIPP's games, KIPP's songs, and, most important, KIPP's expectations. Hayes addressed her audience of eighty-four new students: "Before you get your teachers, I have to give you a present. And as soon as I give it to you, you have to put it in your pocket."

She pulled an invisible object out of her jacket and put it in the hand of each child, leaning down to reach the smaller ones like Jaquan. "This present is my trust," she said. "If you lose it, you cannot go out to the store and get another one. You are going to have to earn it back. I am asking you not to lose it for the next eighty or ninety years of your life.

"Do you want to keep my trust?" Several children nodded. Some said yes.

"How do you think you can lose my trust?"

There were several suggestions: fighting, lying, not turning in homework. She agreed that all of those were ways they could lose her trust.

"I have my back to several people right now," she said. "Another way you could lose my trust is to talk behind my back."

Someone mentioned disrespect. Hayes's eyes widened. "Disrespecting me? Uh! Let me tell you right now. Don't even try. Because it's going to make you look very bad, and you are going to lose my trust.

"There are ways to earn back my trust, but it is very hard," she said. "It is a lot easier just to keep it for eighty or ninety years."

She welcomed them to KIPP once again. The teachers gave each child a dark green KEY Academy polo shirt with the words "Work hard. Be nice." on the back. Their names were called for their homeroom assignment. Each room was named after the teacher's college — Maryland, Rice, and Colorado. Jaquan was assigned to Colorado, the classroom of Mekia Love, the reading teacher.

Three years before, on an opening day when Schaeffler was still principal and was introducing herself and her school to a new fifth grade, she saw a small boy in the back of the room not paying attention, whispering a joke to a friend. He was adorable, small and bright

with a big smile much like Jaquan's. As Schaeffler excused the rest of
the students, she asked the boy to stay. She sat down beside him for
some private counseling.

"You think you're cute, don't you?" she said. "You *are* cute. But you
are a fifth grader now. You are too big for that kind of stuff. From now
on, when a teacher is speaking, you are going to track your eyes on the
teacher and listen to what he or she is saying. You are in KIPP now. It
is time to grow up. I am expecting a lot from you."

Hayes saw no such miscreants on the first day of the class of 2014.
Jaquan listened to every word she said. But there would be difficult
times as the year unfolded, for both Jaquan and the school.

Starting KIPP

11

Getting Permission

FEINBERG GOT RAFE ESQUITH'S address from Sawyer. On his Mac, he typed a letter to the Los Angeles teacher, introducing himself and his friend and fellow teacher Dave Levin.

"Dear Mr. Esquith," the letter began. "It was such an honor to hear you speak at Lee High School. Congratulations on everything you are doing. We would love to know more about it. We wonder if there would be a chance to talk to you some more. We would love to bounce some ideas off you and learn to do more of the type of things you are doing."

Three weeks later, the phone rang in their apartment. Feinberg answered. It was Esquith, calling from California. He said he was pleased to hear from them and would be happy to help: "Tell me about your classrooms. What are you thinking of?"

It was the beginning of a conversation that went on for several years. Levin and Feinberg bounced every new idea or classroom disaster off their mentor in Los Angeles. Levin called. Feinberg e-mailed.

When Esquith began having his students read Shakespeare, as well as John Steinbeck's *Of Mice and Men*, Mark Twain's *The Adventures of Tom Sawyer* and *The Adventures of Huckleberry Finn*, Alex Haley's *The Autobiography of Malcolm X*, Richard Wright's *Native Son*, Amy Tan's *The Joy Luck Club*, Dee Brown's *Bury My Heart at Wounded Knee*, and Robert Louis Stevenson's *Treasure Island*, some of his supervisors at the Hobart Boulevard Elementary School objected to such an adult reading list. They could not understand why he would ignore the basic readers they had provided, since he had such disadvantaged students. Those children had so little preparation in English, and yet he was demanding that they read Shakespeare?

But the students of room 56 liked the books and plays. Their Hispanic and Korean parents had few of the middle-class American qualms about the raw facts of racism and poverty that those classic novels exposed. They did not complain that the homework was too difficult. The students' scores on English tests soared. When Esquith won the Disney Teacher of the Year Award in 1992, he realized he might have an opportunity to share what he had learned with many more teachers.

Feinberg and Levin were no more reticent to drain every last drop of advice out of Esquith than they had been with Ball. Ball was the classroom magician, full of movement and fun and focus, making every moment count. She was Ms. Inside, who helped Levin and Feinberg deepen and sharpen their work with each child. She showed them how to make sure that no student was ignored and how to find something in each lesson that meant something to each student. Esquith was Mr. Outside. His strength was grand strategy — the longer school day, the trips.

This distinction between Ball and Esquith was in some ways artificial, but it helped explain what Feinberg and Levin gained from each. Esquith, like Ball, was a splendid classroom teacher and could keep fifty or sixty students engaged at a time. Ball became as energetic and influential outside the classroom as Esquith did. At this point, though, Ball was still spending all her working days at Bastian. Esquith was starting to go out into the world, lecturing and taking his students to plays and museums and parks. He was turning them into a theater company. It was not a classroom but a club, the Hobart Shakespeareans. At least his students thought of it that way. They happily got out of bed early to get a head start. They asked Esquith if they could open the classroom on Saturdays. They loved hanging around with the teacher who insisted they call him Rafe. More important, they loved being with one another, sharing the bursts of creativity that Esquith encouraged.

The club in room 56 at Hobart Boulevard Elementary School grew larger each year and was self-perpetuating. Long after Esquith's students had graduated from fifth grade, they found themselves drawn back. What impressed Feinberg and Levin most about Esquith was his refusal to accept traditional public school standards and practices, such as six-hour days and basic readers and standardized lessons and compliance with whatever new curriculum the superintendent wanted to try. Esquith won his national teaching award, not because he followed the rules but because he broke them. He thought the public school day was governed by habits no less illogical and harmful and oppressive than those that controlled the poverty-stricken lives of his students when they went home.

He did not think teachers should accept all that. He thought it was awful that so many of his colleagues, faced with the need to get through the day and earn a paycheck, told one another that little could be done with such disadvantaged children. He thought the better course was to solve problems logically, even if no one else was doing it that way. Reason and creativity could help teachers break the cycle of failure, although he admitted that few were capable of devoting the same time and energy that he gave his class. Aside from his wife and stepchildren, the students of room 56 were his life. From the moment he woke up at 5:00 a.m. until he fell asleep at 11:00 p.m., he was usually thinking about them.

In time, as Levin and Feinberg developed their own styles and emphases, their views diverged from Esquith's on issues like discipline, and their relationship with their mentor suffered. The two younger teachers decided that traditional rules of classroom decorum were essential to a healthy learning environment. Although each new KIPP principal set his or her own procedures in consultation with his or her faculty, most adopted the Feinberg and Levin practice of teaching the SLANT rules — "Sit up straight, look and listen, ask questions, nod your head, and track the teacher" — to each fifth grader and making sure mischief received quick and consistent attention. The KIPP founders had their students call them Mr. Feinberg and Mr. Levin. The growing ranks of KIPP teachers were often similarly formal.

Esquith never wanted to start new schools, as Feinberg and Levin did. But he spent much time demonstrating his techniques for many young teachers who visited his class. He had a gift for establishing classroom order naturally. His legendary reputation among parents at Hobart Boulevard Elementary was a great advantage. As the years went on, he would point out to visitors how infrequently he chided a student. He sometimes complained that some of the KIPP people were acting too much like autocrats.

ON THE NIGHT Feinberg and Levin returned from hearing Esquith's presentation, though, they felt completely in sync with what the Los Angeles teacher was doing. They wanted to bring the Word of Rafe to the world. While their chosen name, the Knowledge Is Power Program, seemed just right, they fiddled with the lyrics of the song from which they had taken it. They shrank from the raw, working-class sentiment of Ball's "knowledge is power, / Power is money, and / I want it." To make their proposal more palatable to school bureaucrats, private fund-raisers, and their own values, they changed that to "knowledge is power, / Power is freedom, and / We want it." Feinberg still used Ball's original version with younger students. To them, he thought, money was a clearer concept than freedom. But he would also talk to them about the power of freedom to make choices in their lives, including those that would bring financial success.

Levin and Feinberg wanted KIPP to have a nine-and-a-half-hour school day. Levin was welcoming students as early as 7:00 a.m. and letting them stay as late as 4:30 p.m. Seven a.m., Levin and Feinberg decided, was a bit too early, so they agreed on a schedule of 7:30 a.m. to 5:00 p.m. There would be Saturday sessions too, perhaps two or three a month.

By the Christmas holidays, 1993, their proposal for a fifth-grade KIPP class was in what they considered acceptable shape. Now they had to decide if they were serious about it. Were they really going to do this? Their two-year Teach For America obligation would be over in June. Were they going to stay in Houston a third year? If they tried the KIPP idea, where would they do it? At Bastian, where Levin and Ball were teaching? Could they persuade Ball to join them? If that didn't work, could they start KIPP at Garcia? Would Feinberg's principal agree?

Coming back from the holiday break, Feinberg knew he would not feel right if he left Houston after just two years. He thought he was doing a decent job, but the conversations with his students who had gone on to middle school still depressed him. He could not leave town until he had done something about that.

Levin and Feinberg at first thought they would launch their program at Bastian, since that was where Ball was. They wanted her to be part of it. They tried to arrange a job at Bastian for Feinberg. Joyce Andrews was still principal when they hatched their plan, so Feinberg went to see her and the school's parent coordinator. The coordinator asked about Feinberg's experience with African American students. Garcia, where Feinberg was teaching, was predominantly Hispanic, but Bastian had mostly black kids. The coordinator was not sure Feinberg was ready for that. He described his experience teaching Ethiopian Jews in Israel. He tried to make his stories about the refugee camp vivid and entertaining. It troubled him that the coordinator was not laughing.

After the interview was over and Feinberg had left, the coordinator told Levin and Ball that their friend seemed to be making fun of the Ethiopian children. That was not the kind of attitude African American parents at Bastian would tolerate. Feinberg was not going to be hired. Levin and Feinberg switched to plan B, setting up KIPP at Feinberg's school.

Feinberg was not sure how Verdin would react to the idea. She had raised no objections to Feinberg's ad hoc lengthening of his students' day, but she was impatient with teachers who did not do as they were told. Feinberg had the impression that she was unhappy with him for not being a team player.

He handed her the twenty-seven-page KIPP proposal. "We want to teach a large class of fifth graders," Feinberg said. "We want to put them all in one room."

"How many?" she asked.

"About forty-five," he said.

"And what is your goal?"

"We want to get them ready for the magnet middle schools." A few selective programs had higher standards than the chaotic middle schools that had done so little for the elementary school students Feinberg and Levin had had their first year in Houston.

"Well, Mr. Feinberg," she said, "this seems very interesting." She promised to give him a more detailed reaction once she had had time to read and think about their proposal. Days passed. She kept putting him off. Finally, after many reminders, she told him she had some feedback for him.

"That's great, Ms. Verdin. What do you think?"

"I think the font you chose to print the proposal in is too small. It is too hard to read. You should make the font bigger. But you are going to need district approval for this."

It was difficult to tell from her tone what she thought of the idea, but she had not vetoed it. She was happy to bring Levin to Garcia. Team player or not, Feinberg was to her mind an effective young teacher. She assumed his friend would have some of the same talent. Also, being a brand-new school, Garcia needed some recognition. She thought an innovation like KIPP would help.

As Verdin said, they had to get approval from the Houston Independent School District. Feinberg and Levin put on their best suits and headed for the Taj Mahal, the mocking nickname given the forbidding pile of gray concrete that was the district headquarters, on Richmond Avenue near Wesleyan Street. It looked like something designed by Joseph Stalin rather than by a mournful Indian prince. It was not a welcoming place.

They submitted their proposal to the office in charge of grants. It was the place to start because they wanted to raise money for the lunches they would give students during KIPP's Saturday sessions. There was also the expense of the special outings and trips, what they called the joy factor. Children being asked to work so hard needed something to look forward to. They planned Esquith-inspired excursions to museums, theaters, and theme parks in Houston, and a week-long end-of-the-school-year trip to Washington, D.C. They would raise the money themselves, but they needed the school district's blessing to apply for such grants.

One inconclusive meeting followed the next. Levin and Feinberg struggled to explain an idea that did not fit in the usual spaces on district forms.

"This KIPP plan, it's going to be ed reform, right?

"Well, sure, it's ed reform."

"So what new curriculum are you using?"

"Well, you know, there isn't going to be any new curriculum. You have lots of smart people here in the district who have written a good curriculum. We just want to make sure the kids learn it."

A district official squinted at them. "Well, if there is no new curriculum, how is this ed reform?"

"Well, we plan to have the kids come in at seven thirty in the morning."

"Okay, we understand. You're doing a before-school program."

"Uh, no. We are keeping the kids until five o'clock in the afternoon."

"So it's an after-school program?"

"We're just lengthening the school day."

"You know we don't have a budget for such a program."

"We don't want your money. We don't need district money. If we need some money, we'll raise it ourselves."

They were getting nowhere. They asked Esquith how to deal with administrators. He said that if the bureaucrats were friendly, be polite. "But what if they get in the way?" Feinberg asked. "Work

around them. Do it anyway," Esquith said. Obstructionist administrators were no better than furniture, he said, and should be treated
as such.

Eventually they were ushered into the office of Susan Sclafani, chief
deputy to Houston school superintendent Rod Paige. She was cool
in demeanor but listened respectfully. They were Teach For America
corps members, which she liked. She had helped bring TFA to Houston.
"If you can find the kids, you can do this," she said.

They thanked her. Feinberg's next meeting with her would not be
so friendly. But her endorsement was all they needed to start recruiting students.

Firing Mr. Levin

BY THE END of his second year at Bastian, Levin was convinced of the wisdom of his moving to Garcia and trying to make something happen with the KIPP plan. Bastian was undergoing severe adjustments. Joyce Andrews, the principal who had hired him, transferred to another school just as the spring term began. There had been a rape in the schoolyard, a group of fifth-grade boys assaulting a girl after class. That was too much for the area superintendent. He wanted someone he considered tough, and chose a new principal, a man this time.

About the same time, the Bastian faculty met to select their teacher of the year. Ball appeared to have most of the votes, but there was grumbling. Some people asked in whispers why she always had to be the one. Ball was disgusted by what she considered unprofessional comments. She decided to put a stop to it.

"You know what?" she said, standing up and looking around the room. "I don't even want to represent you. You complain too much. It's not like I was appointed by the principal. I was voted on by the faculty." She paused for breath. "Tell you what. Take my name out of it. I don't want to represent you. Give my votes to Levin or just vote over and leave me out!"

"Are you sure?" said the woman collecting the votes.

"Take it out. Take it out. You all have a good day," she said, and walked out of the room.

In the hubbub, with teachers arguing among themselves and Ball's friends running after her to try to dissuade her, the issue was up in the air. Her recommendation of Levin offended some teachers. They were not at all sure such a novice deserved the accolade. Some appeared to be openly hostile to him. One of them had called him "nothing but a white Ball." Earlier that year, he found someone had slashed his tires in the locked faculty parking lot.

But Levin also had admirers, who shared Ball's affection for the young man. They voted again. David Levin, at the end of his second year as a public school teacher, was declared Bastian Elementary School's 1994 Teacher of the Year.

The new principal appeared to have no problem with that. Like other principals, he was focused on preparation for the Texas Assessment of Academic Skills tests, and Levin's kids were learning their stuff. The TAAS way of evaluating schools would be one of the models for the federal No Child Left Behind Act, signed by President George W. Bush, a former Texas governor, in 2002.

The rule in 1994 was that if fewer than 75 percent of students in each ethnic group passed the TAAS test in any school, that school would be rated unsatisfactory. That posed a problem for the new principal because he had relatively few Anglo and Hispanic students, and there was little margin for error if all of them did not pass. There were only ten Hispanic and one Anglo student in the Bastian fourth grade. All of them were in Levin's class. Levin was told at least eight of the Hispanic students, plus the Anglo student, had to pass or there would be trouble.

Levin later recalled being told by school administrators and special-needs staffers that the best way to avoid an unsatisfactory rating was to exempt those eleven students from taking the test. This could be done if their teacher or their parents signed a statement saying that their language skills were not adequate to take the test or that they had learning disabilities that would make it unfair to judge their progress by that exam. Levin was told to fill out and sign the exemption forms. Other teachers were doing the same. Many of them did not like the state tests. They thought it was wrong to put such pressure on children, particularly if they came from disadvantaged backgrounds.

Levin refused to sign. He was deeply disenchanted with the learning standards at the regular middle schools. He wanted his students to qualify for one of the magnet middle schools, which he hoped would challenge them in the same way he had been challenging them. Some of the magnet middle schools started in fifth grade. If his fourth graders took the TAAS exams and received good scores, they had a chance to move to a magnet right away. He and Feinberg were, after all, starting a special fifth-grade program to qualify students for the magnet middle schools. He would be betraying the KIPP idea before the program even started if he did not do everything he could to prepare his fourth graders for the TAAS tests and make sure they passed.

The Bastian administrators' doubts about the children's chances were well founded. They had been among the lowest-scoring students in the school the previous year. That was why they had been given to the Levin, Harriett Ball's prize pupil. As third graders, only one of Levin's Hispanic students had passed the reading section of the TAAS test, and only two had passed the math section.

Still, Levin thought they were doing well in his class and could pass the TAAS tests if given a chance. His first year at Bastian, 70 percent of his students had passed. Those children had started the year with Ball, of course, but this year he thought he could win the race on this own. At the very least, he wanted a chance to try. He was far more interested in raising their level of achievement than he was in guaranteeing Bastian would avoid an unsatisfactory rating on the TAAS. He was not going to give in to the popular but dispiriting notion that low-income children could not make much progress.

Giving up on Levin, the officials asked the parents of the Hispanic students in his class to sign the form exempting their children. They refused. They explained that that nice Mr. Levin, who was so polite to stop by and keep them in touch with their children's progress, had told them not to sign. Mr. Levin said their children could pass the tests. They knew Mr. Levin. He always told the truth.

Levin would be proved right. All but one of the students passed the math section of the test. All but two passed the reading. The school did not suffer in the TAAS ratings, and Levin's students could apply to the magnet middle schools. But that news came several weeks later. For the moment, the principal appeared to be furious at him. The principal knew Levin would be transferring to Garcia for the next school year. There was no need to take any action to get rid of him. But he decided to send the young teacher an unmistakable signal of his feelings.

The principal, accompanied by a couple of other school officials, personally delivered the letter to Levin in his classroom a week before the end of the school year. He asked Levin to read it, sign it, keep the copy that had been included, and hand back the original. Class was in session. The fourth graders, intrigued by the high-level delegation that was visiting their teacher, were watching. Levin tried to maintain a neutral expression as he read the letter.

It said his services would not be required at Bastian the next school year. He was fired. It gave no reason. (The official word came down later: insubordination.) He signed the original as he was told, and handed it back to the principal, who left. For a day or two, Levin worried that he would not be able to work with Feinberg at Garcia, that he had been fired from the Houston Independent School District in its entirety. His teachers' union representative explained that that was not the case. The dismissal applied only to Bastian. The union wanted to mount a protest. It would make a provocative headline: TEACHER OF THE YEAR FIRED. Levin said no. He did not want anything to get in the way of what he and Feinberg planned to do with KIPP.

On the day he was dismissed, shortly after the principal left, Levin crumpled the copy of the dismissal notice into a tight ball and hit his wastepaper basket cleanly, a nicely arched shot. On the last day of school, when he got into his car to drive home, he noticed that his rearview mirror had fallen off. It was not vandalism, just a rusted screw. Like many athletes, he believed in unseen forces in sport, and in life. Ball had told him many stories about divine intervention. He chose to be like Ball and interpret the fallen rearview mirror as a sign. God was telling him to move to Garcia, and KIPP, and not look back.

It was such a good omen that he did not fix the rearview mirror for several months. He used the side mirrors to make sure nobody was coming up behind him too fast. He kept moving.

13.

Ice Cream and Spinach

FEINBERG AND LEVIN VISITED the fourth-grade classes at Garcia to recruit their first crop of fifth graders for KIPP. They wanted to start with forty-five to fifty students, two full classes that they would teach together in one big room. Any Garcia fourth-grade parents who did not want their child to be taught by Mr. Feinberg and Mr. Levin would be assigned to regular fifth-grade classes.

They rehearsed their recruiting pitch several times. They strode to the front of each fourth-grade class. They were large and loud, impossible to ignore. Feinberg spoke first, since the fourth graders had seen him around the school. "You guys are very lucky," he said. "Normally fourth graders at the end of the year are assigned to a fifth-grade class, but now you guys have a choice. ¡Qué suerte!" (How lucky.)

"This is Mr. Levin, who will be teaching with me. You can, if you want, be in our classroom next year, something we are calling KIPP." Feinberg and Levin had attached to the front blackboard a white banner with KIPP: KNOWLEDGE IS POWER PROGRAM in red and blue letters. They thought this would make their plan more real for literal-minded nine-year-olds.

"Now we are going to explain what KIPP is and see who here is interested in learning more about it and in getting a chance to make this choice," Feinberg said.

"But before we do that, please tell us: If you could go anyplace in the United States to visit, where would you want to go?"

"Disney World!" shouted one child.

"California!"

"Washington, D.C."

Fourth graders liked wishing games. They had more suggestions: New Orleans, San Antonio, Dallas, Alaska, Hawaii. Feinberg and Levin, as rehearsed, waited for the class to quiet down. Then they began to play off each other like drive-time radio-show hosts. "If you could go anywhere in Houston, where would you like to go?" Feinberg asked the class. "Would you like AstroWorld? Would you like roller skating and ice skating, and all those places? What do you think?"

"Next year in KIPP," Levin said, "I don't know if we could do the Florida thing, but we could probably take the kids to Washington, couldn't we?"

"I think we could," Feinberg said. "And all those local things, we could take the kids after school, don't you think? They'd have to earn it, but we could take them there."

Levin's face lit up as if he were hearing this wonderful suggestion for the first time. "Okay!" he said enthusiastically. "All right!"

Feinberg held up a clipboard full of notices to parents. "So if you choose to come to KIPP, there are a lot of things that you would get to do," he said. He could see some interest, at least curiosity, in their faces. Some of the older fourth graders tried to look nonchalant, but the two teachers could see that they were listening too.

"That's the good news about KIPP," Feinberg said. "If you come to KIPP, you get to do a lot of these things. That's the good news. Then, there is the *really* good news. You want to hear the really good news?"

There were several nods.

Feinberg flashed his biggest smile. "The *really* good news, if you come to KIPP, is you come to school at seven thirty and you get to stay until five, and you get to come to school on Saturday for four hours. You get to come during the summer for some weeks, and you get homework every night, all of which will prepare you for college and a great life. That's the really good news."

They had practiced this part of their presentation very carefully. They knew that if they did not give the words the proper tone and spin, they would sound like fools. The recruiting pitch was important. In the years that followed, they would give it many times. They would refine it and polish it and turn it into something very unusual in the annals of American public education — a successful appeal to elementary school students to choose to do more work than they had ever done before.

The first time they tried it, in front of puzzled fourth graders at Garcia, they were not sure it would work. In essence, they had laid out a vision of chocolate cake and ice cream, then dumped a steaming pot of spinach all over it. There was silence for a moment. To their relief, they could see that these children were not rejecting their offer, at least not yet. They were thinking it over. They might be persuaded if given one more gentle push. Feinberg and Levin resumed the scripted dialogue.

"So we'll need to have lunch when we meet on Saturdays, won't we, Mr. Levin?"

"I think we will."

"Well," Feinberg said, turning to the class, "where do you think we should go to lunch?"

These were late-twentieth-century urban American children. Their favorite dining spots were few but enthusiastically embraced: "*McDonald's!*" shouted several voices.

"Well," Feinberg said to his accomplice, "do you think we could do McDonald's, Mr. Levin?"

Levin said he thought they could.

The deal was not closed. They had more sweeteners. At Esquith's suggestion, they had been using something they called paychecks in their classes. These were progress reports designed to resemble a wage earner's weekly salary stub. They had printed out a sample KIPP paycheck on a large, stiff piece of gold-colored cardboard. It had spaces where teachers filled in points — expressed as KIPP dollars — for good work and good behavior. They also gave credit for extra effort, called "ganas" points in honor of the Los Angeles math teacher Jaime Escalante, celebrated in the 1988 film *Stand and Deliver. Ganas* was a favorite Escalante word. It meant the urge to succeed.

The students passed around the paycheck. They were not quite certain how this would ever work in school. Feinberg kept talking, speaking very slowly so that everyone could understand how this strange new class would operate. "That's right," he said. "If you come to KIPP, you also get paid." KIPP dollars could be redeemed for school supplies or candy, or saved to pay for the big end-of-the-year trip. "So the good news is if you come to KIPP, you get the trips, you get McDonald's, and you get paid. Now, for the *really, really* good news."

As connoisseurs of the lower-rated independent television stations, like the one that broadcast *Star Trek* in Houston, Feinberg and Levin had studied the infomercials. The professional TV hucksters who sold cleaning solvent and gadget wrenches gave them ideas for marketing reading and math. In their KIPP pitch, they borrowed several tricks, including the TV host's cheery insistence on topping each fabulous deal with something better. They refrained from using the standard TV come-on — "Wait, there's more!" Their savvy audience might have noticed that and written them off as frauds. But that was what they were doing.

They had learned the power of giving potential customers the impression that no decision was final. If they didn't like the product, they could send it back. "Now, if you're interested," Feinberg said, waving his stack of forms, "and you don't really have to say yes or no right now, we want to know which of you wants to get more information about this. We have a letter we want you to take home. If you're interested, have your parents sign it, then bring it back to us, and we will know where to find you and talk to you more about it."

The response rate for the KIPP marketing campaign of 1994 was encouraging. About sixty-five of the ninety fourth graders at Garcia brought back letters signed by parents. Feinberg and Levin would have preferred to start with seventy-five students and have Ball transfer to Garcia with Levin to be the third KIPP teacher, but she turned them down. Levin spent the next two years trying to change her mind, but she stood her ground. Their new program was exciting for two risk takers without dependents. But it was too big a step for a veteran teacher with four children, a mortgage, and the hard-won respect of the administrators and parents at her school.

So, without Ball, Feinberg and Levin began visiting the houses and apartments of the Garcia families who had shown interest. They went door-to-door after school and into the early evening. They also visited on Saturdays and Sundays. As big Anglo men, they stuck out in those neighborhoods. But word got around that Mr. Feinberg and Mr. Levin really cared. Feinberg's Spanish was bad, of course, and Levin's was no better, but at least they tried to speak it. They were very respectful to the mothers and fathers who were, in many cases, not that much older than they were.

Levin and Feinberg's encouragement of home visits would eventually become one of their most unconventional policies. Many school district administrators, in both poor neighborhoods and rich ones, discouraged the practice. But Feinberg and Levin had discovered that most of their parents considered the visits to be a sign of respect, even when they did not call in advance. This was particularly true in the largely Mexican American homes that sent children to Garcia Elementary. The parents or grandparents had grown up in communities where priests and schoolteachers often dropped in. By blind chance, mostly out of desperation, Feinberg and Levin had adopted that honored tradition.

For the recruiting visits, they had drawn up what they called a Commitment to Excellence form. It was in English on one side and Spanish on the other. The sheet listed commitments for teachers, students, and parents. The teachers' obligations came first:

TEACHERS' COMMITMENT

We fully commit to KIPP in the following ways:

- We will arrive at KIPP every day by 7:15 a.m. (Monday–Friday).
- We will remain at KIPP until 5:00 p.m., Monday–Thursday, and 4:00 p.m. on Friday.
- We will come to KIPP on appropriate Saturdays at 9:15 a.m. and remain until 1:05 p.m.
- We will teach at KIPP during the summer.
- We will always teach in the best way we know how, and we will do whatever it takes for our students to learn.
- We will always make ourselves available to students and parents and address any concerns they might have.
- We will always protect the safety, interests, and rights of all individuals in the classroom.

Failure to adhere to these commitments can lead to our removal from KIPP.

x _____
Please print name(s) here.

PARENTS'/GUARDIANS' COMMITMENT

We fully commit to KIPP in the following ways:

- We will make sure our child arrives at KIPP every day by 7:25 a.m. (Monday–Friday).
- We will make arrangements so our child can remain at KIPP until 5:00 p.m., Monday–Thursday, and 4:00 p.m. on Friday.
- We will make arrangements for our child to come to KIPP on appropriate Saturdays at 9:15 a.m. and remain until 1:05 p.m.
- We will ensure that our child attends KIPP summer school.
- We will always help our child in the best way we know how, and we will do whatever it takes for him/her to learn. This also means that we will check our child's homework every night, let him/her call the teacher if there is a problem with the homework, and try to read with him/her every night.

- We will always make ourselves available to our children and the school and address any concerns they might have. This also means that if our child is going to miss school, we will notify the teacher as soon as possible, and we will carefully read any and all papers that the school sends home to us.
- We will allow our child to go on KIPP field trips.
- We will make sure our child follows the KIPP dress code.
- We understand that our child must follow the KIPP rules so as to protect the safety, interests, and rights of all individuals in the classroom. We, not the school, are responsible for the behavior and actions of our child. Failure to adhere to these commitments can cause my child to lose various KIPP privileges.

x _____
Please print name(s) here.

STUDENT'S COMMITMENT

I fully commit to KIPP in the following ways:

- I will arrive at KIPP every day by 7:25 a.m. (Monday–Friday).
- I will remain at KIPP until 5:00 p.m., Monday–Thursday, and 4:00 p.m. on Friday.
- I will come to KIPP on appropriate Saturdays at 9:15 a.m. and remain until 1:05 p.m.
- I will attend KIPP during summer school.
- I will always work, think, and behave in the best way I know how, and I will do whatever it takes for me and my fellow students to learn. This also means that I will complete all my homework every night, I will call my teachers if I have a problem with the homework or a problem with coming to school, and I will raise my hand and ask questions in class if I do not understand something.
- I will always make myself available to parents and teachers and address any concerns they might have. If I make a mistake, this means I will tell the truth to my teachers and accept responsibility for my actions.
- I will always behave so as to protect the safety, interests, and rights of all individuals in the classroom. This also means that I will always listen to all my KIPP teammates and give everyone my respect.

- I will follow the KIPP dress code.
- I am responsible for my own behavior, and I will follow the teachers' directions.

Failure to adhere to these commitments can cause me to lose various KIPP privileges.

x _____

Please print name(s) here.

Levin and Feinberg pasted a big chart on the wall of their apartment with the numbers one to fifty written on it. Each time they recruited a new student, they crossed out a number. They also tried to raise money. Feinberg applied to more than one hundred corporations and foundations. He did not actually know how to do this, but the Teach For America regional director said it might be a good idea, so he launched his fund-raising campaign with enthusiasm, if little finesse. He went through the telephone book and wrote down the names and numbers of the biggest corporations in Houston. He called each one and got the name of the director of community relations. He wrote letters to those executives, explaining KIPP and asking for an appointment to discuss the program further.

Out of more than one hundred letters, only about a third brought responses. Most said, in polite corporate language, that they had never heard of KIPP and didn't like the sound of it. None promised money. When Feinberg wrote to his friends and his parents' friends, he did better. He raised about two thousand dollars, including many checks for just twenty dollars.

Levin raised about the same amount of money, but he did not need to write so many letters. His contacts were better and his style was more winning, Feinberg concluded. This was to Feinberg a perfect example of the differences between them. Feinberg was a tackle, getting bruised and bloody and muddy in the middle of the line. Levin was a quarterback, nimbly avoiding the pass rush and winning the game with a brilliant pass to the corner of the end zone, his uniform still clean.

Feinberg's frequent suggestions that he was a workhorse and Levin a show horse amused Levin, who did not entirely disagree with his friend's characterization. They realized that compared to the rest of the world, they were both extreme workaholics, but exaggerating their small differences provided a rich source of inside jokes. Levin found an even better, and more literary, metaphor for the story of Mike and Dave. He told Feinberg to read the Larry McMurtry best seller *Lonesome Dove,* about two former Texas Rangers who were also close friends with contrasting personalities.

The book bowled Feinberg over. It was a perfect distillation of what he had been talking about. He saw himself immediately as Woodrow F. Call, the striving but rarely prosperous rancher, who worked from before dawn until long after dark while his friend Gus McCrae sat on the porch of the ranch house drinking whiskey, when he wasn't going to town to visit the prettiest women. Yet when there was a crisis, the lethargic McCrae, as if by magic, was suddenly the hero. He tracked down the villain and saved the damsel while Call watched in astonishment and admiration. Henceforth, whenever Feinberg needed Levin's urgent assistance, all he had to do was leave a message saying it was time to get Gus off the porch.

Whatever the differences in their styles, Feinberg and Levin had managed to raise four thousand dollars for KIPP. What should they do with it? Once again they visited the district's grant officers, the people who had found their idea so perplexing. The grant officials were surprised to see them again. The four thousand dollars caused consternation. The two teachers sat patiently while people whispered and scurried about. Eventually, Feinberg and Levin were informed that a KIPP fund-raising account had been established, and the money was deposited there. As the KIPP founders, they could decide how to spend the money, but Verdin would have to approve each expenditure.

It was exciting to be starting something new. John Lin, the graphic-designer brother of Levin's college girlfriend, created logos for the new program, including a stylish rendering of the four letters, *KIPP,* as if they had been written in chalk on a blackboard. Feinberg and Levin worked on T-shirts and class schedules and curriculum. They traded ideas for setting up their classroom. They would start with a three-week summer session in June to get the students used to their many new rules.

Verdin at first said she might give them one of the kindergarten classrooms, which were bigger than standard size. Then she handed them an even better space: a large multipurpose room on Garcia's first floor, where fifty students would fit comfortably.

Feinberg had FastSigns of Houston make a huge vinyl banner, eight feet long and four feet high. Against a white background, it said KIPP: KNOWLEDGE IS POWER PROGRAM. "KIPP" was in red; "Knowledge Is Power Program," in bright blue. The Garcia janitor let them borrow the automated ladder he used to change the lightbulbs in the school's two-story-high lobby. They hung the banner forty feet in the air. It looked like a championship flag at the top of a high school gym.

Verdin called Feinberg into her office. "Mr. Feinberg, who gave you permission to put up that banner?"

"Oh," he said. Such conversations with his principal had become routine. He always said the same thing. "I didn't realize I needed permission to put up a banner."

She gave her standard instruction: "Well, from now on, ask for permission."

"Yes, ma'am."

14.

Money from Mattress Mack

In their search for financial backers, Levin and Feinberg thought about approaching Jim McIngvale, better known in Houston as Mattress Mack. McIngvale owned Gallery Furniture. Over the years, the store had grown from a few tents on I-45, a popular commercial strip, to one of the most successful businesses on the north side, where Garcia Elementary School was located, as well as in all of Houston. Feinberg had written to McIngvale but got no reply. It occurred to him, watching the man's television commercials, that a visit to the store might be a better way to reach him.

Many American cities have entrepreneurs like McIngvale, in love with the power of television and unafraid to look foolish on the tube. Levin and Feinberg watched Mattress Mack with fascination. They were selling reading, writing, and math to often reluctant buyers and were happy to learn new techniques.

"Come to Gallery Furniture, where we *really* will save you *money!*" Mattress Mack shouted at them from the TV screen. He threw a fistful of money at the camera, making the point as strenuously as he could that customers who visited his rapidly growing business would find it worth their while.

Would he throw any money at KIPP? Feinberg and Levin drove over to see. They expected someone that outgoing would not be difficult to find. McIngvale was on the showroom floor, with a loudspeaker microphone nearby. "Hi, Mr. Mack," Feinberg said. "We're two teachers from Garcia Elementary, down the road."

"Teachers!" he said. "I love teachers. Education is the most important thing to fix to help our country. Hang on a sec."

He grabbed the loudspeaker microphone. *"Attention! Today only, today only. Couches twenty percent off. Make sure you grab the couches."*

He turned his attention back to his visitors. Feinberg jumped right in, not certain what would happen next. "We're starting this program with fifth graders," he said.

"Oh, fifth graders!" McIngvale said enthusiastically. "A very important age. Just before middle school. Hang on a second."

He pushed the microphone button again. *"Recliners! Recliners! Go see the recliner section."*

Levin and Feinberg diagnosed a bad case of attention deficit disorder, or at least its commercial variant. They were going to have to speak in ten-second sound bites. "We're starting a program called KIPP," Levin said. "It stands for Knowledge Is Power Program. We believe there are no shortcuts."

McIngvale's eyebrows went up. "What did you say?"

"We believe there are no shortcuts."

The furniture dealer's livelihood depended on communicating essential information quickly and attractively. He was a fanatic on the subject of great quotes. "You know what?" he said. "That is *absolutely right.* There are no shortcuts. It's all about hard work, right? So again, what are you here for, boys?"

Feinberg talked fast. "Well, we're starting this program and having the kids come from seven thirty to five and having summer school for everybody this summer—"

McIngvale smiled broadly. "This is *great!*" he said. "This is exactly what public education needs. So what can I do to help?"

"Well," Levin said, "we put this proposal together." He handed the businessman a copy of the KIPP plan. "We wondered if you know anybody who could help. We need to raise some money for some things, like lunch on Saturday, and field trips, and—"

"Well, boys, I really like you," he said. "I'll tell you what. I need to run this by my education mentor. You ever heard of Thaddeus Lott?"

They said they had. There been a story about him on ABC's *20/20* magazine show. He was well known. "Lott, Thaddeus Lott," McIngvale said. "He was principal of Wesley Elementary School in Houston. He has kids walking in lines and he has all the phonics and he knows how to do the basic-skills stuff. He's my education adviser. He will know what to do. Follow me."

They walked through the store to the parking lot. "Here is my car," McIngvale said. "You follow me."

The drive to Wesley Elementary in Feinberg's pickup truck took fifteen minutes, with Feinberg shaking his head in wonder. "Dave," he said, "this is the strangest life we have ever led."

At the elementary school, they followed McIngvale as he waved at the secretaries and walked into Lott's office. "Thaddeus," he said to the tall man sitting behind the desk, "how are you doing?" He slapped the KIPP proposal on the principal's desk. "Dr. Lott, these boys came to me. They have a program called Knowledge Is Power. They want my support. I want you to tell me if this is a good program or not."

McIngvale sat down and helped himself to candy in a jar on the desk. Feinberg and Levin waited while Lott skimmed the proposal. He asked a series of questions. How many students had they recruited? What was their curricular emphasis? Would they be using phonics? What did Ms. Verdin think of their program? How much money did they need? How did they plan to use it? The questions were more intelligent and more practical than the ones they had gotten at school district headquarters. After a while, Lott signaled McIngvale that these two boys seemed to have thought it through and might be worth his time.

Mattress Mack greeted this news as if he had just gotten an order from the Marriott Hotel chain. "We're going to change the world!" he said. "We're going to change the world!"

"Boys," he said, "I'll tell you what. I think what Dr. Lott here says is fantastic, and I think you should use the SRA reading program, the same one he uses. If you agree to use SRA in your reading program, I will pay for it."

The two teachers had not thought about a reading curriculum. Their lessons would be focused, as Esquith's were, on reading and analyzing novels. It did not matter much to them which reading program they used to supplement that. They said they would be happy to use SRA. That sealed the deal. From then on, no one in Houston was a bigger supporter of Levin, Feinberg, and KIPP than Mattress Mack, who enjoyed throwing money at them as much as he liked tossing it at television cameras.

All Will Learn

IN EARLY JUNE, the first KIPP students walked into Feinberg and Levin's classroom at Garcia. They were curious and excited and a little worried about the extra work. Their new teachers feared that some of them would not show up, since their families were in the habit of visiting relatives in Mexico during the summer. But nearly everyone was there the first day.

Levin and Feinberg would remember those three weeks of summer school in 1994 as one of the best times in their teaching lives. They had an extraordinarily large class, to be sure — twice as large as any class they had taught before. But they were team-teaching, playing off each other's strengths. It worked even better than they had expected it would.

They compared it to basketball, their weekend passion. Two people who played well together could do anything. There were classroom equivalents of no-look passes, monster picks, behind-the-back feeds, alley-oop dunks — their options were infinite. Their first year as teachers had been a mess. Their second year, they understood what they had to do. Now, at the beginning of their third year, all that was coming together. They wanted the students to understand that KIPP would not be like anything they had done before. Feinberg called it the "Toto, we're not in Kansas anymore" moment. That first day, they both wore suits, not the usual elementary school teacher attire. They planned to give the students their KIPP T-shirts later, as a rite of passage.

The sign over the door of the classroom said WELCOME TO MR. LEVIN AND MR. FEINBERG'S FABULOUS, FANTASTIC FIFTH-GRADE

CLASS. As apprentices of classroom decorator Harriett Ball, they had resolved to make their new space a masterpiece. They had lovely bulletin boards. One had Ball's motto: ALL OF US WILL LEARN. On another was a drawing of dolphins diving into the three Ds: DESIRE, DISCIPLINE, and DEDICATION. There were fifty little dolphins in the picture, each with the name of a student in the class. In the air above the childrens' heads were the word clouds, suspended from the ceiling with fishing line. Everywhere a student looked in the room, she or he would be learning something. At least that was what the two teachers hoped.

Only one of the fifty students who had signed up for KIPP did not appear the first day. Feinberg and Levin visited her home that evening and discovered she had changed her mind. She did not want to do it. She preferred a class with normal hours. Of the forty-nine students in attendance, forty-two were Hispanic, six were black, and one was Anglo. They came from the two regular Garcia fourth grades and the two classes for students who were still making the transition from Spanish to English.

Feinberg and Levin knew it was unusual to start a new program in the summer. They could have waited until August, when the regular school year began. But they wanted to lengthen both the school day and the school year and to do it right away. They hoped to rescue summer school from its tainted reputation as remedial education for slow children and show that it could raise learning standards for everyone. They would get to know the students. The students would get to know them and their methods. When the regular school year began, they would not need to spend the first few weeks orienting everyone to KIPP.

The big KIPP banner hanging from the lobby ceiling drew some notice, but few people made much of a fuss over the KIPP class. There was a regular summer school session at Garcia the same three weeks. From a distance, what Levin and Feinberg were doing did not seem very different from what the other summer school teachers were doing. Team teaching? That was old hat. All that singing and chanting?

Feinberg had been doing that at Garcia for nearly two years, ever since he began meeting regularly with Ball. Other Garcia teachers did not see it as a big deal.

The students sat in blue plastic chairs at two-person tables, arranged in two U shapes, one U inside the other. The open ends of both U's pointed toward the front of the classroom. Feinberg or Levin would stand in the center and give instruction when not moving around the room. It was crowded and seemingly chaotic, a two-ring circus led by the six-foot-three ringmasters.

That June they kept regular summer school hours, 8:00 a.m. to 2:00 p.m. They wanted to create an atmosphere of teamwork and family before they switched to the longer day. They wanted students to grow comfortable with their expectations from the beginning and learn the routines. The first day, Feinberg, Levin, and the students read aloud Dr. Seuss's *Sneetches,* a lively introduction to the concept of team and family. Then they read some historic speeches, including Martin Luther King Jr.'s "I have a dream" address. The second day, they read more books, including *The Polar Express.* The teachers gave homework each night, one or two hours' worth. As they expected, many students did not complete their assignments. That gave them their first opportunity to demonstrate that unlike in other Houston schools, such lapses would not be tolerated at KIPP.

On day two of the Knowledge Is Power Program, a girl with long dark hair, named Melissa, informed Mr. Feinberg and Mr. Levin that she had not done her homework. She did not say why. Feinberg was standing at her desk, discussing this with her. He called Levin over to join the conversation. "Mr. Levin, you remember the contract everyone signed, right? The Commitment to Excellence?"

"I certainly do, Mr. Feinberg."

"Melissa, you signed that, didn't you?"

She nodded.

"And didn't that contract say you would work and behave in the best way you know how and do whatever it takes for you and your fellow students to learn?"

She stared with some puzzlement at the two men in suits. Where was this going? She sensed she was in trouble, but was having difficulty figuring out why. Nobody had ever talked this way to her before about homework.

"Remember, Melissa," Levin said, "there are no shortcuts."

"Right!" Feinberg said, his voice rising. "We talked about this! We're working hard to teach you every day, and we need you working hard to learn and do your homework . . ."

He stopped because Melissa had started to cry. The teachers switched to more comforting voices. Feinberg sat down next to her. He began to go over the assignment. She could do it, he said. All she had to do was set aside some time. But he continued to press the point that there was no other option in this class. "Melissa, honey," he said, "we expect you to get your homework done." She stopped crying and listened.

Each day at 8:00 a.m. when class began, they gave the students thirty minutes of thinking-skills work, usually a couple of word problems in math as well as other tasks relevant to what they were doing. While the students worked, Feinberg and Levin moved around the room, checking homework.

They taught the classic Ball exercises. They used her lesson on place value up to thirty-three digits, what they called Texas-size numbers. Fifth graders loved the idea of trillions and quadrillions. They went home and demonstrated their new knowledge to their brothers and sisters, who had never before heard anyone correctly recite the gross national product of the United States. They worked on short vowel sounds and long vowel sounds. They sang "Read, Baby, Read." They rolled all their numbers. The nines were particularly popular.

Teachers: I heard from a li'l ole bird that KIPP was great in math.
Students: No brag. Just facts!
Teachers: Then can you count by nines?
Students: *Yes!*
Teachers: KIPP, KIPP!

Students: Good as gold, let me see your fingers roll. (very quickly) Nine, eighteen, twenty-seven, thirty-six, forty-five, fifty-four, sixty-three, seventy-two, eighty-one, ninety, ninety-nine, one hundred eight. Whoomp, there it is!

They learned life skills: how to behave in difficult situations, how to persevere, how to be kind, how to help others. They learned the Esquith mottos, such as "There are no shortcuts" and another one that would become popular as KIPP grew: "Work hard. Be nice." Feinberg and Levin thought this part of their program was the most important. It made all the other learning possible. They remembered their conversations with their former students in middle school. Those children's attitude toward school, their sense of purpose and responsibility, had deteriorated rapidly, making progress in reading, writing, and math more difficult.

Homework was important to Levin and Feinberg. They wanted students to call them at home if they had any questions about their assignments. About forty of the families had telephones. Some students used pay phones on the street outside their apartments. They called often. Their questions were about everything. "I can't understand these instructions, Mr. Levin." "I can't read this, Mr. Feinberg." There was only one phone in the teachers' apartment, so they took turns answering, usually ten to twenty calls a night.

Much of the KIPP plan had been borrowed from Ball and Esquith, but having students call them about homework was their own idea. It became KIPP's most original feature. The practice appeared to reduce the stress of homework for their students and made it far more likely they would get it done. It also helped Levin and Feinberg see which homework assignments were clear and effective and which needed tweaking.

Nearly every evening, they gave a few children a ride home and stopped to chat with the parents. They got back to their apartment at about 7:00 p.m. and worked until they fell into bed at 11:00 p.m. They had to stop watching *Star Trek*. There was no time.

Building the KIPP culture was a struggle. Sometimes Feinberg and Levin did not explain clearly what they wanted. Sometimes they were misinterpreted, given the language barrier in a classroom with many students whose grasp of English was imperfect. And sometimes, to intrigue their students and occasionally to transmit information not for children's ears, they resorted to a secret language, a collection of words that sounded like non sequiturs but made sense if you strung together the first letter of each word.

The first weeks of KIPP brought many discussions of lost homework. Where had it gone? "I did it," a student would say, "but I don't know where it is." The Kippsters, as Levin and Feinberg began to call their students, came to understand that they were expected to turn in homework every day. But they were recently promoted fifth graders, ten-year-olds. Children that age lost things. So their teachers taught lessons on how to find lost homework as well as anything else in their lives that had mysteriously disappeared.

"You don't know where your homework is?" Feinberg said. "Well, I do. I know exactly where it is."

The children had grown accustomed to their teachers' claims of magic powers. Sometimes they turned out to be true. They were not going to automatically dismiss anything Mr. Feinberg or Mr. Levin said. "Where is it?" a child asked.

"It is where you last left it," Feinberg said.

The students looked puzzled. "Where you last left it," he said. "Think where you last had it, and go there. It's not magical. It didn't disappear and fly away. Go to the last place you put your homework sheet, and that is where it is."

They noted the advice and tried to follow it. It was hard to remember the last places they had put things. But many of them discovered that when they sat and thought quietly about this, likely spots occurred to them. Often the homework was found, just as Mr. Feinberg and Mr. Levin said it would be.

Cynthia, a Kippster whose English was not very good, went on a school field trip that summer with other fifth graders who were not in KIPP. One of the teachers on the bus was rummaging through her purse, complaining that she could not find her keys.

"I know where your keys are," Cynthia said.

The teacher looked surprised. Had some student taken them? "You know where they are?" the teacher said. "Where are they?"

Cynthia repeated the advice Mr. Feinberg had given them, exactly as she remembered it: "It's where your ass left it."

"*What?*"

"It's where your ass left it," Cynthia repeated, a little worried by the teacher's reaction.

The teacher did not think this was funny. "*Why did you tell me that?*" she yelled.

Cynthia, astonished, began crying. "But Mr. Feinberg says that all the time!" It was not until Verdin called Feinberg in for an explanation that the adults realized what had happened.

There were other mishaps that summer of 1994, but the word on KIPP was encouraging. The other students at Garcia could see that the KIPP kids were having fun. One of them was so excited with the new program that she decided to enroll without benefit of parental consultation. Her name was Vanessa. She arrived at Garcia very late in the spring of 1994, after the KIPP sign-up was complete. Her English was almost nonexistent, but she had seen the word clouds in the KIPP classroom sky and heard the happy chatter of children in the class. She came into the classroom and told Levin and Feinberg that she did not want to go to the regular summer school class for non-English speakers. She wanted to be in KIPP.

They told her the class was full. She would have to be in another class for that summer and the new school year as well. She did not understand. At 2:00 p.m. that day, after the end-of-school bell rang, she walked into the KIPP classroom. Without a word to either teacher, she went to the back of the room, knelt by one of the bookshelves, picked out a book, and started reading. At least it looked as if she was reading. She couldn't understand the English, but she was obviously eager to give it a try. Levin and Feinberg exchanged looks. They went to the main office. The principal was resistant at first. Did they think they could break all the rules? But they were allowed to add Vanessa to their fall roster.

They could not wait to see what would happen when August came and KIPP went to its nine-and-a-half-hour daily schedule. Then Verdin betrayed them — at least that was their interpretation. When they returned from a short post-summer-school break, they discovered she had given the large ground-floor classroom to an art teacher. Feinberg tried to talk her out of it. He pointed out another classroom that would work just as well for teaching art. But the principal had decided that she did not need to justify every decision she made to a twenty-five-year-old with just two years' teaching experience. Her enrollment was increasing. The fire codes said younger children had to be on the ground floor, so all fifth-grade classes would have to go upstairs.

"Mr. Feinberg, I have made my decision."

"But Ms. Verdin — "

"Mr. Feinberg, we are done talking about this."

"But Ms. Verdin — "

"Mr. Feinberg, not another word."

"But Ms. Verdin — "

"Mr. Feinberg, I'm warning you."

He gave up. Discouraged, he and Levin walked upstairs to inspect the classrooms they had been given. It was even worse than they had thought. They had been assigned rooms 210 and 220, which were at opposite ends of the hallway, much too far apart for team teaching. They noted that room 218, next to 220, was not in use. There was some equipment stored there, but they could move that to room 210 and have two rooms next to each other. Verdin remembers vetoing their plan to knock down the wall between the two rooms in her brand-new school.

It was not what they wanted, but they saw possibilities. They could stuff all twenty-five two-person desks and fifty chairs into 220 and use 218 as a room for special projects and storage. They gave each room a name. Room 220 was Big, and room 218 was Dog.

Big, their main room, had just one blackboard. They needed more than that. They priced dry-erase boards — the white boards that teachers wrote on with colored markers. The cheapest were $180 at Office Depot. Their debate over whether to spend that money lasted two hours. It seemed very expensive to them, but eventually they made the purchase and put the board up on a side wall of the classroom. They did not ask Verdin for permission.

Big Dogs on the Porch

THE REGULAR SCHOOL YEAR for the first KIPP class in Houston began in late August 1994. Feinberg and Levin were flying high. By October they were certain their experiment was a success. They could tell from the enthusiasm shown by their kids, from the quality of the completed assignments, and from the rising scores on the reading and math tests they gave to keep track of each child's progress. The fifth graders became so fond of the Ball songs that they sang them without prompting on the playground. At lunch, Levin and Feinberg could hear "Read, Baby, Read" bursting out from some part of the schoolyard.

Word of this spread to the Teach For America regional office in Houston. New recruits were sent to watch Levin and Feinberg run room 220, with the help of Lisa Medina, the classroom aide assigned to them by Verdin. The corps members came so frequently, sitting in the corners and along the walls of the jammed classroom, that after a while the two teachers barely noticed them.

One morning, with several Teach For America trainees present, the two teachers found themselves in the zone, the mystical realm of perfection athletes and actors talk about. They were on top of their game. It was what Ball meant by being touched by God. They gave an energetic lesson, followed by singing in rounds, and then dancing. It was wonderful, but they were having many days like that. They cooled the class down, got them lined up to walk to lunch, and then, as the students were leaving, heard an odd sound. They looked around and saw that the Teach For America rookies were applauding, a standing ovation.

But the reality of teaching children from distressed families, even on days full of fun, was rarely so sublime. It was still a struggle to keep students focused, to keep them interested, to keep them from treading on the feelings of other students. Levin and Feinberg needed all kinds of disciplinary tools. The most effective, at least at the beginning, were their enthusiasm for their jobs and their willingness to move quickly to divert outbreaks of hostility or boredom.

One of the techniques was suggested by the Ball slogan "If you can't run with the big dogs, stay on the porch." It meant that a good education was for students who were trying hard, who had high expectations for themselves and their classmates. If a student did not want to be with those academically ambitious canines, then the only place for that student was the porch, an unexciting place where life rarely changed and nobody had much fun. Even before KIPP began, Feinberg and Levin had experimented with isolation as a disciplinary technique. The idea was to use the Porch — a place separated from the rest of the class — as a motivator. Students who were not working hard or not behaving would be removed temporarily from the ranks of the big dogs but remained in close touch with their teachers, who would show them how to overcome their frustrations and deficiencies.

The device was very old and had many progenitors, including some as old-fashioned as putting a child in the corner of a classroom with a dunce cap. At first glance, KIPP's version looked similar. The Porch was a single desk with a single chair in an empty space at the back of room 220, formed by a cabinet that jutted out from the center of the wall. The Commitment to Excellence form said KIPP students promised to protect the safety, interests, and rights of the students in the classroom and to do whatever it took to make sure everyone learned. Anyone who got in the way of that effort risked being put on the Porch. Once they were on the Porch, they could not talk to any other students. During lunch they would have to sit at a separate table, away from their friends. They could speak only to the teachers. Indeed, speaking to the teachers was essential for getting off the Porch. Doing schoolwork and obeying school rules would earn them the right to rejoin the team.

Feinberg and Levin knew one of the most powerful forces in their class was peer pressure. Students wanted to be with, and be like, their friends. To cut them off from their friends was a useful motivator. At least that was what Feinberg and Levin thought. They began an endless series of experiments with the Porch and other forms of passive discipline; none of them was entirely satisfactory, but each helped to point some students in the right direction. Years later, as the number of KIPP schools grew, the Porch evolved in several different ways. Some schools — including the ones founded by Levin — dropped it altogether. But at the beginning, the Porch was just a way to mark a line that students could not cross without ending up in isolation from their classmates.

Porching offenses were often academic. But it was a student's effort, not the number of answers he got right, that was judged. Kippsters would not be porched for getting a bad grade on a test. They would be porched for not doing homework or for taking an ill-advised shortcut, like copying answers from another student. Students were also porched for bullying other students and for disrupting class, showing disrespect to a teacher, stealing, lying, and other standard classroom offenses. If more than one student was on the Porch, they sat at other desks in the back of the room.

The first year of KIPP, the Porch was a sporadic thing. Being porched usually lasted only a day. As 5:00 p.m. approached, Levin or Feinberg would ask questions of whoever was sitting at the Porch desk. The questions would be about the student's work and the student's attitude. The conversation always ended with the student's being asked, "All right, have you learned your lesson?"

Usually the student said yes.

"And if we take you off the Porch, are you going to show us by your actions that you have learned your lesson and it is not going to happen again?"

Again, a typical answer was in the affirmative.

"Fine, you are off the Porch."

For some students, the chastening effect wore off quickly. Homework was a major issue. Levin and Feinberg wanted it done each night so that everyone would be ready for the next day's lesson, but some children would go days without bringing it in. For them, time on the Porch became longer. "You haven't completed this homework," the teachers would tell the student, "so you are going to be on the Porch all next week. But if you turn in your homework each of those days, at the end of the week you will be off the Porch."

The teachers experimented with individualized Porch modifications. "It seems like every time we let you have normal freedom, you screw up," Feinberg said to one boy. "You wind up on the Porch, but on the Porch you do much better, and then we say you are off the Porch. Maybe next time you come off the Porch, let's keep a couple of things in place. Maybe you can talk to friends at lunch but not in class. Or maybe we will seat you on the other side of the room from your friends. We want to set you up for success."

Among the most frequently porched Kippsters that first year was Howard. Levin and Feinberg considered him the slowest person on the planet. He rarely got his work done on time. He was easily distracted. During thinking skills, the written exercises students did while eating their free breakfasts, Howard was so slow that they put an egg timer next to him. That did no good. They took the clock off the wall and set it on his desk to remind him he had to keep working on the problem. They put a stopwatch around his neck. They invited classmates to put their watches on his desk. If the campaign had upset him, they would have tried something else. But Howard was a sunny child and liked the attention. He accelerated his pace, but not by much.

Another regular Porch resident was Larry. He lived with his mother and a younger sister. He had not been asked to do very much by his former teachers. He was accustomed to getting away with misbehavior, like speaking out of turn and insulting other students. Levin and Feinberg jumped on such offenses. The idea was to keep children such as Howard and Larry focused on the lesson. If they let any misbehavior go unnoticed, that would increase the likelihood of further bad behavior, distract from the lesson, and slow down the class. If they let some students tease others, resentments would fester, an even more corrosive undermining of a learning environment.

For those reasons, both Feinberg and Levin disliked the standard school recess. It was a prime distraction. It interrupted the flow of their teaching. They had to line everyone up to go outside and then line them up again to return to class. Recess inspired fights that affected the classroom for the rest of the day. Levin and Feinberg refused to take their class out for recess in the morning, when the energy and concentration of their students were at a high point. Verdin did not like such departures from the schedule. But fewer students at recess meant less disruption, so she let it go.

As a substitute for recess, Feinberg and Levin had a forty-five-minute dodgeball game just for their students every afternoon. About 3:30 p.m, after the regular Garcia students had gone home, the KIPP class would take a snack break and then head for the gym. They used the basketball court. The class divided itself into two large teams, one on each side of the midline. Teachers and students tried some new rules. If you sank the ball in the basketball hoop from the other side of the line, everyone on your team could come back into the game. Some players were ghosts and could not be killed by being hit with a ball because they were invisible. It was a good assignment for players who were small or weak or very new to the game.

By Thanksgiving, the class was going so well that Levin and Feinberg began to wonder if their initial goal, qualifying students for the magnet middle schools, was too modest. Could their students soar ahead of even the magnet kids? First things first, they decided. They worked on getting their students ready for the entrance exam for the Vanguard magnet middle schools. The Vanguard programs were embedded in regular middle schools, just as KIPP was embedded at Garcia. The test was given in February. Feinberg and Levin studied old tests and introduced similar questions to their morning work.

This was teaching to the test, a practice that would become increasingly controversial as states like Texas, and then the federal government, required annual examinations for all public school students. Critics said tailoring lessons to what was going to be on a state test narrowed the curriculum and hurt students. Supporters, including Levin and Feinberg, said the practice was simply review of skills and concepts that state test makers — most of them teachers — had decided were important for students to learn. No one ever complained when classroom teachers had students review topics that were going to be on their own tests, so what was wrong with preparing students for state tests? Repetition was one way that people learned, including pilot trainees, novice golfers, foreign language students, and fifth graders.

The reading section of the magnet school test, Feinberg and Levin noticed, usually included a jumbled-sentence problem. Inside a box were ten words out of order. Students had to arrange the words into a coherent sentence and mark their answer sheet with the last letter of the third word in the reconfigured sentence. The math questions included number patterns and number sense. All of those testing approaches were added to the morning work. Levin and Feinberg did not know any other teachers who were going to such trouble to get their students into Vanguard. In one sense, that was upsetting because it showed how low expectations were, but in another sense it meant that their kids were more likely to beat the competition.

Their expectations were fulfilled. The test results showed that almost every KIPP student had moved up two grade levels in just one year. Most of them were eligible for Vanguard programs. Feinberg and Levin asked Verdin if it might be possible to add a sixth grade to the school the following year. They wanted to keep their fifth graders together as rising sixth graders and make KIPP a fifth-and-sixth-grade program. They suggested she add a couple of portable classrooms to the edge of the playground so there would be room.

"Well, I think that is a really great idea, and I think we should explore it some more," she said. Nothing happened. When they pressed her, she said such a program would have to be endorsed by the north district superintendent. They went to see him. "It sounds like a good idea," he said. "Let's keep thinking about it and exploring it." That was what Verdin had said. The words, they realized, were meant to be a polite no. They had gotten out of the habit of accepting any no, polite or otherwise. They looked around for some other way to take their students to the next level.

A Room in Motion

THE MOST VIVID RECORD of what went on during the first year of KIPP is an amateurish but revealing eighteen-minute and twelve-second video shot by classroom aide Lisa Medina sometime in late 1994 or early 1995. The video was designed to give future KIPP teachers, parents, students, and financial supporters a look at what Feinberg and Levin were doing. It shows Feinberg, Levin, and forty-seven students chanting and singing and moving about despite being stuffed into a classroom that would ordinarily hold half as many people. With the two-person desks pushed together and students sitting side by side, there was just enough room for the students to do their work and the teachers to move around the classroom.

In the middle of the gray-carpeted room were four rows of desks, five students in the front row, six in each of the next two rows, and seven in the back row. That made twenty-four students, all of them facing the long blackboard at the front. Along the right side of the classroom, from the perspective of a teacher standing at the front blackboard, were two more rows of desks, perpendicular to the rows in the middle. Eight students were in the row against the right wall, and six students in the row in front of them, all facing the middle of the classroom. Along the left side was a single long row of desks, behind which sat eight students, also facing the middle of the room.

That made forty-six students. The forty-seventh student in the video, a lean boy, sat in a chair behind a desk at the back of the room in an empty space between a pillar and a bookcase. Above his desk a large sign said THE PORCH.

Medina's camera showed the students bent over their desks, working on an assignment. There was no noise, no chatter. The two teachers were no longer in the suits they wore the first days of summer school. Feinberg, wearing jeans and a white KIPP T-shirt, with "Knowledge Is Power" on the back and "KIPP" on a blackboard on the front, sat in a chair in the front of the classroom near the doorway. Levin, also in denim and an identical T-shirt, was crouching next to him. The two were having a whispered conversation.

There were several large windows along the right side of the classroom, from the teachers' perspective. All of the shades were drawn. Some of the shades were covered with more posters and slogans. Some, but not all, of the students were wearing KIPP T-shirts identical to the ones their teachers had on.

In the video, the students finished working and began to run through several Ball chants and songs, with a great deal of waving of arms, pounding of desks, and snapping of fingers. At one point, several rows of students stood on their chairs and desks and kicked their feet into the air in time with a chant about the seven continents.

Feinberg paced in front of the class, shouting, *"What room is this?"*

All of the students shouted back:

> This is the room
> That has the kids
> Who want to learn
> *To read more books*
> *To build a bet-ter*
> *To-mor-row!*

Feinberg, still moving, smiled and said, "Give me the beat!"

The students began to slap their desks with their hands. Slap, slap, *slap*! Slap, slap, *slap*! They sang Ball's song:

You gotta read, baby, read.
You gotta read, baby, read.

Feinberg and Levin walked around the classroom, keeping the rhythm with two slaps on their thighs and a loud clap of their hands. They were still using the original Ball lyrics, for practical-minded fifth graders.

The more you read, the more you know.
Knowledge is power,
Power is money, and
I *want* it.
You gotta read, baby, read.
You gotta read, baby, read.
No need to hope for a good-paying job.
With your first-grade skills you'll do nothing but rob.
You gotta read, baby, read.
You gotta read, baby, read.
You'll rob your momma, you'll rob your friends.
Don't you know you can learn?
Don't you know you can win?
You gotta read, baby, read.
You gotta read, baby, read.

High on the right wall was the slogan: IF YOU CAN'T RUN WITH THE BIG DOGS, STAY ON THE PORCH. On the wall in front, above the black-board and below the clock, was another slogan in large capital letters: ALL OF US WILL LEARN. All of the words were in black except "will," which was in red. On the back wall was a large drawing of Humpty Dumpty and an accompanying rewrite of his nursery rhyme: HE READ SO MANY BOOKS / HE FORGOT TO FALL.

The class rolled its nines, then its eights, then its sevens. Feinberg cupped his hand over his right ear, as if he couldn't hear them clearly. Much louder, they rolled their sixes.

"Excuse me, sonny," shouted Feinberg, standing in front of the class. "Does anyone know where I can find some" — he paused for dramatic effect — "*big dogs?*"

"Whoop! Here we are!" the students shouted back. They switched to state capitals, prompted by Feinberg.

"Austin?"

"Texas!"

"Santa Fe?"

"New Mexico!"

"Sacramento?"

"California!"

"Olympia?"

"Washington!"

"Juneau?"

"I know!"

"What do you know?"

"Alaska!"

He asked about Lincoln and got a weak reaction. He tried again and got a stronger "Nebraska!" Jackson stumped many of the students. Feinberg had to do it twice before they came back with a loud "Mississippi!" The lesson kept going, a festival of mnemonic devices. Levin took over as lead cheerleader by shouting, "How many ounces in a cup?"

"Eight!"

"How many ounces in a cup?"

"Eight!"

"Drink it up!" Each student pretended to drain a drinking glass. Levin did the same as he walked up the aisle. Everyone counted to eight. "A cup of soup I ate" — the memory key was there. "Eight ounces in a cup!"

Both teachers walked up and down the aisles, making the same hand gestures as the students. "On your feet, please!" said Feinberg. Many stood on their chairs. In most classrooms that would be a no-no, but no one told them to get down. Some students did not have enough floor space to stand anywhere else.

"How many continents are there?"

"There are seven! There are seven!"

They named them in succession, raising their arms, jumping into the air, and kicking their legs to the side. It looked dangerous, but no one fell.

Almost as quickly, after a review of the number of cups and quarts and gallons, too fast and complicated for an inexperienced ear to follow, the rush of chants ended.

"The number is five, you will be sitting down," Feinberg said. "One, two, three, four, five."

Levin was at the blackboard. "Eyes up, please," he said. He took them through a long-division problem using Ball code words for each stage of the arithmetic process — "at the door," "pull down the shade." Then Feinberg wrote a huge number on the board — thirty digits. Feinberg asked them to help him mark off each group of three digits by chanting, "One, ten, hundred, hook it!"

"Very good job," said Feinberg. "In order to read a number, Try Big Mac Tonight — *trillion, billion, million, thousand.*"

They read it off as the teacher pointed to each group of digits. They took deep breaths as they prepared to shout out the correct name of each three-digit group. They went much higher: "Say what you see, say the comma's name: Quarked, Quastar, Sexy, September, October, November, December" — the mnemonics for *quadrillion, quintillion, sextillion, septillion, octillion, nonillion, decillion.* There was little time in the short video to show the teaching. It was one disposable crutch after another, but the teamwork was evident. They were hemmed into a small classroom with too many classmates, but they were acting as one. On the jerky video, which sometimes bumped up and down to the sound of their singing, they seemed happy to be doing so.

Investigating New York

ONE DAY IN THE SUMMER of 1994, Sy Fliegel, a former New York City school administrator, received a telephone call from Levin. He said he had heard of Fliegel's work for the Manhattan Institute. In an unusual partnership, the conservative-leaning think tank was paying the liberal-leaning Fliegel to set up small and innovative public schools in the city. Fliegel had founded the Center for Educational Innovation, a leading educational reform organization.

Levin said he was interested in talking to Fliegel about establishing a school in New York. He and a friend were starting a program in Houston, but they weren't sure it would have room to grow there. Would Fliegel be willing to talk to them the next time they were in town?

"Fine," Fliegel said. "When are you coming up?"

"Sometime in the fall. We are really busy now," Levin said.

"Let me know," Fliegel said. "We'll have a meeting. We'll sit down."

It wasn't until October that Levin, still in the first semester of the KIPP experiment, made it to Fliegel's office at the Manhattan Institute, on the third floor of a building at Vanderbilt and Forty-fourth streets. Feinberg had not come with him but would be there on subsequent visits.

Fliegel was a legend in New York education circles. As a public school administrator in the 1970s and 1980s, he had engineered the creation of several successful schools in East Harlem. The most famous was Central Park East Secondary School (CPESS), whose principal,

Deborah Meier, became one of the most respected educators in the country. She and her teachers raised the achievement of inner-city teenagers by treating them like graduate students. Instead of work sheets and multiple-choice tests, CPESS had research projects and oral exams. To make sure Meier could pick a congenial team of teachers, Fliegel violated several staffing rules, particularly the one that required him to post any job openings so that the most senior eligible teachers could apply for them. The school's success gave him a reputation for daring effectiveness and led to a book, *Miracle in East Harlem,* about how he had helped that subdistrict move from thirty-second to fifteenth place in reading and math achievement in the city.

Levin and Feinberg's approach to teaching inner-city children was different from Meier's, but Fliegel was willing to help anyone with an idea that worked. The two teachers felt that KIPP might be smothered in its crib before its first birthday if they stayed in Houston. They wanted to keep the fifth graders they were teaching, promote them to sixth grade, and recruit a new fifth grade. They wanted to hire at least two more teachers and eventually establish a full-scale fifth-through-eighth-grade middle school. Verdin had finally told them she did not have the space or the authority or the money. Hoping to change her mind, Levin remembers asking her on a date but being turned down. Verdin says that never happened.

Fliegel did not ask Levin for any data on his program. He just wanted to hear the young man talk. He had favorite responses for the two kinds of situations that New York school administrators — and school-reform entrepreneurs like him — most often faced. If someone complained about something, he nodded gravely and said, "Thank you for bringing this important matter to my attention. I will investigate it right away and get back to you." Even when his wife complained about his leaving socks on the floor, he would smile and say, "Thank you for bringing this important matter to my attention."

His second standard response, offered whenever someone brought him a new scheme to save American schools, was to probe the petitioner's soul. "What is your dream?" he would ask. The question did not work as well with the conservatives who ran the Manhattan Institute. He asked them instead, "What are your goals?" But Levin responded enthusiastically to the dream question. That won Fliegel over.

"Well," Fliegel said, "I think I can get you two fifth-grade classes in the South Bronx." He had no guarantee that Levin and Feinberg would be successful, and they were certainly nothing like the much older, more experienced, and more cerebral Meier, but he believed what they were saying about low-income kids' potential for success. He was also impressed that two Ivy League graduates who had completed their Teach For America obligation still wanted to stay in the inner city.

Fliegel felt his usefulness at this stage in his life was in employing his reputation as a miracle maker to put bright and eager educators in the right environments. Fliegel knew that District 7, the part of the New York school system that included the South Bronx, had an area superintendent, Pedro Crespo, who was friendly to experiments like this one. He also knew that whatever Levin and Feinberg's fancy plans, New York principals would have the same practical view of them that Verdin had had when she accepted their idea for a new kind of fifth grade. They were smart and energetic teachers who would probably do better in the classroom than anyone else who might apply. And they were tall, athletic males, a rare and valued commodity in schools full of restless boys.

Fliegel believed that the success of educational enterprises depended as much on leadership as on the quality of the concept. People came to him with ideas that they assumed would succeed simply because of their obvious merit. Fliegel thought that was nonsense. An idea had no chance unless there was strong leadership. Levin went to see Crespo and his top staff in District 7. They said exactly what Fliegel said they would say. They thought the KIPP idea was interesting. They could certainly give him and his friend two fifth-grade classes in an existing K-5 school. District 7 officials knew Fliegel's track record. His relationships got KIPP New York started, but Levin soon learned that surviving in the South Bronx was going to take much more.

19.

In the News

AT 8:30 A.M. ON SUNDAY, December 18, 1994, the telephone rang in the bedroom of Anne Patterson, the west district superintendent of the Houston Independent School District. It was her friend Cathy Mincberg, a member of the city school board. Patterson, a tall, red-haired woman, liked to sleep in on Sundays. She was only half-conscious. She wondered why anyone would call her at what was to her such an early hour. But Mincberg was very excited. She was shouting into the phone.

"Anne, *have you read the Post yet*?"

"Uh, no."

"*Go! Go read it!* There are these two guys on the north side. They want to start their own school, but nobody will help them out. They're going to move to New York. Why don't you give them a call?" Mincberg had heard something interesting about two teachers at Garcia Elementary and had mentioned this to a *Houston Post* writer, Susan Besze Wallace, who at twenty-four was about the same age as the subjects of her piece. The story Wallace had written about Levin and Feinberg reminded Mincberg of how she had felt when she was a new biology teacher trying to change the world.

Patterson had learned that Mincberg's instincts were often very good. So maybe this story was worth something. But first she would get some coffee. Coffee was very important. And then she would read the paper.

The story was on the front page, part of a three-part series on the significance of male teachers in the inner city. The headline said FEW

GOOD MEN, just above a photo of a KIPP fifth grader, Raymond Garcia, at a pay phone outside his apartment, discussing his homework with his teacher. The caption below the photo said, "2 male teachers driven to change young lives for the better." Beside the photo in large type was this explanation: "Across America, there's a growing movement to lure men back into the classroom. Some hope it will provide the father figure millions of our children don't have. David Levin and Michael Feinberg are two who answered the call in Houston."

Wallace, the reporter, had gotten a grant from the national Education Writers Association to spend three months working on the series, which included stories about a male state teacher of the year and a charismatic coach. Feinberg and Levin never made much of their gender. Within a decade, the majority of KIPP teachers, like teachers in general, would be women. But Feinberg and Levin were as happy as Mincberg was to see the article. They hoped it would give them some credibility and maybe revive their plan to stay in Houston.

The story began:

> On a windy Wednesday night, 12-year-old Raymond Garcia makes a collect call from a pay phone near the rusty Coke machine in his apartment complex.
>
> He raises a piece of notebook paper above his head so he can read it by streetlight and waits for a familiar voice to approve the charges.
>
> Physical science is the topic of the conversation tonight. Sometimes it's social studies, lots of times math. Often, he calls just to talk.
>
> Neighbors are waiting their turn for the phone, so he has only a few minutes. Usually that's all it takes. Tonight the complexities of solids, liquids and gasses are explained, and Raymond signs off.
>
> He walks home past the patch of grass that used to be a swimming pool. He and his younger brother Ruben aren't allowed to leave the apartment unless their mother is home.
>
> But she won't be back from work until 10 or so, and his father died four years ago. The last grownup Raymond talks to tonight isn't a parent.

It's a teacher.

"G'night, Tiger," Mike Feinberg tells him at the other end of the phone 15 miles away, before clicking over to another call, another student. Between rings, Feinberg and teaching partner Dave Levin grade yesterday's homework, plan tomorrow's and try to decide on which Christmas play their fifth grade will perform.

The story was very long, 2,799 words, giving Wallace enough space both to chronicle the lives of the students and to describe Feinberg and Levin's teaching methods. Patterson read the classroom descriptions carefully. She knew what good teaching looked like. Unlike most newspaper stories about schools, the account gave her enough details to judge for herself if the two young men knew what they were doing.

The story continued:

> Often, these teachers — Feinberg in his Chevrolet pickup and Levin in his Ford Taurus — provide wake-up and taxi service to a student or two. The men have dug into their own pockets to buy alarm clocks for families without them . . .
>
> They pace back and forth in their cramped classroom, pointing, clapping, inspiring. Every day is approached with fourth quarter, do-or-die urgency.

Wallace made the point that Mincberg had noticed: Houston might lose these fine young men to New York City. Patterson had seen enough. These were her kind of guys.

Patterson had grown up in Westfield, New Jersey, influenced by her obstetrician father's social conscience. She did her first teaching in inner-city San Diego, then moved to Houston with her husband, a banker, and began training other teachers to inspire disadvantaged children. Eventually she was made principal of a school that had had three principals in three years, near Rice University. She recruited a talented faculty, using her teacher-training knowledge of who was good and who wasn't. Test scores soared. By 1994, she was the west district superintendent. She was still eager to find great teachers, even if they were babies like Levin and Feinberg.

She got Feinberg's number and left him a message: "I'm really interested in this business," she said. "Why don't we get together?" Feinberg called back and suggested they meet at a microbrewery on Richmond Avenue, one of his and Levin's favorite recreational neighborhoods. Patterson hoped they could help solve the problem of Gulfton, a beehive of apartment buildings with low-income families from Central America. The neighborhood was not technically part of her district, but Gulfton children eventually found themselves at Lee High School, which was on her turf. If she could create a model middle school program for some of those kids, it would be a good example for other middle schools and eventually raise the level of achievement at Lee High. It would not be easy. Gulfton was known for its poverty and gangs. It was one of the ten zip codes in Texas with the highest rate of juvenile crime.

She told Feinberg and Levin that she thought there was space for their middle school on one of the Lee High parking lots. They could set up modular classrooms and move Gulfton middle school students into them. They would need special buses, but that was doable.

The idea sounded promising to Feinberg and Levin. Their KIPP proposal had four principles for success, what they called the Four Factors: more time for instruction, high-quality teaching, parental support, and administrative support. Levin and Feinberg felt they had the longer school day and the quality teaching under control. They were not perfect, but they had at least proved they could keep a class going for nine and a half hours a day and teach well enough to increase student achievement significantly. They also knew how to build parental support.

But administrative support was beyond their competence. If they did not find powerful allies soon, they were not likely to last very long. The north district people had turned them down. The Bronx school officials seemed sincere, but that turf was new to them. Feinberg did not know New York well, and Levin, child of the Upper East Side, was no expert on the Bronx, its school leaders, or its political peculiarities.

They knew how harmful administrative sloppiness or resistance could be. For their Saturday morning classes at Garcia, they had asked Verdin to give them a set of keys to the school so they could let themselves in. She said no but promised that a janitor or an assistant principal would be there. Twice so far, the key holder had not appeared and they had had to conduct Saturday school in the parking lot.

There were also misunderstandings about the money they had raised. Every month, Feinberg called the school district office to check the KIPP balance. Each time the numbers made less sense, to the point where he was sure the fund was several hundred dollars below where it ought to have been. When he investigated, he discovered that Garcia administrators had requisitioned some office supplies and library materials from the KIPP account. The amount missing was nearly eight hundred dollars. He vowed to expose the office thieves, but Patterson told him to shut up. She did not want to get into any fights with headquarters over her stealing Feinberg and Levin from the north district. If Feinberg turned the missing dollars into a cause célèbre, one of the accused officials might strike back by vetoing the teacher transfer. She told Feinberg and Levin that once they were safely part of her west district team she would have the money they needed. Years later, Verdin said it was an inadvertent error, money being deposited in the wrong account, and she said she had quickly corrected it.

Both Feinberg and Levin liked Patterson. About aggressive teachers with new ideas, she said, "Let the stallions run." She thought it wrong to micromanage educators who had a passion for results. They thought Patterson might be able to back up her promises, but they had to keep the New York City option open. They had agreed to go to the South Bronx if District 7 gave them the space. It seemed wrong to toss away that opportunity. They also wanted a chance to stay in Houston. They owed it to their students, the ones from previous years who kept in touch with them, and the ones who were in their KIPP class. They had told those children they were going to help get them into college, and many parents were counting on them.

20

One on One

It was becoming clear to Feinberg and Levin, owing to the efforts of Patterson and Fliegel, that they could soon have not one school but two. If both Houston and New York came through, Feinberg would stay to start a new KIPP at Lee High, and Levin would open a second KIPP in the Bronx. But they were still locked into their daily Houston routine. They taught together ten hours a day and lived together the rest of the time. They were getting on each other's nerves.

Basketball provided some escape. They played weekends with several Teach For America friends. Usually they were on the same team and could work out their aggressions on other people. But when no one else was available, they played against each other one-on-one.

They were, to be sure, best friends. The success of their joint project had strengthened that bond. But it was sometimes annoying to live one's life as Mike and Dave rather than as two separate, independent, proud entities. They were American males, so they never discussed this, but they both knew what was going on. Their similarities far outweighed their differences. But the irritations of daily life often led them to fixate on the ways they did not connect. The two characters in *Lonesome Dove* were one fascination. Another useful metaphor was *The Odd Couple*. Levin had a bit of Felix Unger in him. He was the more meticulous of the two. Their arguments often revolved around Levin's wanting to make something perfect that Feinberg thought was good enough. When they differed over the decorations for the KIPP classroom, it was usually Levin insisting on the precise artistic values Ball had taught him.

Just as their first KIPP class began, they squabbled over where students should put their headings on their papers. To many teachers, including them, this was important. The heading was the first thing a student wrote on any piece of work. They had to agree on how it should look. Feinberg wanted the student's name, the date, and the subject on separate lines in the upper right corner. Levin preferred all that information on one line at the top — student's name on the left, date in the middle, and subject on the right. They fought about this for more than two hours. Feinberg finally won because, as he later put it, "Dave was a little more mature and realized this was just stupid."

They also had a long dispute over how students should show they were balancing both sides of an algebraic equation. Fifth-grade teachers at that time rarely tried to teach algebraic concepts, but their mentors Esquith and Ball had convinced them that it was a useful challenge for this age group. If the formula was $x - 7 = 20$, students were told to isolate the variable, x, on one side of the equation by adding 7 to both sides. That would produce the answer, $x = 27$. So far, so good. Feinberg wanted students to write the plus 7 on each side above the equation and draw a line through both the plus 7 and the minus 7 on the left side of the equation so that it was clear they had canceled each other out. On the right side, the plus 7 would float above the 20 and be added to produce 27. Levin thought it was better to put the plus 7 below each side of the equation. That would show more clearly that the statement on the right was a simple addition problem, with the larger number at the top as fifth graders were accustomed to seeing.

In that instance, Feinberg gave in. He could see that their students would be more comfortable with Levin's method. Feinberg also agreed to Levin's request that they upgrade their problem-solving catchword, UPSLOB (*u*nderstand, *p*lan, *s*olve, *lo*ok *b*ack) to the more sophisticated DR QFOSAC (*d*o, *r*ead, *q*uestion, *f*acts, *o*peration, *s*olve, *a*nswer, *c*heck).

They made the necessary compromises, but that did not ease the stress of coordinating every move with another person. They realized it would be disastrous if they ever had an argument in front of the class, except for the rehearsed disagreements they sometimes used to dramatize a lesson. It was draining to hold themselves so tight. When it came time for some one-on-one basketball, they both thought a little competition might be therapeutic. They did not tell themselves that, of course. It took a while before they realized that even on the court, going after each other might not be a good idea.

Their favorite playground was in Grady Park, a half block up York-town Street from their apartment. The cement basketball court was in a corner of the park, surrounded by trees. It had a metal roof, to allow play on rainy days, but it was open on the sides. The court was well maintained, with cloth nets on the baskets.

They both loved the game. Both knew Levin was the better player. But Feinberg thought his stolid Captain Call might beat the gifted Gus McCrae if the game became a contest of endurance rather than skill. One Sunday afternoon in early 1995, when no one else was avail-able for a game, Feinberg suggested they go one-on-one. This time, he said, just to make it interesting, why not say the loser was whoever quit first? Feinberg kept to himself his theory that he might win a war of attrition.

It was chilly as they walked over to the court. Despite the weather, they were dressed in their usual T-shirts and shorts. The game was half-court, one point per basket. If a player scored, he kept possession of the ball. The first hour was good exercise but uneventful. So was the second. Levin had pulled ahead, about 100 to 60. They were not en-tirely sure of the precise score, but the numbers, under the endurance rule, had lost their meaning, and neither of them wanted to quit.

Feinberg kept his mental process as simple as possible. I am just not going to quit, and I am going to kick the shit out of him, he said to him-self. He did not have Levin's speed and agility, but he was as tall, had more muscle, and could force Levin to shoot from the outside. When Levin drove in for a layup, Feinberg stood in his way and bumped him back. No matter how or where Levin shot, Feinberg tried to make him pay—a shove in the chest, an elbow in the ribs, something.

Levin's unspoken response was, The harder you hit me, the more points I am going to score. He kept sinking jump shots. He could summon his dwindling energy for occasional bursts of speed that let him slip past his lane-blocking friend and go right to the basket. Take that, Mike!

They were both proud but also had senses of humor and analytical habits that allowed them to put the game in context. It was, they thought, a primal moment — two stags banging antlers at the top of a mountain. There was no woman involved. They were glad of that, because otherwise they might have killed each other. But the clash of wills was still exhausting, and painful. They passed the three-hour mark. When they reached four hours, they were only vaguely aware of the time or anything else. They were getting groggy, almost sleepwalking. Feinberg was still trying to be physical, getting in the way, looking to block shots, hoping to wear Levin down. But inertia had taken over. Neither of them was thinking clearly.

Completing their fifth hour, it began to dawn on them, dimly, that they might do serious damage to themselves if they let this go on much longer. Feinberg had a bloody lip from one collision. He was losing feeling in his legs. Levin had bruises all over his torso — marks of Feinberg's elbows. Levin was leading by more than 80 points. Feinberg was fixed on his mantra: Don't give up, don't give up, don't give up. But Feinberg was not surprised when his friend suggested a truce. Once again, he conceded, Levin was a bit more mature.

"Uh, Mike, this is getting a little ridiculous," Levin said, breathing hard. "We are really good friends, but this could turn into a fistfight. It could go on forever."

Feinberg smiled wearily and agreed. He wasn't going to claim victory. But at least he had not quit. "Let's get some wings," he said. Off they went to their usual postgame protein uploading at Wings 'N More on Westheimer Road.

It was a game to ponder and to tell ever more exaggerated stories about as the years went on, but they were glad it was over. They might soon be in different cities, never again having a chance to teach together or enjoy their time together as they did after the game, digging into the chicken wings as they slumped in their chairs.

Recruiting in Gulfton

THE DISTRICT 7 OFFICIALS in New York said they had a place for KIPP in the South Bronx. Patterson was moving ahead with her plan for KIPP at Lee High. But the school year was far from over. They had a heavy obligation to the forty-seven students they were still teaching at Garcia. Even if Feinberg stayed in Houston, it was unlikely his new school would have any place for their current fifth graders. They had to find good sixth-grade middle school classes worthy of these kids. Maybe there would be a way to bring them back to KIPP if Patterson kept her promise to let the program grow. Feinberg resolved to keep his eyes on his babies, as he called them, and make sure they were not mistreated if they had to leave his daily care.

Feinberg needed to find space and recruit students for next year's fifth grade. He liked the idea of relocating to Lee, but he did not want to put fifth graders in a classroom next to eleventh graders. It would make their parents uncomfortable. Instead, Patterson said he could get the space he needed, and separate his little kids from the big kids, by starting the new KIPP school in two modular buildings — sometimes called mobile or trailer classrooms — on a bare patch of land in back of the school.

Each of the two modulars would cost $22,000 and have space for two classrooms, a total of four rooms. Unfortunately, other schools in overcrowded Houston were fighting for the same equipment. The district had set up its own modular construction unit, cranking out buildings at a rapid clip, but that did not mean there would be enough for KIPP. Patterson had difficulty insisting that her request have priority, because she had some of the city's most affluent neighborhoods and her schools were less crowded than many others.

Recruiting students for KIPP looked simple. There were two elementary schools in Gulfton, Cunningham and Benavidez, with many children of the sort they wanted for KIPP. In March, Feinberg visited four fourth-grade classes at Cunningham and five at Benavidez. Most of the children's families had originated in Central America. There were also children of Mexican descent, like the Garcia students, as well as some from Vietnamese American and African American families.

Remembering the two students Esquith had brought with him when he spoke in Houston, Feinberg recruited two KIPP girls for his recruiting visits. They spent about twenty minutes with each fourth-grade class. Feinberg didn't want to bore his audience or overstay his welcome. He was trying to convey excitement and intrigue, using the script he and Levin had written the year before. Feinberg again cast himself as Mr. Feinberg, the talkative one. The two girls substituted for Levin, the helpful sidekick.

Feinberg asked where the fourth graders might like to go on a trip. He wrote on the blackboard their fantasy destinations — Disney World, AstroWorld, New York, Washington. He asked his student accomplices their opinion. "What do you think? If these guys came to KIPP, do you think we could do a trip to San Antonio?"

"Sure, Mr. Feinberg, we can do that," they said in confident voices.

"My favorite food is hamburgers," Feinberg said. "Do you think once a week we can grab McDonald's or something for lunch?"

The girls looked puzzled, as if dealing with a forgetful uncle: "Mr. Feinberg, we do that right now!"

The infomercial had the desired effect. The fourth graders at first looked bored, then disbelieving, then hopeful, then excited. The room began to buzz. The presence of the two older, worldly-wise fifth graders impressed them. Recruits later told Feinberg that what they remembered most vividly about their introduction to KIPP was not him but the two Garcia girls. They gave the exercise an authenticity that the fourth graders were not used to when visitors tried to sell them something.

Feinberg handed out the forms in each class. "This is not a sign-up form," he said. "We just want to see who is interested. I will come talk to you some more about it."

"What do you mean, you will come talk to us?" one girl asked.

"I will come to your homes," he said.

Some of the fourth graders seemed skeptical.

"Yeah, I will come to your homes," he insisted.

More than one hundred parents signed forms. Some of the fourth-grade teachers told Feinberg they'd recommended KIPP. This was not, he learned, always a selfless gesture. In some cases a teacher thought a child had gifts that would not be properly nurtured in a regular school. But in other cases a principal would sing the praises of KIPP because she wanted that kid out of her school as soon as possible.

Feinberg had room for three classes, about seventy-two students. He and Levin had decided, after much discussion, that this was the right size. If they had been able to persuade Ball to join them their first year at Garcia, they would have had seventy-two students right from the beginning. If there were many more than that, they thought, the personal connections between students and teachers would be harder to forge, particularly if their schools grew as planned to four grades, fifth through eighth. Significantly fewer students than seventy-two per grade would weaken their argument that KIPP could be a full-size school, with enough of an enrollment to justify its costs, rather than just a little program in a couple of rooms.

Feinberg planned to have two classrooms in one modular, and one classroom plus space for an office and individual tutoring in the other. He wanted to rotate three groups of twenty-four students each between the three classrooms, one for reading, one for math, and one for science and social studies. To do that, he needed at least two more teachers.

Levin could not help. There was too much to do in New York. Feinberg visited the Gulfton parents on his own, finding his fractured

Spanish sufficient for the task. If a parent asked him a question he did not understand, he looked at the prospective student and asked, "So what did your mom just say?" The more visits he made, the smoother his pitch in Spanish. To his surprise, he was beginning to feel awkward with his English-language pitch for those few black and Asian families, and one Anglo family, who needed it. It was a relief to crank up his much-practiced Spanish sales talk.

Gulfton had seventy-five thousand people jammed into three square miles. It appeared that both of Feinberg's roommates, Levin and Frank Corcoran, who was going to New York with Levin, were abandoning him. He would need a new place to live, something he could afford on his own. Why not Gulfton? In May he rented a ground-floor apartment in Lantern Village, a complex full of immigrant families. He moved into unit 4109 in Building 41. The apartment had five hundred square feet, with one bedroom, one bath, a kitchen, and a living room, all for $440 a month.

He liked the cheap rent. Both he and Levin were teased for being excessively frugal, which pleased them. Feinberg also found his new address useful in recruiting. His apartment was across the street from Burnett Bayland Park, known for gang activity and drug dealing. As a resident, he had credibility when he said he wanted to help local kids. "Our neighborhood needs to be better," he told parents.

The parents, more often than not, smiled and nodded. They were happy to make the acquaintance of a teacher who thought so much of them that he had moved into the neighborhood. They and their children signed the Commitment to Excellence forms. KIPP Academy Houston was in business.

Serenading Bill

ESQUITH TOLD FEINBERG and Levin to prepare their students for travel—the big trip to Washington, D.C., in May 1995—as if they were a network crew about to cover the Olympics. They had to learn protocol and decorum for what was, to disadvantaged urban children, a foreign land of airplanes, hotels, museums, and national monuments. The two teachers taught lessons on the paintings in the East Room, the statuary in the Capitol, the functions of the federal departments, and the words emblazoned on the monuments to Mr. Jefferson and Mr. Lincoln.

As they had warned, not everyone qualified for the trip. About a half-dozen students had spent too much time on the Porch and too little time on their studies. The week their classmates were in Washington, they were assigned to sit in the back of classrooms of other Garcia teachers and read more about the places the class was visiting.

The forty excited fifth graders who made the trip discovered that school was still in session even after they landed at Baltimore-Washington International Airport on Continental Airlines, which had given Feinberg and Levin a good deal. The teachers would henceforth call these journeys field lessons, not field trips. On the bus from the airport to their hotel in Arlington, Virginia, they encouraged students to observe, reflect, and learn. "Look at what different types of trees grow here, compared to Houston," Feinberg said as they rumbled south on I-95. "This is the mid-Atlantic region, so different from our Gulf Coast."

It was an expensive venture to take so many children so far. The teachers did everything they could to save money. For instance, the ghosts of their afternoon dodgeball games reappeared once they got to the hotel, with a different purpose in mind. Their reservation was at the Embassy Suites Hotel in Crystal City, a strip of commercial and office properties along Jefferson Davis Highway in Arlington County, close to National Airport. Each room cost $119 a night. The suites with two beds in the bedroom and a pullout couch in the living room were supposed to have no more than six guests. The king-size single-bed suites were supposed to have no more than four guests. But Levin and Feinberg, remembering their crowded college dorms, decided that was a waste of useful space. When Embassy Suites declined their request to put more students in each room for the same price, they did it anyway. They assigned seven students, plus an adult chaperone, to each of the larger suites, and six students plus a chaperone to each of the smaller suites.

The excess students in each room were told that they were ghosts, just as in dodgeball. They were invisible, but they had to act like it. No booing or chain rattling was allowed. They were to be quiet and unseen. Vanessa Ramirez's mother, Sara, was uncomfortable with this. Her daughter saw her cringe as the ghost system was explained. But Ramirez was ready to follow Mr. Feinberg and Mr. Levin anywhere, so she said nothing.

Feinberg told the students and the chaperoning parents that stuffing more kids into each room was just an economical way to travel. It would also, he said, make the group more cohesive and less likely to get into trouble. "We are going to show you how to behave in a hotel," he said. "If we walk in, and there is a lot of noise, the hotel people are going to ask themselves, how many kids are in that group? Instead, we want them to think of us as a party of one. If we make no more noise than just one person, it will work fine."

He saw skeptical looks. "We have had to raise money for this trip," he said, "and we would love to give everyone his or her own luxury suite, but that's not affordable." Feinberg and Levin had also calculated that the fewer rooms they had, the fewer chaperones they needed, cutting their costs even more. Years later, asked if defrauding an innkeeper fit with KIPP's emphasis on doing the right thing, Feinberg and Levin said it was a gray area. They continued to feel the hotel could have done more to welcome them, but they agreed that they could be said to have stepped over the line. But, they added, if they had paid the full bill, they would not have been able to take as many students, and that would have been, in their minds, a great loss.

Esquith had recommended Embassy Suites. Hotels in that chain were relatively inexpensive. Each was built around a central courtyard with dining tables that offered a huge money saver — free breakfast. Feinberg advised the students to take advantage of this nutritious opportunity. Add to their breakfast tray a couple of bagels and an extra apple, and they would have a delicious snack for later.

That wasn't enough of a lunch for hungry ten-year-olds, of course. The class's midday meal was an even more elaborate project: the peanut-butter-and-jelly-sandwich assembly line. It was a Feinberg and Levin idea, for which they endured many jokes. Buying lunch at restaurants would have killed their budget. Instead they found a local discount supermarket and loaded up with plastic sandwich bags, brown paper bags, bread, peanut butter, jelly, apples, and small bags of potato chips. Different rooms took turns each night making bag lunches for the entire class. Embassy Suites kitchenettes became assembly areas for the sandwiches and bagged lunches. One child put peanut butter on one slice of bread. The next child spread jelly on the other slice. The next child assembled the sandwich and put it in a plastic bag. Sandwich, apple, and chips were dumped in the paper bag, and the process began again. The sandwich crew played a radio or boom box for inspiration. The assembly line rocked on.

The children in each hotel room, ghosts and otherwise, were supervised by kings and queens, the Levin-Feinberg terms for parent and teacher chaperones. Mothers liked being called queens. Whenever the KIPP group arrived at or left a destination, the children were instructed to gather around their king or queen. Each sovereign counted his or her subjects. If none were missing, they gave Feinberg and Levin the thumbs-up sign and the group moved on.

Transportation in Washington was by the Metro, the students' first time in an underground train. They practiced subway etiquette. Going up and down the big escalators, they were reminded to stand on the right and walk on the left. Levin and Feinberg stood in front of each turnstile and inserted the fare cards themselves. Kings or queens would grab the fare cards as they popped back up at the end of the turnstile and keep them in their wallets or purses.

The fifth graders were excited, and yet there were disappointments. They had looked forward to seeing the White House. Their teachers had devoted many lessons to the famous building. There was speculation that they might even see President Clinton. But Feinberg and Levin had not anticipated the crucial difference between tourists, accustomed to being hustled from one sight to another, and KIPP students, taught to observe and reflect on what they had observed.

The group waited patiently in the long line for the White House tour. Levin and Feinberg reviewed for them what they would see, including the historical significance of each sight. But once they were inside, everything went too fast. Their guide kept telling them to move along, move along. In the Red Room, Levin and Feinberg tried to slow it down.

"Remember this from our studies?" Feinberg said. "Who remembers about this furniture? Who used to work in this room? What presidents are on the wall? Can you look at the wall and tell me which person there was *not* a president?"

Several hands went up. Levin pointed to one boy who said, "Benjamin Franklin?"

"Very good."

The official guides were disapproving. Lessons were cut short. The students made the best of it. Later they climbed to the top of the Washington Monument. They looked for the statues of Sam Houston and Stephen Austin in the Capitol. They tested the strange echo effect in the Old House Chamber, which had allowed John Quincy Adams to overhear what his legislative adversaries were saying.

But it was all rush-rush. The Supreme Court was particularly bad. They had only thirty minutes to view the busts of the chief justices, peek at the court chamber, and move on. Out in front of the building, Levin and Feinberg tried an impromptu lesson on the architectural traditions represented by the columns along the massive front portico. Feinberg was testing them on the difference between Doric and Corinthian when he noticed a familiar-looking man in a suit walking by. It was Stephen Breyer, one of the newest justices.

A teachable moment! Feinberg was thrilled. He caught up with Breyer and began talking very fast. "Justice Breyer, Justice Breyer, you've got to come over here. You've got to meet our kids from Houston."

Breyer gave Feinberg a polite smile. "I'd love to," he said, "but I have a meeting in my chambers."

"You don't understand. These are the hardest-working kids in the country. They go to school from seven thirty to five, four hours on Saturday, summer school every summer." Breyer realized he wasn't going anywhere, short of knocking this frantic person down and running for the door. "Okay," he said. "I'll come over for a minute."

"Boys and girls, this is Justice Breyer, a member of the U.S. Supreme Court," said Feinberg, proud of his catch. "You know the Supreme Court justices. How many are there?"

That was an easy one. "*Nine!*" said every child.

Breyer gave his small audience a twenty-second greeting. "I hear you boys and girls work very hard in school. I am very pleased to hear that. Good job. Please keep that up." He turned to leave, but Ruben Garcia, the little brother of the boy who had been pictured in the *Houston Post* article, raised his hand.

"Ruben?" Feinberg said. "Do you have a question?"

"Yes," he said. Breyer stopped and looked at him.

"Were you here in 1969 when the court voted on *Miranda v. Arizona*?" the ten-year-old asked.

Breyer's eyes widened. Who were these kids? "Why, no," he said hesitantly. "That was before my time."

"Oh," Ruben said. He thought about this for a moment and then raised his hand again. "Well," he said, "if you had been here, how would you have voted on that case?"

Breyer shook his head in astonishment. Feinberg and Levin high-fived each other. The justice decided that for such an appreciative audience, his appointment could wait. He answered questions about habeas corpus and the rights of prisoners and the Bill of Rights. It was a minilecture on the Constitution, and it would not be the last time he received a group of fifth graders from KIPP.

On the last day, a Friday, Levin and Feinberg told the group that as a special treat they could visit the National Peanut Butter and Jelly Factory. It was an incredible place, the teachers said. "You can get crunchy peanut butter or creamy peanut butter, and as for jelly, there is strawberry and apple and grape and apricot," Feinberg said. "And what about the bread, Mr. Levin?"

"Every kind you can imagine," Levin said. "Rye, sourdough, wheat, pumpernickel — anything."

The students nodded wearily. This sounded odd, but they were accustomed to their teachers' peculiar tastes. They were sick of peanut butter and jelly, but they had to be polite. There was a national everything else in Washington, so maybe a national sandwich factory was not so far fetched.

At 5:00 p.m., at the corner of Eleventh and Pennsylvania, Levin and Feinberg told them to organize themselves into proper groups. Those who wanted sourdough bread had to line up in one spot. Those who preferred rye had to be in another. There was a crunchy-peanut-butter group and a group for those who preferred the smooth variety. Some students noticed that Levin and Feinberg had strange looks on their faces. They could not keep it up anymore. They confessed it was all a joke. They were standing a half block from Planet Hollywood, and that was where they were going to have dinner. There would be hamburgers and fries, to erase their students' peanut butter and jelly memories.

After a loud and happy dinner, as the sun was setting, Levin and Feinberg thought everyone needed quiet time to reflect on all they had seen and heard. In a few weeks they would learn that KIPP had been judged an unqualified success, based on its TAAS scores. Only about half their students had passed the state tests when they were fourth graders. After a year of Feinberg and Levin, more than 90 percent of them had passed both the math and the reading tests. This news pleased the teachers, but it was not a surprise. Like all good educators, they could tell well before the tests were given that their students had come a long way.

"This is our last time to be in a place away from Houston," Feinberg said to the group as they gathered outside the restaurant. "We want to soak up all the sights, the sounds, the smells, in this different place. This is our last stroll through D.C. We are going to walk in complete silence and take everything in."

The forty children, plus kings, queens, and teachers, walked up Pennsylvania Avenue. They passed the Old Post Office building, the old Willard Hotel, and the Treasury Department and finally reached the White House. It was not difficult to keep quiet. There was much to see. It was a pleasant, warm evening. Their stomachs were full of restaurant food. They stopped in front of 1600 Pennsylvania Avenue. Some stood on the little brick ledge of the White House fence, holding on to the iron gateposts as they peered at the president's house.

Two girls, Melissa Johnson and Danielle Malone, began to lead a serenade of their favorite songs and chants. They did "Read, Baby, Read." They did "This Is the Room." Harriett Ball's words soared into the soft spring air.

They were not in school. They were in Washington, D.C. But it was Friday, the day when KIPP often had songfests. What better place to show who they were? They sang songs like "I'm Just a Bill" and "No More Kings" from *Schoolhouse Rock,* a popular video series used at KIPP. Passersby stopped and listened. What was this? A demonstration? A protest? In the spring of 1995, there were many things to be upset about, but these children were singing happy songs. The growing crowd inspired them to sing louder. Between songs, the Kippsters would chant: "We want Bill! We want Bill!"

A Chevrolet Suburban with Secret Service markings pulled up, but the agents seemed just to be enjoying the music. Feinberg saw on the White House roof a security guard who was waving his hands, as if he were leading the choir. And in one window of the executive mansion, several students saw what appeared to be a man waving. There was no way to tell if it was the president, but the consensus that night was that Bill had heard their concert.

The students completed their repertoire to loud applause. Levin and Feinberg guided them toward the Metro stop for their return to the Embassy Suites. That night's sandwich-assembly team prepared another fifty lunches, then went to bed, more than ready to get up the next morning and go home.

Changing Places

PLANS FOR THE SECOND year of KIPP moved ahead, a tale of two cities. Levin was going to New York. Feinberg was staying in Houston. Feinberg would have preferred to keep their Garcia KIPP class with him as sixth graders, but he had neither the space, the transportation, nor the administrative support to make that happen. Feinberg said he would look for a way to bring the sixth graders back, a promise he eventually kept.

For the seventy-two new KIPP fifth graders, Feinberg planned three teachers besides himself, one for reading, one for science, and one for social studies. Feinberg would teach math for half of each day and do management chores the rest of the time. Patterson said she would provide the modular classrooms, the food, and the payroll services and have an allotment of $2,200 per pupil for everything else — primarily salaries. That was enough for four staff members at standard Houston salaries. Feinberg had made $21,500 his first year and as a third-year teacher had reached $24,500. It was not much, but he was young and had no dependents. He planned to hire people just like himself.

Each of his teachers would be paid what Feinberg was making, plus an extra $5,000 for the longer school days, Saturdays, and summer classes. With the cost of benefits, that left no money to pay himself for his extra time, so from the beginning he was the lowest-paid teacher at his school.

Finding the right teachers turned out to be more difficult than he had expected. His former college girlfriend, Allison Bieber, had a twin sister, Laurie, who was teaching high school in the upscale Philadelphia suburb of Cherry Hill. She had a master's degree in education from the University of Pennsylvania and some useful classroom experience in rugged parts of West Philadelphia. She agreed to work for Feinberg in Houston.

He was still two teachers short, with KIPP summer school scheduled to begin in a month, when disaster struck. The modular classrooms Patterson had promised were suddenly unavailable. The two she had ordered had been shipped to someone with more clout. Two more were being built, but they would not be ready until August, too late for the KIPP summer session. If Feinberg was going to have summer school, it would have to wait until just before the regular school year began in August.

Feinberg responded to this crisis by giving himself more things to do. Teach For America officials in Houston asked him to be a faculty director during their summer institute. He agreed, a decision that made no sense but turned out well anyway. At the institute, he found his second teacher, Mike Farabaugh. He had been part of the Texas House crowd at the summer institute in 1992, then taught at a school in the Rio Grande Valley. He had a sense of humor and an energetic classroom style.

Feinberg's third hire was Jill Kolasinski, who had completed just one year in Teach For America. She thought KIPP was a wonderful idea, but her supervisors at her Houston middle school were not happy with her forsaking them for an untested and unpredictable experiment. If Kolasinski went to KIPP, she would be counted as a Teach For America dropout. She went anyway and would eventually run her own KIPP school. Before long, many TFA corps members were cleared to work at KIPP.

Feinberg was excited. He had his teachers. He had his space. He had what he considered a brilliant new plan for reading instruction. His students would be two or three years below grade level, so he would make the first few months all about reading. Bieber would teach reading along with history. Farabaugh would teach reading along with science. Kolasinski would teach reading along with language arts. Feinberg himself would teach reading along with math. They would talk about college every day. Feinberg decreed that they would each put their college diplomas on their classroom walls.

One afternoon, Feinberg showed Farabaugh the Lee High facilities. During the week, Feinberg said, they would have to stay in their modular classrooms. Their students could not mix with high schoolers. But for Saturday class, they would have the run of the high school building. They could use the computer labs. They could give swimming lessons in the pool. And then that dream died too. Patterson called to say that Lee was overenrolled by more than four hundred students. It would need the new modulars for its own students. "There is no room for us at the high school anymore," she said.

Feinberg went into denial. "What are you talking about?" he said. "This is completely unacceptable! We had this all arranged."

"Mike, Mike. I am *not* leaving you hanging. Slow down, slow down. I am committed to this."

"What are we going to do?"

"I don't know," she said. "But we are going to figure this out somehow. I am going to find you a place." She did, three days later, at Askew Elementary School. "They have three extra modular classrooms they don't need," she said. "And they have a supply closet full of junk that it looks like nobody has touched in twenty years. If somebody cleaned it up, you could turn it into an office."

Feinberg asked how far away Askew was from Lee. Thirty minutes, Patterson said. In which direction? The wrong direction. It was in an affluent neighborhood with few immigrant families. That was why it had extra space. It was thirty minutes farther away from Gulfton than Lee High was. It would be a forty-five-minute bus trip for the KIPP students.

Feinberg wondered how he could feel any worse about the turn of events, but then he realized what an embarrassing blow this was to his credibility with the Gulfton parents. He had dismissed their fears about sending their nine- and ten-year-olds to a high school campus.

He had told them it would be perfectly safe because their children would be arriving before the high school students and leaving after they left. He had sold the parents on the wonderful facilities, the pool, and the computers.

But with Lee no longer available, he had to go back and tell each family that the high school plan had been scrapped. He developed an entirely different pitch. He told them he had found space in an elementary school far to the west, in one of the best parts of town. There were no drugs, no gangs, no fighting, no distractions. He promised them terrific bus service, which would pick kids up at nearly every Gulfton corner and take them to and from Askew with the ultimate convenience.

He feared this would all sound false to them, but no one objected. He was their neighbor. He had shown them respect and trust by visiting their homes. Yes, Mr. Feinberg, they said. That sounded fine. Thank you very much for telling us.

24

Harriett and Herman

A DECADE BEFORE she encountered Levin and Feinberg, Harriett
Franks had met her future second husband, Herman Ball. It was 1983
and she was still working in Austin. She was an elementary school
counselor, a lively divorcée with four children. Herman Ball was a
school district maintenance supervisor. He was a big, shy man who
often came by to ask if she needed anything.

"How you doing, Ms. Franks?" he would say with a small smile.
"We need to fix those shelves of yours." Or he might be bolder and
say, "We are leaving for lunch, Ms. Franks. Would you like us to bring
you back lunch?"

He and his crew would sometimes sit with her and other staffers
having lunch or a soda break in the teachers' lounge. Harriett and
Herman never spoke like boyfriend and girlfriend. He did not have
the confidence for that. But with each conversation, he gained courage. One day, while he installed new shelves in her office closet, he
took a deep breath and tried to tell her how he felt about her.

"I know you don't have time for much," he said. "You got your kids,
but I've been watching you. I know the church you attend, and I watch
you sing in church."

"How do you know that?"

"I followed you," he said. "I always sat where you wouldn't see me.
Then I left after the sermon."

Her eyes widened. She had never had a stalker before. He did not
seem very dangerous.

He kept talking, trying to get it all out before he lost his nerve. "I never did want you to know that I liked you. I was in the room that day you sang those songs, and remember when you tripped?"

"You were there? Why didn't I ever get to see you?"

"As soon as I saw you standing at the end of the sermon, I would walk out. I always sat in the back at the opposite end so I could get to watch you."

Amazed, she smiled at him. "Well, I'll be doggoned," she said.

He seemed delighted that she was still talking to him. She had not called the police. "I was there at Christmas too," he said. He named the times and places he had gotten a glimpse of her. It was hard, he said, to feel about a person that way but only be able to see her by sitting in the back of her church. He could not believe she could have any feelings for him. She was nice to him, but she was that way with everyone. He was a maintenance man and she was a counselor. She had a college degree and he did not.

She smiled at that. He was a good man, and he loved her. She continued to see him but realized she no longer wanted to stay in Austin. Her ex-husband and many bad memories were there. She had to move. She regretted that she would not be able to see Herman anymore, but she had made up her mind. She told him she was heading to Houston.

He was quiet for a moment, then spoke up: "I will go up there with you."

She was astonished. "You can't leave your job, and I have to take my kids."

"No, really," he said. "I know you don't believe me, but I want to help."

He drove her to Houston to look for a house. After she moved, with all four children, he made the two-hour drive from Austin to Houston several weekends to see her. Her children adored him. He was more like their father than their real father, she thought. He took time to read to them and carry them on his back. He taught them how to ride bicycles. He taught them how to swim and protect themselves from bullies.

So in 1985 she married him. He moved to Houston and became

more a part of her life than any other man she had known. She wondered how she had gotten so lucky. Before she married him, every morning had been rush, rush, rush, getting the children ready and off to school, figuring out what to do about dinner. He insisted on taking over much of that burden. "You're older than me, and I want to preserve you," he said. "You don't need to cook."

"But I need to —"

"Sit down," he said.

"But I need to —"

"Sit down."

"But I got to get the clothes washed."

"I will take care of it." He had difficulty breaking her of the habit of handling everything, but he kept at it. "Just lay back, just lay back," he said. "Get some rest."

He cooked for the children. He combed their hair. He gave her son haircuts. Each morning he drove the two oldest to high school and returned to walk her younger children to the neighborhood school. He escorted them across a busy street, hoping she would sleep in. Then he brought her breakfast. "Look what Daddy got you," he said, and laid out her clothes for work.

One day in 1990, Herman told Harriett he was going over to his sister's place in southwest Houston for a fish fry. At some point that night, Herman was on his way back to his sister's apartment in his sister's car, which was being recklessly driven by an eighteen-year-old who had been invited to the party. Harriett was later told that somehow Herman put his foot on the brake and stopped the car. Herman got out. When the driver didn't get out, Herman went over to the driver's side to talk to him. The eighteen-year-old didn't want to talk. He had a gun. He shot Herman in the arm.

One of Herman's nephews, who was in the backseat, later told Harriett that Herman fell to his knees, clutching his arm. "Why did you shoot me?" he asked, hurt and astonished. "I was just trying to protect the car."

The eighteen-year-old got out and shot him again. Herman slumped over. The driver ran away. Passersby called police and an ambulance. But it was too late.

Several hours passed before Harriett found out. Herman had spent the night at his sister's before. When he didn't return that night, she was not alarmed.

When his sister called the next morning to tell her Herman had been shot dead, Harriett didn't believe her. The woman was always playing crazy jokes. "Let me talk to Herman," Harriett said. But he was gone.

KIPP Today:
Jaquan Climbs the Mountain

When Susan Schaeffler opened the KIPP DC: KEY Academy in the summer of 2001, she had one teacher for fifth-grade reading and writing, one for math, one for science, and one for social studies. When Jaquan Hall arrived at the school five years later, Schaeffler's successor as KEY principal, Sarah Hayes, had more money from D.C. charter school funds and donations. She could afford a fifth-grade team with five teachers: Mekia Love for reading, Andrea Smith for math, Julia Buergler for writing, Emily Foote for social studies, and Irene Holtzman, who doubled as the school's operations director, for science.

The first Feinberg and Levin KIPP class had been made up of fifth graders because that was the grade their principal wanted them to teach. They decided to create fifth-through-eighth-grade middle schools in their respective cities because they wanted to take advantage of their experience with fifth graders and because eighth grade in Houston and New York was usually the last step before high school.

There were other fifth-through-eighth-grade middle schools around the country, but that model was less common than sixth through eighth or seventh through eighth. Over time, Levin and Feinberg came to see their fifth-grade starting point as a fortunate accident. Fifth graders, they felt, tended to retain a child's desire to please adults. The hormonal and cultural pressures of preadolescence had not yet made them more of an instructional challenge. With ten-year-olds, teachers had a chance to instill habits of learning and classroom behavior, a team and family spirit, that could carry their students through the restless preteen years and establish a foundation for high school and college.

Charter schools like KEY were public schools, paid for with tax dollars, but they didn't have to follow the rules of their school districts, such as sending students home at 2:00 or 3:00 p.m. The five fifth-grade teachers at KEY had enough time in their nine-hour day to meet regularly and discuss individual students like Jaquan. They also had time to give those students extra instruction in their weakest subjects.

Most public schools had only a six-and-a-half-hour day. Some experts were suggesting that all schools increase instructional time. But it was expensive. Studies showed the time would be wasted if schools were not well run. KIPP officials had estimated that their schools were spending on average 13 percent more money than regular public schools, mostly because of higher teacher salaries to pay for the longer day. The extra funds came from private donations and government grants.

The fifth-grade team's conversations about Jaquan Hall were usually upbeat, even though he started the year at the bottom of his class in most subjects. He was cheerful and cooperative. They were confident he would rise to the level of his obvious intelligence, as soon as he developed the habits of mind and behavior they were there to encourage.

To their minds, his mother was sometimes a problem. Sharron Hall was very busy, with a job and three other children. At times she found it difficult to get to the school when Jaquan was put on the Bench, the KEY version of the Porch. There were not many parking spaces on the commercial strip where the school was located. Hall wondered out loud if some of the meetings were necessary. But once she got to the school, she was very supportive of the teachers' decisions about her son and had useful ideas for motivating him.

By November 2006, three months into Jaquan's fifth-grade year, his five teachers had gathered a great deal of data about him. Each of them had a laptop computer with test scores and class exercise results. They exchanged ideas on how to adjust their approach with each student in order to have the best effect.

Smith, the math teacher, was a slender woman with a crown of curly blond hair. She thought Jaquan's main handicap was that he was young for his grade. He had just turned ten in the middle of November. She blamed his restlessness and lack of focus on that. He had to be reminded frequently to SLANT — the KIPP acronym for "Sit up straight, look listen, ask questions, nod your head, and track the teacher." He rushed through his assignments, failing to answer some questions, particularly those that required him to read a few explanatory sentences. He made careless errors. The team agreed to give him an extra hour a day of math in one of their Climbing the Mountain classes, designed for students who needed extra help.

Smith's math classes were fast paced and complex. She had games, competitions, and short quizzes to see where every child stood. The Ball chants that had launched KIPP were still there, but Smith had added her own touches. This was typical of KIPP teachers. The year before, at the AIM Academy, KEY's new sister school across the Anacostia River, a twenty-five-year-old fifth-grade math teacher named Lisa Suben had asked if she could use an approach different from the standard KIPP curriculum. She had had success in Mississippi teaching math with a different sequence and more reliance on projects — what some educators might call a constructivist approach. Schaeffler, the director of all KIPP DC schools, and the AIM principal, Khala Johnson, were astonished that a newcomer would have the brass to discard the Ball-Levin-Feinberg playbook, but teacher creativity was part of the KIPP creed, as long as the results were good. Johnson and Schaeffler gave their permission. At the end of the year, Suben had produced one of the biggest one-year achievement jumps in KIPP history, from the 16th to the 71st percentile on the Stanford Achievement Test 10.

Smith's record for raising student achievement was also good. One of her tests in early November was a subtraction speed drill. She handed out sheets with 100 simple problems. Each student had just three minutes to complete them. At the beginning of the year, most students got no more than 20 or 30 correct in that short time. Jaquan's score then was 22. In the November exercise, he had 52 correct. Several students in the class were in the 90s. Smith had begun to give similar speed drills in multiplication and division. Her goal was to help the class do better each week than they had the previous week. Once the algorithms were ingrained, they could move on to more advanced topics. At KIPP, all students started first-year algebra, usually a high school course, in seventh grade and in most cases had completed it by the end of eighth grade.

Much of Jaquan's problem, Smith thought, was conceptual. He needed to improve his reading and writing before he could improve his math. If he had to explain what he was doing on one of her quizzes, he left that question blank. She focused on helping him think more about concepts, while the entire team worked on his reading.

Holtzman, a woman with long brown hair and a firm grasp of the KIPP approach in all subjects, was delighted to find Jaquan full of excited questions in her science class. Like most of her students, he was free of preconceptions, or any conceptions at all, about her subject. The D.C. schools that fed into KEY did not have much time for science. They had to focus on reading and math scores. Jaquan was excited about Holtzman's plans to mix chemicals and breed animals. He was keeping up with the best students in the class in absorbing scientific facts, but he had difficulty expressing in writing what he knew.

Foote, a fun-loving instructor who had transferred from a KIPP school in Philadelphia, discovered that, as with many of her social studies students, Jaquan's low reading level slowed his progress. Her class was for him an extra hour of reading practice, with nonfiction texts that she hoped would stretch his literary muscles. But the vocabulary was very difficult for him.

Buergler's writing class became one of Jaquan's favorites. A slender woman with long, dark hair, Buergler often had students stand and wiggle and sing and dance, waving their arms about. Jaquan's writing was as rudimentary as his reading, but by November he had improved. He still sometimes forgot to capitalize the word at the beginning of a sentence, to write in complete sentences, to include all punctuation, and to have his subjects agree with his verbs. But when Buergler pointed out such errors, he corrected them quickly.

He made no secret that he loved Love, his reading teacher. She was a tall woman, gentle and patient. The other team members teased her about the soft spot she had for the little boy who gave her a hug each morning. The team knew that reading was the key to everything. KIPP students, and elementary students in general in the United States, were improving more in math than in reading. Learning theorists said good teaching could have an immediate effect in math, since it was a subject that children usually learned only in school. Reading, by contrast, required them to overcome language lapses they had picked up at home and to recover from the lack of early exposure to books.

When Love gave Jaquan a fifth-grade reading passage, he could decode—that is, pronounce correctly—most of it. But his comprehension was considerably less. She worked on showing him how to analyze what he had read and how to predict what came next. He was easily distracted, so she worked on his stamina. She wanted him strong enough to sit and read a book for fifteen minutes without stopping.

Habits of behavior were crucial. Each child had to find a way to stay focused on learning, obey the rules, and develop the spirit of consideration for other students that the KIPP teachers felt would pay benefits for the rest of their lives. The fifth-grade team at first worried that the extremely social Jaquan was becoming friendly with older boys who had behavior problems themselves. But this became less of an issue, even as his homework problems grew.

He was benched for missing too many assignments. It took two weeks for his mother to find a place in her schedule when she could meet with Smith and Jaquan after school to discuss the matter. Smith explained to Hall that not only did Jaquan miss homework assignments, but much of the work he turned in was of poor quality. His mother looked at him: "Jaquan, I have responsibilities as your mother, and you have responsibilities too. One of those is to complete your homework." He had started playing peewee football, his mother told Smith. "If you want to keep playing football," she said to her son, "you will have to keep your grades up and complete your homework."

Jaquan was fidgety. His mother more than once told him to keep still and look at Ms. Smith while she was speaking. Smith liked what the mother had said. "This is not something we take lightly, Jaquan," the teacher said. "We take homework seriously here because it is how you practice, how you practice the skills that you learn, just like you practice football."

The boy was not accustomed to this kind of conversation with teachers. In his previous schools, the tendency had been to give little homework and to shrug off failure to complete it. He did not cry during the meeting with his mother and his teacher. He said he was sorry. He admitted he had been wrestling with his brothers the night before, when he should have been spending more time on his homework. He promised to do better.

Starting Two Schools

25

"Them Jews Are
Stealing Your Stuff"

IN HOUSTON, EVERYONE Levin knew was a teacher or was involved in education in some way. His whole world was the KIPP kids and Feinberg and their Teach For America friends. He was committed to teaching, but he wanted to be where his life could be more than that. By moving back to New York, he would have that chance.

Feinberg came with him to the South Bronx during spring vacation in 1995 to help recruit students. With them was Frank Corcoran, their latest roommate in Houston, who had agreed to join Levin as the other teacher at KIPP New York. Levin was going to start with just fifty students, twenty-two fewer than Feinberg was planning to have in Houston. He thought it was better to start smaller in a school system that was so new to him and in which KIPP had no track record. He thought he could do it with just the two of them teaching, plus an administrator to handle paperwork and other details.

If there was ever an odd couple, it was not Levin and Feinberg, but Levin and Corcoran. Corcoran was Catholic. Levin was Jewish. Corcoran was quiet. Levin always had something to say. Corcoran was Notre Dame. Levin was Yale. Corcoran was passive and self-effacing. Levin was aggressive and ambitious.

Corcoran had been intimidated by his two roommates. To him, they were big, loud dynamos, full of plans and schemes and energy. At first he had been more familiar with Feinberg, since they had been teaching at the same school for two years. For the first few weeks living with the KIPP boys, he barely spoke to Levin at all. But Levin liked him and made a point of talking to him every day. Their conversations about what was happening in their classrooms became a daily routine. They grew close and were to live and work together for the next ten years.

Maxine O'Connor, the principal of P.S. 156 in the South Bronx, had given Levin permission to set up a KIPP fifth grade in two of her classrooms. Her dark-brick elementary school drew students from several nearby housing projects. To encourage her cooperation, Levin and Feinberg had paid to fly her to Houston in January to watch them teach. She appeared friendly and supportive, an attitude that would seem to Levin to change drastically after he established his program at her school.

During their spring visit, Levin, Feinberg, and Corcoran looked for KIPP recruits in the fourth-grade classrooms at local elementary schools. Levin and Feinberg put on their usual show, with Corcoran watching and taking notes. They promised a trip to Disney World. They promised Saturdays at McDonald's. They guaranteed all kinds of fun for those students who agreed to a longer school day and more homework. They distributed leaflets in both English and Spanish in the housing projects. They visited students' apartments.

But the reception was cooler than in Houston. Many South Bronx parents indicated that they thought the three young men were insane to believe they were going to do much in this part of the nation's biggest city. They were called crazy white boys and other words to that effect. Some parents considered them one more intrusion by the system, something to be tolerated rather than embraced.

Levin, Corcoran, and Feinberg saw depressing differences between the poor but hopeful culture of the families they knew in Houston and the more cynical and apathetic attitudes of many families in the South Bronx. The Mexican American and Central American parents in Houston saw themselves on the way up. Their apartments were cramped and their jobs low paying, but they were better off than they

had been before they came north. The environment for African American, Dominican, and Puerto Rican parents in the South Bronx was
less hopeful. Entire buildings had been abandoned to rats and drug
dealers and vagrants. Police were sometimes abusive. The schools were
disappointing. They had seen programs like KIPP come and go.

Feinberg had no more time to help in the Bronx, but Levin and
Corcoran kept trying. When Garcia closed for the summer in May,
they went back to New York and resumed recruiting. They wanted at
least forty-six students, and soon, so they could start summer school.
Despite the widespread skepticism among local parents, some families
were still willing to take a chance with KIPP, since the program would
be in the same building as P.S. 156, which their children would attend
anyway. The longer school hours, plus the Saturday and summer sessions, would in some ways make their lives easier. If these young men
wanted to provide what amounted to free after-school care, plus free
child care every other Saturday morning and for three weeks each
summer, why not? It would be helpful while it lasted, which was not
likely to be very long.

The only advantage the South Bronx had over Houston, from the
KIPP perspective, was that Levin did not have to worry about getting
his students to school. Back in Gulfton, Feinberg was tearing out what
little hair he had left trying to arrange the bus routes. P.S. 156, on the
other hand, was located in one of the most densely populated neighborhoods in the country. Levin and Corcoran's students could mostly
walk to school. Even the short trips had their dangers, with bullies and
gangs, but Levin would not have to worry about buses.

That advantage would be meaningless if he did not find enough
students. A week before his summer school was to start in June, he
had forty-three recruits, three fewer than he needed under city staffing rules to be able to pay both himself and Corcoran. One of his
last recruiting opportunities was a student registration meeting for
all grades at a nearby high school. He made sure he was there on time,
but at the door to the auditorium, an event organizer armed with a
clipboard would not let him in.

"I'm Dave Levin," he said. "I'm a teacher and the principal of a new program at P.S. 156."

"I'm sorry," the woman said. "You are not on our list. We don't really know who you are. Where were you teaching last year?"

"Uh, well, in Houston, but I'm all set up for here this year. I just need to find a few more students. I'm sure the parents here would be glad for an opportunity to get one of our flyers. I don't plan to pressure anyone."

"Sorry, can't do it. You're not authorized."

Levin had been sneaking into New York public school gyms and playgrounds since he was fifteen. Auditoriums usually had other entrances. He found one and slipped inside, trying to be inconspicuous. He approached likely parents with a whispered pitch: "Listen, I am starting a new program for fifth graders at a public school near here. We take the kids from seven thirty to five, and every other Saturday morning and three weeks in the summer. Would you like to sign up? Do you know any other fifth graders?"

He stuck out like a streetlamp. Eventually he was spotted and escorted out. Just barely enough parents contacted him to fill out the class, but each new day revealed how hard this was going to be and how few of the promises made to him were being kept. His three-week summer school was blocked by O'Connor, who had seemed so friendly when she came down to Houston in January. Unlike Garcia, which had a regular summer session when KIPP began in 1994, P.S. 156 was closed for the season. There would be no security, no janitors. Levin was told to forget it.

Levin had made his decision. There was no turning back. But before he left Houston for good, he had one more important duty. Harriett Ball was getting married again. She asked Levin to give her away.

Levin was fully aware of the amusement among both his and Ball's friends at the sight of the lanky twenty-five-year-old standing in as the father of the forty-eight-year-old bride. He didn't care. He could not contain his delight. His relationship with Ball was one of the anchors of his new life as a teacher. She had gotten him started. She had shown him how even he, as awkward as he had been his first months at Bastian, could reach those kids. She had taught him all her secrets. He was overjoyed to return the favor, at least in part, by playing a major role in one of the big scenes of her life.

Feinberg joined him at the small wedding in the backyard of Ball's house. Throughout the ceremony, Levin could not stop grinning. Feinberg had never seen him so happy. Neither of them knew much about the groom, but whatever Harriett wanted was fine with them.

The ceremony went well. The marriage did not. The man turned out to be different from what Ball had thought. He was nothing like Herman. Within a year she was determined to get him out of her life. That proved to be difficult, but she knew to whom she could go for help. Levin paid for the divorce.

Levin tried once again to persuade Ball to become part of KIPP. He spoke to her several times, but she had not changed her mind. "I can't do it, David," she said.

"But Harriett, it was all your idea. You created this."

"I can't do it. I have four kids. I have a mortgage and no child support. I need a salary of at least what I make now before I can do this."

"We could work something out."

She looked at him. He was such a fine young man, but what did he know of life? "You and Mike can always get help from me. I'll be here for you. But if it doesn't pay my bills, I have no one to go to. You're young and can start over. I don't have that luxury." She couldn't go to New York. Her son was in his last year of high school.

"I'm going to let you use it," she said, meaning the Harriett Ball playbook, the songs, the chants, the games. It was all theirs, with one condition. "If anyone asks you where you got it, you tell them you got it from me."

KIPP's initial success had nonetheless planted a thought in her head. Just a year after Levin left for New York, Ball had an about-face. She decided she no longer wanted to remain a classroom teacher in

Houston. It was not Levin but a much higher power who made the key argument. The potency of her methods, and the bankruptcy of the notion that poor kids couldn't learn much, had become startlingly apparent in the first two years of KIPP. Clearly she had something valuable that could be passed on successfully to other teachers.

She was out taking a smoking break in the parking lot behind Bastian on a spring day in 1996. She finished her cigarette and walked back toward the building. The voice came down from above, as it had before. "I gave it to you," the voice said. Just five words.

She stopped and listened. She felt sorry. She hadn't trusted in God. She knew how well her teaching methods worked. She had passed them on to Dave and Mike. She had trained other people in the school district. That was fine. That was generous. But God wanted her to go further. He wanted her to stop what she was doing and spend all of her time sharing this with more children.

She took a deep breath and walked into the building. Standing beside the double doors was the principal. She looked at him. She was at peace. The decision had been made. "This is my last year," she said.

"Ball, you ain't going anywhere. You're gonna stay here and keep our scores up."

"No, this is it," she said.

When Ball left Bastian, there was no official farewell, no thanks from the principal for all she had done. That only made her more determined to set her own course. She vested her pension, borrowed money on her mortgage, and started her own business. She began to travel, training teachers all over the country. She was excited by how many people wanted to hear her. She found she could make more money than she had as a classroom teacher. She visited Levin and Feinberg at their schools. She made suggestions. But they were growing up, doing their own thing. She was proud of them, but she had her own work to do.

A few years later, as Levin and Feinberg began to acquire a national reputation, appearing on television with their students singing Ball's

songs, she heard the talk from people she knew. "Them Jews are stealing from black folk," they said to her. "Them Jews are stealing your
stuff."

"Baby, it's free advertising," she said.

"That's what them Jews do, they take it."

"Sweetheart," she said, "have a good day."

"What's With This Guy?"

COLLEEN DIPPEL, AGED FOUR, was in the car in 1976 when her mother lost control on an icy winter road and hit a tree. Colleen had been playing on the floor of the backseat, something her mother often let her do. She heard and felt the crash. The backseat, thrust forward, fell on top of her. When she pushed her way out from under, she saw blood everywhere. She found her mother crumpled in the front seat. She tried to open the woman's eyes, but it was no use. Patricia McCafferty Dippel never recovered consciousness and died four days later.

Dippel's father was a construction worker, a good provider without a college degree who sometimes struggled with the demands of raising his very social daughter. Dippel went to parties instead of studying. Most of her friends in Gardiner, New York, were going off to college. Dippel assumed she would too. But in her senior year, her father told her he would not pay for it. "I can't trust you," he said. "I don't believe you are going to go and really study and be there for the right reasons."

She shouted at him, "You are ruining my life!" But years later, she realized his decision was a turning point. He was right. She only wanted to go to college to be with her friends. She was forced to think about what else was important. Working several jobs — Planned Parenthood office clerk, lifeguard, swimming teacher, waitress — she put herself through Dutchess County Community College and the State University of New York at Albany. She had planned to be a lawyer, but a string of administrative jobs with the Teach For America program, in New York and then in Houston, led to a different life from what she had imagined.

At the beginning of a staff meeting during her second week in Houston, in the summer of 1995, a Teach For America institute faculty director she didn't know walked into the room. He was big. He was wearing what Dippel considered a ridiculous outfit, a Colonel Sanders string tie, a vest, and a black cowboy hat. She wondered how anyone would have the guts to dress like that and not be self-conscious.

They went around the table introducing themselves. The urban cowboy said he was Mike Feinberg, a Teach For America corps member overseeing a group of new teachers in training. When it was Dippel's turn, she smiled and said, "Hi. I'm Colleen. You've probably received several e-mails from me. I'm running the workshops this summer. You don't need to know my title, but you do need to know that you all have to turn your course descriptions in to me, and if you don't turn them in to me, I'm going to become your worst nightmare."

Right after the meeting, Dippel found Feinberg looming over her, trying to introduce himself. He liked sassy, attractive women. Dippel had the lean, healthy figure of a swimming instructor and resembled the actress Julia Stiles.

"Oh, yes," she told him. "You're on my list. You haven't turned in your paperwork yet."

Feinberg seemed delighted. "Oh," he said, "I would *hate* to be *your* worst nightmare."

What a smart-ass, Dippel thought, but she was undeniably intrigued. Her doubts about the cowboy guy increased when Feinberg turned in his project description, nearly identical to the one she had received from her friend Mike Farabaugh, another corps member adviser that summer. She went to see Farabaugh.

"Mike, what's with this guy? You wrote his course description."

"I did not write his course description."

"You're lying, but what's his deal?"

"Well, why?"

"Well, he's kind of cute."

Farabaugh smiled. Teach For America summer institutes had their romantic side. "I'll set you up with him."

"No, I have a boyfriend."

She still found reasons to talk to Feinberg. At a Teach For America institute social event, she cut in on several female corps members who were telling him in great detail how they were freaking out because they didn't have their lesson plans done. Dippel chatted with him a bit, then said she was leaving.

"I'll leave with you," he said.

She wanted to go back to her dorm room at the university and get some sleep, but they stopped for ice cream and walked around a bit. He finally dropped her off at her floor before he went up to the room he had been assigned so he could avoid the long trip back to his Gulfton apartment. Half a minute later, after looking for her room key, she realized her roommate back at the party had it. She went upstairs and knocked on Feinberg's door.

"I know you'll think I am making this up, but my roommate has my key. Can I crash here tonight?"

Feinberg welcomed her in and made her comfortable on the bottom bunk. Like a gentleman, he took the top bunk. Ever after, he would tell Dippel, and all their friends, that he knew if he didn't make a pass at her at such a vulnerable moment, she would be unable to resist him in the future. As much as it irked her to hear him repeat this story, he was proved correct.

The next night, they went to the movies. "Want to come over to my apartment with me?" he said as they left the theater. "I have to fax something tonight."

She thought this was the lamest come-on she had ever heard, but she agreed. She discovered that his Gulfton apartment was indeed loaded with office equipment and books for the school he was about to start. The Xerox machine was almost blocking the front door, forcing them to squeeze into the apartment sideways.

Their romance began for real that night, as did a very long and inconclusive argument over whether he had actually had something that needed faxing.

Off the Porch

LEVIN HAD NOT BEEN allowed to have the three-week summer school he had wanted at P.S. 156, but he hoped he could at least start the new KIPP class a week or two early. As July turned to August, he begged to be allowed to bring in his students. The word came back that he could have a two-day, not a two-week, head start. Each of those days, his students would only be allowed in the school for two hours.

Levin's solution was to hold a week-long summer school on the concrete blocks outside the front entrance of Intermediate School 151, the middle school just down the street from Public School 156, an elementary school. Students sat on the flat-topped blocks. He put up a huge sign, TEAM ALWAYS BEATS INDIVIDUAL, on the outside wall of the school. He and Corcoran did their best. The new students of KIPP New York learned to chant, very loudly:

> This is the room
> That has the kids
> Who want to learn
> To read more books
> To build a bet-ter
> To-mor-row!

They liked the rhythm of the words, even though they were not in a classroom, but sitting in their white shirts and beige shorts on concrete blocks outside 250 East 156th Street in the Bronx.

Levin was having trouble keeping his spirits up. He had to be enthusiastic and energetic when he greeted his new class. The students had to see that KIPP had nothing of the ill-tempered listlessness that characterized many big-city classrooms. But he was having difficulty feeling it.

At least his P.S. 156 space was better than what Verdin had provided KIPP at Garcia. They had a double classroom on the second floor. He and Corcoran decorated it colorfully. They welcomed with smiles and happy words the children who appeared, as instructed, two days before school started. The fifth graders were subdued but made little trouble. They seemed pleased by what they had experienced in their abbreviated summer school. Some took an interest in the new games and chants and stories. Others looked on with apprehension and puzzlement, not sure what this was about.

Corcoran had no experience with the KIPP system, so he and Levin had been practicing, thinking, and talking of little else. Levin's mother had found them a walk-up apartment on the third floor of a building on East Thirty-third Street. It was a pleasant neighborhood. By living together, Levin and Corcoran, like Levin and Feinberg the previous year, could spend their evenings planning for the next day and take turns answering telephone calls from students about the homework.

Their conversations the first few weeks were often about how hard it was to teach in the Bronx. The big KIPP idea that all students were going to college seemed to many of these children like one of those fairy tales they had been forced to read in fourth grade. Their quizzes came back full of mistakes and unanswered questions. Many resisted doing the homework. In contrast to KIPP's first weeks in Houston, when Feinberg and Levin felt their class rising like a brightly colored balloon, the Bronx class often seemed glum and weighed down.

Levin thought of the situation in baseball terms. He was playing in a tougher league. The speed of the pitching was faster. The outfield fences were farther away. He had been hitting the ball out of the park in Houston, but in New York he was swinging and missing.

He tried to adjust. When KIPP was born, Levin and Feinberg, without much discussion, agreed that they would never be satisfied. They would change their model as they discovered parts that did not work or parts that worked better with some adjustments. That was how they had come up with the KIPP idea in the first place, trial and error. They had learned from Ball and Esquith, but they had to tailor their mentors' methods to their own styles and circumstances.

Feinberg was still making changes as he started his Houston school. Levin and Corcoran had to do the same in the Bronx. That commitment to change in response to bad results became a KIPP axiom. Each school, each team of principal and teachers, would take what worked for them in the KIPP tool kit and toss out the rest. Classroom results, confirmed by test scores, would be their lodestar. If their adjustments did not raise achievement, they would junk those changes too and try again. They wanted KIPP to be both resilient and fresh, adjusting to a changing world and to new information but never losing sight of the need to help children learn better.

In their second-floor classroom in P.S. 156, the first thing Levin and Corcoran got rid of was the Porch. Levin had seen it work in Houston for some students, but he had never liked it much. It seemed too static, too hard to administer. The Porch motivated students who were usually well behaved and well motivated. They needed only that relatively painless bit of temporary isolation to remind them that they had to avoid lethargy and other sluggish habits.

With children who had more serious behavioral problems, who would tell a teacher to fuck off without feeling any remorse, the Porch had little power. Those students went on the Porch and never got off. They were not bothered by their change in status. For them the Porch, Levin thought, was like purgatory. They stayed in it until they were consigned to hell, which in Levin's mind meant being kicked out of KIPP. But Levin was resolved to expel students only in the most extreme circumstances, which, it turned out, happened only once or twice a year, far less than in many regular public schools that forced students to transfer to special programs for discipline problems. Levin and Feinberg considered each student they could not teach a failure on their part. They kept looking for ways to get the number of dismissals down to zero.

Pondering what to use instead of the Porch, Levin decided the most effective disciplinary technique he and Feinberg had employed the year they taught together was instant and overwhelming response to any violation of the rules. If a student insulted a classmate or failed to pay attention to a lesson or lied about something he had done, Levin and Feinberg would stand on either side of the student and direct all their physical size and conversational energy on that one target.

"So you think you are better than everyone here, is that right?" Or "Is that the kind of language you would use with your mother?" Or "Do you think this kind of activity will help you at all later in life? Will it help you get to college?" Or "Do you have that little respect for yourself, and for everyone else in the class?"

Levin thought he and Corcoran needed to practice that approach and look for ways to augment it. He preserved a bit of the Porch, the practice of making offenders eat lunch by themselves. He also tried keeping some misbehaving children after 5:00 p.m., extending their already long day. For a while, a student who broke the rules had to sit in a little kindergarten-size chair in class. The idea was to have different disciplinary measures for different students and not be bound by the rigidity of the Porch. Levin wanted to give misbehaving children the special attention they craved. They would not be ignored in the way that they often were at home. The methods Corcoran and Levin developed were fluid, which they liked. They were also not much more effective than the Porch, which they didn't like.

They needed a name for what they were doing. Labels were useful because they helped students organize what they were learning and gave teachers a shorthand way of communicating. What should they call their new, multifaceted approach? It was, they thought, the anti-Porch, but that was too negative.

Corcoran shared Levin and Feinberg's taste for science fiction. He and Levin watched *Star Trek* or space movies occasionally in their apartment. One weekend their video store rental was *Starship Troopers*, a simpleminded version of Robert A. Heinlein's novel. There were references in the film to "administrative punishment" for misbehaving troopers. New recruits to mankind's war against galactic adversaries thought it sounded like a bureaucratic slap on the wrist. Some learned too late that it actually meant being taken out behind headquarters and shot.

Levin and Corcoran smiled at each other. Okay, they would call their new disciplinary system Administrative Punishment. They agreed that they would never, ever tell anybody what had inspired the name.

Each night they talked about ways to break down their lessons into more vivid and comprehensible parts. They wanted to help each student master each concept. It was laborious work, trial and error. Levin had little time left for the day-to-day administrative work that was also his responsibility. He looked for someone to handle counseling, paperwork, and administration, a person who could become the school's director. He did not want that title, because he feared it would take him out of the classroom. He would still make the major decisions about the school, but he wanted somebody else to do the office work. He hired a well-regarded Teach For America veteran, twenty-seven-year-old Gillian Williams, who seemed to fit the profile.

She came highly recommended by other educators, but her style did not match his. She felt teachers should act like friendly relatives, not taskmasters. She asked students to call her by her first name. She was not comfortable correcting a child the second he broke a rule. She found many of the Administrative Punishment methods too harsh and Levin too demanding.

By November, both Levin and Williams had had enough. He did not feel he could create the culture necessary for learning if he did not have everyone in the school, particularly the adults, on the same philosophical wavelength. At the same time, she had gotten a job at another New York City school and told him she was giving him two weeks' notice. Neither was feeling very kindly toward the other when she delivered this news in the narrow storage room they used as an office. He told her he wanted her to leave right away.

She was surprised and angry. "No, I'm not going to," she said.

He thought about this. "Okay," he said. "You don't have to go immediately, but you won't be allowed around the kids at all."

"Are you serious?"

"Yeah," he said. "You can just sit in this room all day."

So she packed up that day and wrote Levin a long letter explaining why KIPP was a mistake. She said he was embarrassing the children. He was much too direct. He was too honest with them about their deficiencies, almost to the point of abuse. She said he was hurting them more than helping them. He had better change or suffer the consequences.

Years later, after having achieved success as a South Bronx elementary school principal and an independent school-improvement specialist, Williams remembered that part of her shrank in horror from some of the methods Levin used, but that both of them had changed. He had become a better teacher. "I have gotten more militant about getting results, and plenty of people shrink in horror at what I do now," Williams said. "What appealed to me about Dave is what he did worked, and the kids loved him" — even when, after breakdowns in discipline, he preached forty-five-minute sermons on proper behavior while the class ate their lunches silently, amazed at this white man who was carrying on as if they were in church.

In time Levin would admit that Williams had been right to say he had much to learn. But she had been attacking the pillars of what had worked for Harriett Ball, and that made little sense to him. He continued to listen to criticism, of which there would be a great deal, and tried to learn something from it, just as he hoped his students would do when he criticized them.

Starting Again in Houston

BUS TRANSPORTATION FROM the Gulfton homes of Feinberg's students to their new school at Askew Elementary was a problem. District policy was to punch in students' addresses on the computer and choose street corners that served most of them. Many still had long walks to bus stops. Feinberg thought that could kill his program. It would be dark those mornings. His school was starting so early. He had promised his parents that the buses would be convenient.

He knew the building on McCarty Drive where the school district bus schedulers had their offices. He showed up one morning with breakfast taquitos for the entire staff and offered to help them get the new KIPP bus stop locations just right. "Could we put the computer on manual override?" he asked. "I would like to punch in my own times and locations." The man in front of the computer, munching on his taquito, told Feinberg to go right ahead.

Askew was a kindergarten-through-fourth-grade school. The two-story brick building was fifty-six years old, with a dozen yellowish brown modular buildings clumped together in back. KIPP would use three of the modulars — a large one with space for two classrooms, a smaller one with space for one class, and a third with a two-hundred-square-foot storage room, which would serve as Feinberg's office. Piles of broken furniture, old books, and cleaning equipment filled most of that space, but Feinberg managed to push them to one side. He had a desk and chair.

Unlike Levin in New York, Feinberg had gotten permission to

conduct a summer session. It was shorter than he wanted, just two weeks. It finished a week before the regular school year began. He still needed to arrange for lunches and a hundred other details. He pushed the FileMaker program on his Mac to the limit getting the paperwork ready for opening day. He wrote schedules and homeroom lists and letters to parents. His teachers tried to remove, or rearrange, the piles of debris in the previously occupied modulars. There was not much time for pedagogical debates or detailed lesson plans. Feinberg told his team to focus on essentials: "Get your classrooms ready, get your materials ready, tell me what you need, start doing your planning for what you are going to do when the kids get here. Those first couple of days we're going to have them all together, and don't worry about it. I am going to take care of everything."

As his teachers discovered, Feinberg's idea of taking care of everything sometimes meant doing things they thought they had already done. Each night, after they went home exhausted, Feinberg slipped into their classrooms and made changes. Some of their posters were not, in his view, properly hung or well chosen. Some of the lettering on their bulletin boards was crooked. Feinberg knew he was going too far, but he could not control himself. He blamed Levin for his fixation on classroom arrangements. His friend demanded the best possible displays, as Ball had done. Feinberg had picked up the perfection bug from them. Feinberg loved what he called Las Vegas lettering, glittery characters in colors so bright they could not be ignored. He wanted every wall of every classroom to radiate excitement.

But rearranging teachers' classrooms behind their backs was not a good management technique. He rationalized his intrusions by saying he had hired them just to teach. They could not be expected to share his twenty-four-hour-a-day obsession with every detail at the school. He knew what he wanted but lacked the time and skills to communicate his vision clearly and completely. So he just interfered. It hurt some feelings, but he was quick to blame himself. He was full of jokes and compliments. That helped preserve, just barely, his image as a happy-go-lucky big dog who knocked over the furniture but was fun to have around.

For the first day of the shortened KIPP summer school, Feinberg made a large gold poster that said THINK LIKE A CHAMPION TODAY. He had stolen the slogan from an inspirational football movie, *Rudy*. He rode the first bus to Gulfton, arriving at 6:30 a.m. Farabaugh was in the second bus. At each stop, Feinberg hopped out and held up his poster so that everyone would know this was the KIPP express. He shook hands with the parents. He shook hands with the fifth graders. "Welcome to KIPP!" he said.

He talked very fast, like a coach before a big game. "This is great!" he said. "This is going to be fun. Please touch the poster and *say* what is on the poster, then get on the bus."

In *Rudy,* an undersized Notre Dame undergraduate through heroic effort makes the university's football varsity and is allowed to join the other players in slapping a poster that says PLAY LIKE A CHAMPION TODAY in the tunnel on the way into the stadium. Few if any Gulfton children had ever seen the movie or been asked to slap a sign before they climbed on a school bus. Some were confused and passed by without touching it. Some had trouble reading the words. But they all got on the bus. By 7:15 a.m., they were at the school.

There were seventy-one students the first day. They included one Southeast Asian, two South Asians, one Anglo and two African Americans. The rest were from families that had originated in Central America or Mexico. As Feinberg had requested, the KIPP teachers had cleared all the desks out of one of the classrooms so that all seventy-one students could crowd in for an opening-day orientation. The teachers stood along the walls while Feinberg worked the room. He had the teachers introduce themselves. He tried some icebreakers. Who has two brothers and sisters? Who has three? Who has four? Five? Six? Who is left-handed? Who has seen the ocean?

He taught them some of the Ball songs, starting with "Read, Baby, Read." He taught them how to roll their nines. It took them several tries to pick up the beat. They could clap, but when asked to sing at the same time, they lost the rhythm. Feinberg thought this was hilarious. He kept the mood light. They liked practicing "Read, Baby, Read" at full volume. The more they sang it, the louder they got.

Feinberg wanted to prove this was a fun school, but only because learning was fun. He knew there was a fine line between entertainment and engagement. He did not want his new students to think KIPP would be all games and candy and McDonald's. He wanted to weave those thrills into mastering thirty-three-digit numbers, reading novels, and acquiring an intimate knowledge of the White House, the Congress, and the Supreme Court before the spring trip to Washington, D.C.

"It's going to be fun if we work hard for you, and you work hard for us," he told them. "As long as you play by the rules, then we are going to go out of our way to do all kinds of cool things for you. But it all has to be earned."

The first two days, with the entire school still gathered in the one classroom, Feinberg and his teachers read *The Sneetches, The Polar Express,* and other books. Feinberg interrupted to ask questions, seek opinions, and make observations and connections to relevant parts of his students' lives. He wanted everyone involved in the magical act of reading. That would be the heart of what they would do the rest of the year.

His message was the same one Levin was using in New York: We are a team and we are a family. Not only do we respect one another's differences, but we celebrate them. We live together, learn together, take care of one another, and have fun together. In *The Polar Express,* he emphasized the moment when the children hear the bells, a sign of their faith and belief in what has happened to them on their journey to the North Pole. Feinberg hoped that family feeling would guide their long days at school and their hard work to learn. He introduced them to parts of the KIPP credo that he and Levin had been polishing for months:

"Work hard. Be nice." (This was an Esquith slogan. He preferred the "Be nice" to come before the "Work hard," but Feinberg thought it read better the other way. In New York, Levin used "Be nice. Work hard.")

"There are no shortcuts." (Esquith's signature slogan, eventually the title of his autobiography.)

"Assign yourself." (That meant students should take responsibility for doing whatever they needed to do to get an education and support their team and family.)

"If there is a problem, we look for a solution. If there is a better way, we find it. If a teammate needs help, we give it. If we need help, we ask."

They were simple aphorisms. In the affluent and well-educated neighborhoods where Feinberg and Levin had grown up, they would be dismissed as unfashionably banal. But in Houston, among families seeking to rise out of poverty, they made sense.

In the middle of the third day, Feinberg called an end to the group orientation and sent the students to their respective classrooms. It was time to let his teachers teach. Feinberg and Levin believed, based on their own clumsy beginnings in Houston, that teachers should be judged not by style or philosophy but by results. If their students were excited and engaged, if test scores rose, if KIPP alumni went on to succeed in high school and, most particularly, got to college and did well there, then that was all that they needed to know about those teachers.

Feinberg and Levin would, of course, closely monitor teachers' performance and interfere when they saw fit. They were not reluctant to reteach something a teacher had already covered. When students arrived for Feinberg's math class, he never confined himself to math. He had reading exercises. He discussed science and its relationship to math. He would say, "You just learned about the water cycle, right? So talk to me. What is evaporation? What is condensation?" If he saw blank looks, he would tell Farabaugh, the science teacher, "Hey, the kids don't know the water cycle."

Every afternoon, the KIPP fifth grade was reorganized into three groups, each at a different level in reading. They read novels from 3:30 to 4:15 p.m. They began with Roald Dahl's *Charlie and the Chocolate Factory*. By the end of the school year, they had completed six books. In class, each child would read a half page to a page aloud. Their teachers would often interrupt to provoke a discussion. From 4:15 to 5:00 p.m., the time that Levin and Feinberg had devoted to dodgeball their first year, Feinberg had a study hall period so that students could start their homework. They were assigned about two hours a night, including their forty-five-minute head start at school. KIPP teachers supervised physical education for their homerooms during the same period after lunch that the Askew students got their exercise.

Unlike Levin, Feinberg had a good relationship with his building principal. Elaine Allen did not see him as a threat or an annoyance. He never had trouble getting into the school building, as he had had at Garcia. KIPP Saturday classes were at Lee High, closer to Gulfton and with those enriching extras, like the computer lab and the swimming pool.

Feinberg encountered — not for the last time — parents who despite signing the Commitment to Excellence contract did not like the strict discipline and long homework. One mother called Jill Kolasinski, Feinberg's reading teacher, on the telephone and complained loudly about her daughter's being put on the Porch. "My daughter is just fine," the parent said. "She doesn't need to be treated this way."

Feinberg's response to such complaints was to visit the home and show the parents their child's fourth-grade TAAS scores. "Your daughter is very bright," he said to the mother who had yelled at Kolasinski. "She's got a lot of potential, but before she got to KIPP, this is how she was doing. If you say you want her to be treated the way she was at her old school, this is the result of her old school." That parent calmed down. But others continued to complain. One or two each year would be so unhappy they would not send their children back the next year.

J. R. Gonzalez, a Gulfton student recruited in 1996, remembered years later what it was like to be a fifth grader at KIPP Houston. He was tall and athletic, good in math, and weak in English. When he did not do his homework, his teachers were in his face, marking off points and putting him on the Porch. Feinberg could be frightening. He might scream at J. R. and then, in a suddenly quiet voice, explain that such behavior was not acceptable.

Homework was a huge issue every day. Feinberg experimented with making students stand the entire period in any class for which they weren't prepared. "You haven't brought your ticket with you," he told the students, "so you can't sit down." J. R. did not like it. But he did not tell either Feinberg or his father how he felt. He was afraid of what they would say to him. He was also beginning to think that despite the school's annoying rules, it might be the best thing for him, and he was making friends with the other KIPP students.

Feinberg thought the first year went well. His teachers were gaining confidence and adding new techniques. The school's standards remained high. But the future did not look good. There was no room at Askew to create a sixth grade the following year. Patterson had promised to find the space, but she was taking much longer than Feinberg had expected.

When no expansion plan materialized, Feinberg unleashed on the central school administration his advocacy-in-democracy lesson. All of the fifth graders called officials downtown to complain about not knowing where they would be going to school the next year. Hours later, Patterson was frantically trying to repair the damage, while Feinberg, not the least contrite, continued to ask her exactly when he was going to get his new facility.

Patterson had to explain to everyone she worked with that the rash of student calls was indeed, as they had suspected, the work of that overgrown adolescent Feinberg. She also had to tell them she was going to put a stop to Feinberg's misbehavior once and for all. Patterson told Feinberg to report to her office immediately after school. She knew that was unlikely to happen, since he was never prompt for any appointment with her. She had lost count of the times he had promised to be at her office by 5:30 p.m. and then kept her waiting past her usual time to go home. It was often not until 7:00 p.m. that she would see him, through her office window, pulling into the parking lot in the blue Chevy van he had bought to transport children. She would give him a stern look. "I'm sorry, Anne," he would say, "but there were some kids I had to take home."

When he arrived the evening after the advocacy lesson, she dispensed with all pleasantries. She had to get through to him. She talked about being a team player, about not cutting the ground out from under her, about being patient, about not acting as if he were the only school principal in the city who cared about children. She could tell he was not buying it. They both knew she was not good at dressing down subordinates. It was mostly playacting. Feinberg was a gifted classroom performer when it came to being stern with his students, and he could tell she was going through the motions.

He stood his ground. He said he would do what he had to do to cut through the apathy that was strangling Houston and a lot of other school districts. His school was doing great. His kids deserved a chance to achieve. He was going to continue to fight for that any way he could.

Patterson leaned forward on her desk and rubbed her temples. It was time for action. So for the first time, she wrote Feinberg up.

Writing somebody up is a popular method of administrative discipline in American school districts. Patterson gave Feinberg an official letter, to be placed in his personnel file, telling him what he had done wrong and directing him to act differently in the future. She told all of the officials who complained to her about Feinberg that she had written him up. In their culture, where many actions were taken for the sake of appearance, this was a satisfactory punishment. People at headquarters thought, She really stuck it to Feinberg this time. He'll think twice before he does something this outrageous again. It's in his permanent record now.

What actually happened was that after Feinberg signed the reprimand, adding the smiley face he and Levin used in almost all KIPP communications, Patterson tossed the letter into one of her drawers. It did not go into Feinberg's file, and she forgot about it.

Climbing the Fence

THE KIPP FIFTH GRADERS were chattering with excitement the day they returned to class after their advocacy exercise. Feinberg congratulated them on their fine work. He did not tell them that his supervisor had yelled at him and written him up. They would eventually learn the rules for working inside a large organization. An explanation of the penalties for rebellion, he thought, was not appropriate for their grade level.

"You are doing what no other fifth graders in the country are doing," he said. For once, he was fairly sure he was not exaggerating. "Knowledge is power. You are not sitting back being spectators and letting people drive you around. You are taking charge for yourselves. This is what we mean by team and family. *Viva la KIPP!*"

"*Viva la KIPP!*" the class shouted happily.

It looked as if his stunt had worked. Within a few days, Patterson told him KIPP had been approved to move to Sharpstown Middle School. She could provide enough modular buildings for both a sixth grade and a fifth grade at that site. Sharpstown was only fifteen minutes from Gulfton, much less time than it took to get to Askew.

More people were noticing KIPP. The article in the *Houston Post* had been followed by an article in the *Houston Chronicle*. The Channel 13 correspondent Don Kobos had visited. Local activists and educators had adopted Levin and Feinberg. Karol Musher, a speech and learning specialist, and her physician husband, Dan, had invited the two teachers to their family's Passover dinner. The Mushers had many influential friends, including Barbara Hurwitz, whose husband, Charles, was a leading financier. Karol Musher had helped the Hurwitzs' son Shawn deal with his reading disability, much as Jeannette Jansky had helped Levin when he was a child. Years later, Shawn would become interested in KIPP, make friends with Feinberg, and serve first as KIPP Houston's board chairman and then as a member of the national KIPP board. But in Feinberg's first year at Askew, the most important thing Karol Musher and Barbara Hurwitz did for him was to persuade the mayor, Bob Lanier, to visit.

The mayor's appearance was set for February. When Rod Paige, the Houston school superintendent, heard about that, he added his name to the mayor's entourage for that day. School public relations and protocol officers rushed to make the arrangements. They collided with the KIPP Academy's twenty-seven-year-old principal, who did not feel he had to follow the usual protocol.

Feinberg and Elaine Allen, the Askew principal, met with Patterson to plan the visit. Feinberg said he wanted to meet the mayor in the school library, explain to him how KIPP worked, then take him to the classrooms. Feinberg thought the best way to learn about KIPP was to watch the students and teachers in action.

"But we should serve him something first," Patterson said. "He's coming out in the morning, so we need to have some breakfast. What are we going to serve?"

"What are you talking about?" Feinberg said.

"Well, you've got to have orange juice and muffins. We've got to serve something."

"Well, no, we *don't* have to have that. That's not what I am serving."

"What are you serving, Mike?"

"I am serving inspiration."

There was a silence. Patterson was not sure if he was kidding or just being his usual high-minded, annoying self. Patterson decided not to argue. "Whatever, Mike," she said. "This is your show."

"Look," he said. "I want this to be a different visit. The thing that makes KIPP KIPP is that it is about the kids. It is not about me. It is not about the danishes. It is about the kids. That is what we want. That is what we preach about. That's what the literature says. When people come out, that's why I want them to see it's not who we are, it's what we do."

He was getting excited. The snacks issue might sound trivial to them, but it exposed something vital and too often overlooked in districts like Houston. "I want them to see what we're doing. They are not coming out to visit KIPP because we have the best fresh-squeezed orange juice in town. I want them to see the kids do their thing."

"Whatever, Mike," Patterson repeated, her tone weary. "Barbara Hurwitz is running this for you. It's your show. I can't stop you. But I think you are making a mistake."

The visit, Feinberg thought, proved her wrong. Lanier and his wife seemed to enjoy the no-nonsense, content-rich, snack-poor briefing he gave them in the library. They spent more than an hour watching his teachers and students in the three classrooms. At one point, the mayor even read with the class. The students did some Harriett Ball chants, which were becoming the standard KIPP greeting for visitors. On his way back to his office in his car, Lanier told his education adviser he wanted to know how they could make more schools like KIPP. Paige also appeared to be impressed.

Feinberg still worried about the move to Sharpstown. Workmen were putting up the modular classrooms in a field in back of the middle school. He found it difficult to get good information by telephone. He persuaded KIPP teacher Laurie Bieber to drive with him there in her car one evening to survey the progress.

It was still March, not yet daylight saving time. It was dark when they arrived. Feinberg peered through the chain-link fence. He saw some buildings in the gloom, but he wanted to get closer. He climbed up the fence.

Like many other people working with Feinberg and Levin, Bieber considered herself part of the family. It was a communal feeling that the two founders thought was their schools' greatest strength, and it saved them from disaster time and again. In this case, Bieber thought of herself as Feinberg's sister and acted accordingly.

"Mike," Bieber said, "please don't do that. You'll hurt yourself." The field lesson to Washington, D.C., would start in a few days. She could see him in the hospital with several broken bones, unable to make it.

Nonsense, Feinberg thought. He pushed himself up and over. On the way down, his left hand snagged on a sharp chain link at the top of the fence. It hurt. He was bleeding.

"Uh, it looks like I'm going to need some stitches. Can you take me to the hospital?"

Bieber played the annoyed big sister one more time. "I am *not* driving you to the hospital. You'll get blood all over my car." But she didn't mean it. It was a teacher's car, so there was plenty of notepaper in the trunk. Feinberg wrapped several sheets around his wound. At the hospital, he got ten stitches, which he displayed proudly at work the next day. There was no time for recuperation. He was adding a sixth grade, and he wasn't going to miss the D.C. trip.

30.

Taking Away the TV

AMONG KIPP FIFTH GRADERS at Askew was Abby Hernandez, who liked to watch television. As a result, she rarely completed her homework. Putting her on the Porch had no effect. Feinberg visited the Hernandezes' third-floor apartment, not far from his own building, to ask about this.

"I want her to do her homework, Mr. Feinberg," Abby's mother said in Spanish, "but Abby will not leave the TV. She is a TV junky. I have found her late at night, after the station has signed off and there is nothing but snow on the screen. Abby is still watching."

The apartment was small — a living room and a dining room, a tiny kitchen, two bedrooms, and a bathroom. The thirty-six-inch television set dominated all human activity in that confined space from its lordly perch on top of the living room cabinet.

The TV was on all the time. The family did not have cable — almost no one in Gulfton did — but there was more than enough over-the-air broadcasting to fill a ten-year-old's day. Abby watched *telenovelas* (soap operas) on the Spanish channels. She watched cartoons on the English channels. She watched comedies. She watched celebrity news. She watched everything, as did her mother, father, and two cousins.

Abby was a bright child. Feinberg was sure of that. She had chubby cheeks and long, dark hair braided in a ponytail. She was bubbly and social. She participated in class but wasn't learning nearly as much as she was capable of. As Feinberg listened to the mother, he thought about what to do. Television addiction had been a problem for Ameri-

can children, both rich and poor, for nearly a half century. Feinberg
had tried some approaches and read about others.

"We should start to limit the TV," he said. "Take it away until it is
earned. She has to get her homework done, and when it is done, you
are going to reward her by giving her an hour or so of TV a night. But
you are going to limit it to an hour or so because too much of anything
becomes a bad thing."

The mother smiled. She said she thought that was a fine idea. They
called Abby in and told her what they had decided. Abby said she
understood. All was well.

Except that the next day, Abby arrived at school with her homework once again incomplete. "You've got to be kidding me," Feinberg
mumbled to himself. That night he went back to their apartment.
Bieber, Abby's homeroom teacher, went with him. The front door was
slightly ajar. When he knocked, it opened wider to reveal Abby on the
couch, watching TV.

"¿Qué es esto?" (What is this?) Feinberg asked the mother, who was
in the kitchen.

She looked at him and shrugged her shoulders. "What can I do?"
she said. "She won't leave from in front of the TV."

Feinberg could think of only one more option. "You know what
you're going to do?" he said. "You're going to give me the TV."

"I can't give you the TV. It is the only one we have."

"That's fine, but you tell me you are powerless to stop your daughter from watching it, so it seems to me the only way to make sure she
doesn't watch TV is to take the TV out of the house."

"That's true," the mother said, "but I'm not going to give you the
TV."

Feinberg decided to go for broke, play his last available card. "I
don't want to do this, but you give me the TV, or your daughter is not
in KIPP anymore."

Bieber was knocked askew when she heard that. It was a radical
move, but she could see its logic. She decided it was revolutionary but
necessary. She held her breath to hear what the mother would say.

The woman did not react at first. She was quiet for a few seconds. She did not seem upset, just thoughtful. Then she said, "Take the TV."

Abby, who had been listening intently, began to cry. Feinberg unplugged the set and reached down to pick it up. He stopped for a moment to talk to his student. "Abby, you can earn this back. You do your homework great for three weeks straight, and I will bring the TV back."

Bieber offered to help, but Feinberg insisted on carrying the TV himself. He stumbled out of the apartment, straining his back with the weight of the thirty-six-inch monster. He managed to get it down the two flights of outside stairs and into his van. The next day, he lugged it into Bieber's classroom and put it on a side table. Several students regarded this as the ultimate act of insanity by the demonstrably addled Mr. Feinberg. They said to Abby, "I don't want him taking my TV."

Feinberg kept pushing. The rule for the next three weeks was that when Abby brought in her homework each morning, she had to put it on top of the television set. The routine offered Abby some notoriety among her classmates, which she liked. She kept to the bargain. She completed her homework every day for three weeks.

So Feinberg put the television set back in his van, drove to her apartment, and carried it back up the stairs for its ceremonial return to the living room. He plugged it in and congratulated her. "Remember, now," he said, "this is something that is earned. For everything there is a time and a place."

Abby had her good days and her bad days after that, but her homework was usually done. She learned how to focus on what was important. She was valedictorian of her class at the Bootstrap Ranch School in Montana and got into Texas A&M on a full scholarship. Carmi Wells, the Bootstrap superintendent, later remembered Abby as "a great kid" in both academics and character.

The story of Feinberg and the television set would be retold many times. Feinberg said he was never entirely sure it was the right thing to do. He was not against television, just its overuse. He admitted he had intruded into Abby's family life far deeper than he should have.

But he thought the rash act of a desperate teacher had a beneficial effect on his staff, who congratulated him on his reckless courage. It also sent the message to students that he would go to crazy lengths to make sure they had the time and opportunity to get a good education. If it was that important to him, then maybe it would become more important to them.

31.

Going to Utah

AT THE END of their first year apart, Feinberg and Levin decided they would do the Washington, D.C., field lesson together. It was an unwieldy undertaking: 120 fifth graders unleashed on the nation's capital. The teachers' memories of the first trip to D.C., kings and queens and Justice Breyer and peanut butter and jelly sandwiches, gave them confidence they could pull it off.

The guides and docents still rushed them through the exhibits, but this time they warned the students that that would happen. Justice Breyer welcomed them to the Court. Senator Paul Simon of Illinois and Representative Gene Green of Texas greeted them at the Capitol. Planet Hollywood was once again a pleasant surprise. The two teachers felt that they had the fifth-grade trip solved. While munching hamburgers and studying the Arnold Schwarzenegger memorabilia on the restaurant's walls, they discussed next year's sixth-grade trip.

Where to go? They invited Corcoran, Farabaugh, Bieber, and other teachers to join them at their table for a brainstorming session. Many possibilities occurred to them. They wanted something big, really awesome. What would be the greatest attraction they could offer these city kids? It seemed obvious: the Grand Canyon.

The idea made sense to all of them. They decided to announce their choice in front of the White House, right after the silent walk and serenade. Corcoran found a white board and markers and drew a spectacular rendering of the canyon. Feinberg and Levin announced their decision. Corcoran held up his picture. There were gasps and cheers from the students. The teachers all congratulated themselves on another brilliant idea. Levin and Feinberg were so excited that when they got back to Houston and New York, they placed a conference call to Esquith to tell him what they had done.

On the telephone, their mentor was silent for a moment. Feinberg sensed disapproval. Esquith assumed his warmest classroom voice. "I think there would be better places to go," he said.

"Uh, what do you mean?" Feinberg said.

"Well, first of all, unless you go take the kids down into the canyon, all you are doing is getting a quick look from the rim, not much more educational or exciting than that Chevy Chase scene in *National Lampoon's Vacation*. You know, okay, here's the Grand Canyon, now let's quick get back in the bus."

"Yeah," Feinberg said.

"So," Esquith said, "it's a nothing trip unless you go down into the canyon, but it's a real strenuous hike, far too hard for the kids. You can take mules, but the mules need a two-to-one adult-to-child ratio. That's expensive. So why are you going to the Grand Canyon?"

It was Feinberg's turn to be silent for a moment. "Oh, shit," he finally said.

Esquith was always ready to help even his slowest pupils. "A good concept," he said, "is to go to Utah, go to Zion, go to Bryce, go to Moab, much more kid friendly."

"Okay, yeah," Feinberg said. "Thanks, Rafe."

Feinberg and Levin agreed they had to make a change. They felt sheepish as they announced the great trip to the Grand Canyon had become the great trip to Utah, but the fifth graders, soon to be sixth graders, remained excited about going anywhere unfamiliar. The next week, Corcoran and Levin drove to Utah to check out the scene and called a surprised Esquith to compare notes.

The excursions — both large and small — connected school learning to the real world in ways educational theorists like John Dewey had been recommending for a century. Feinberg took large groups of students to Broadway road productions in Houston. There was usually an awkward moment when they walked into the theater, a hundred

Hispanic and African American children. Feinberg saw the faces of the adult ticket holders. Eyes rolled at the thought of titters and tears. Then, at intermission, audience members approached him with looks of astonishment. "Where do these kids come from? They are *so* well behaved."

"We are from the KIPP Academy in Houston."

"And did we see them mouthing the words of every song, quietly singing along?"

"That's right. They know the words to every song. Our kids are going to college, and they learn to appreciate different things."

Field lessons also had bad moments, immediately transformed by Levin and Feinberg into topics for lengthy discussion. The KIPP founders jumped on grade-school mischief like revival preachers discussing bars and bordellos. On one Washington, D.C., trip, Feinberg sent two boys home for punching each other in their room. "What makes me the most angry," Feinberg told the whole class, assembled in the hotel corridor, "is that this started with a pillow fight *last* night. You two must have been thinking about this the whole time today, thinking about what you were going to do tonight. So while we were at Arlington National Cemetery, at President Kennedy's grave, reading those wonderful quotes, looking at that beautiful skyline, you were thinking about pillow fights. When we were at the Korean War Veterans Memorial, you were thinking about pillow fights. When you were at the Lincoln Memorial, reading the Gettysburg Address, you were thinking about pillow fights.

"We are a team and a family," Feinberg said. "This gets earned." He looked at the two miscreants. "And you have shown that you do not appreciate where you are, you do not appreciate the learning, and therefore you don't deserve to be here. You don't deserve to have a celebration of learning with us. You will be on the next flight home to Houston."

Field lessons should not be just sightseeing, Levin and Feinberg thought. Esquith said they were rich opportunities for critical thinking. Wherever they took their students—Washington, Utah, California, New York, Orlando — when the group returned to the hotel each night, they sat together and reflected on the day. Feinberg and Levin and their teachers tried to involve every child. What did you like today? What didn't you like? What was exciting? What was disappointing? How about tomorrow? They used the reading teacher's tool: predictions. What were they expecting to see the next day?

The first Utah trip in 1997 acquired its own magic. The Houston students went by bus — cheaper and more educational than an airplane flight. They left in the morning and were still in the Texas Panhandle, with little to see but gas stations and billboards, when night came and they dropped off to sleep. As the eastern sky began to lighten early the next morning, the students snapped awake in wonder.

They were in the Great American Desert, near the Four Corners, where the boundaries of New Mexico, Arizona, Colorado, and Utah come to a point. The landscape looked like Mars, not Earth. Feinberg so enjoyed seeing their surprised faces that he made sure to wake himself up just before dawn on subsequent trips so that he would not miss a moment of eleven-year-olds from the big city transported to a different universe. They woke, looked around, and said, "Whoa!" They nudged friends awake. It was a perfect start to a journey Feinberg would take many times.

Banished to the Playground

LEVIN AND FEINBERG had their flaws, but Esquith loved their energy and charm. During spring vacation, in 1994, they found time to go to Los Angeles, see Esquith's class, and meet his wife, Barbara Tong. At their first lunch together, the young teachers shared their vision, so grand and so naive that Esquith and Tong started laughing.

"You know," Esquith said in a friendly tone, "you guys are nuts."

Feinberg and Levin looked at each other. They looked at Esquith and Tong. They said in unison, perfectly timed, "We're on a *mission from God!*" It was a reference to the comedy film *The Blues Brothers,* which Esquith and Tong had seen. Maybe these guys would go nowhere, the couple thought, but they were fun to have around. And they were hard workers. They knew that they could not expect too much in just a year or two.

That was clear to Esquith, even as his celebrity grew in the wake of his national teaching award and other honors. His life at Hobart Boulevard Elementary School was still full of rules that made no sense to him. The most salient example was hard for friends and visitors to believe until they saw it with their own eyes. Since 1989, Esquith had been teaching his class on the school playground for four months of every year. Rain or shine, he and his students were there each morning, learning Shakespeare and economics and math on a patch of concrete within sight of room 56, up on the second floor, which was being used by other teachers and their students. The school had become so crowded that officials had instituted three different vacation schedules. When Esquith and his students were on vacation, another class used room 56. But Esquith did not take vacations, and thus many of his students didn't either. Without a classroom, the only place for them was outside.

An assistant principal had announced the new system at a meeting. Esquith approached the woman afterward to see if he could make a deal. "I've got something going here," he told her. "The kids have been meeting me on vacations and stuff. Can we keep the room? Can we work something out?"

"No, Rafe. The thing is, we're all the same here. You have to understand, if we gave you special treatment, we would have to give everyone special treatment."

"But everyone is not like me. I am volunteering to work during vacations for free. So doesn't that get me something? Shouldn't we be giving special credit to these kids who want to come in here and work on their vacations? Isn't that amazing?"

The conversation took place three years before he began to win national awards. But becoming an educational celebrity did not help. As the administrator had said the first day, rules were rules. He could use the lunch benches and tables on the other side of the school, but only for an hour in the morning. Otherwise, from 6:30 a.m. to 6:30 p.m. he and his large entourage were camped out on the concrete. Sometimes they dragged over a bench that had not been chained down, but most times the students sat on the ground.

It went on that way for more than a decade. One day, after he had begun to collect some support from interested local businessmen, one of his patrons called to check on him. "Bill," Esquith said, "these kids are so great. We were reading *Huck Finn* today. We were sitting on the cement, and they were crying over the book."

"They weren't crying over the book," the patron said. "They were crying because their asses were hurting."

He and his students were often outside in April and May, when it was hot in Los Angeles. There was some shade under the stairway leading up to room 56. He brought cold water and other drinks. His outdoor class grew as the Shakespeare plays caught on, but it was very hard to rehearse outside. The children's voices evaporated in the open air. Feinberg and Levin listened to Esquith describe his routine. They realized that as long as they had something to offer their students, they should be able to find some space to teach somewhere, even if it was a concrete sidewalk.

No principal tried to stop Esquith's open-air lessons. In a school with two thousand low-income children, they had many other things to worry about. Some administrators liked Esquith and cheered him on, even though they lacked the power to give him his room back.

One Friday, when Esquith had his class in the school library, he told them that a show of Shakespeare moments was about to open in Los Angeles. The tickets were going on sale at UCLA on a Sunday morning. It would turn out to be Esquith's first encounter with Ian McKellen, the famous actor who would become the Hobart Shakespeareans' most important patron. During the performance, McKellen would notice the large group of children in the audience, quiet, absorbed, and in some cases mouthing his words as if they had already memorized the plays. He would invite them and their teacher backstage and become part of the life of room 56.

Before the performance, Esquith had no idea such a thing could happen. He just wanted his students to see a real Shakespearean actor. He urged his students to bring in any spare change, and he would find some way to fund the rest of the forty-dollar-a-seat tickets. They had to be at the front of the line at UCLA to make sure the tickets didn't sell out. "What time should we catch a bus here to get in line?" he asked the class. The students agreed that 4:00 a.m. would be about right. He wrote on the library blackboard, "Meet Rafe at 4 a.m."

The next Monday morning, there was a teachers' meeting in the library to discuss class assignments for the next year. Esquith didn't have to attend the meeting because he was, technically, on vacation. Some other teachers didn't understand why he insisted on coming to school every day, but they did covet his vacation schedule, even if he didn't go on vacation, because he got Christmas off. Someone asked, "Why does Rafe get that schedule? We've been here longer."

The principal, Jim Messrah, had seen the note still on the black-board, "Meet Rafe at 4 a.m." He pointed to it. "That's why," he said.

Eleven years after Esquith began spending his vacations on the playground, Hobart Boulevard's enrollment began to decline. Many neighborhood families were moving to better neighborhoods. An assistant principal, Mercedes Santoyo, later the school's principal, realized she could reduce the number of teachers who had to share classrooms.

Esquith was in her office one day. They were having one of their spirited discussions. He considered himself her loyal opposition, explaining the problems he saw in some of the district's policies, like the requirement that all teachers use the Open Court reading series, several levels below the Shakespeare he was giving his kids.

During a pause in the conversation, she gave him a small smile, as if she knew a secret. "So, Rafe, do you want your room the whole year?"

He looked at her carefully. This did not appear to be a joke. "For that," he said, "I'll do anything you need. I'll read Open Court books. Anything."

With that, room 56 became once again the year-round home of Rafe Esquith's fifth grade and the Hobart Shakespeareans. He did attend Open Court training and asked polite questions, but he continued to shun the program in his classroom.

Ambushing the Superintendent

FEINBERG'S SECOND YEAR of KIPP Houston was going well except for the facilities. Feinberg wished he could persuade the Sharpstown Middle School administrators to give his students access to the auditorium, or the gym, or, most important of all, the library. When it was time for them to choose their next novels, he had to bus them to the public library several blocks away. It occurred to him, however, that going out of their way to get books might be a plus. When his students boarded the library buses, they could not fail to understand how important, and in some ways exciting, the act of reading was at their little school.

The second year was in fact going so well that Feinberg's always active imagination was in overdrive. Why stop at just adding a seventh grade in KIPP Academy Houston next year? Why not realize his and Levin's dream of bringing the Kippsters from Garcia back into the fold? Where would he find the space? He did not even know where he could put his seventh graders. He had spoken to Patterson about adding more modular classrooms at Sharpstown, but that seemed unlikely. Patterson mentioned plans to buy a building in southwest Houston for another school project. Maybe KIPP could get space there.

As usual, Patterson urged Feinberg to be patient. As usual, he ignored her advice. Winter turned to spring. Nothing was settled. One day in March, Patterson asked him to come to her office. Her eyes had the puffy look Feinberg associated with bad news. She rubbed her temples, another sign of trouble.

"Mike, there is something I have to tell you. I cannot . . ." She gulped and tried again, looking straight at him this time. "There is *no* space, no space. There is no way to get you anything above and beyond the space you have now. I think you are going to have to stay where you are next year."

"So you're not going to give me more modulars?"

"No, we already lost that battle."

"Well, then, that's not acceptable. How can we stay at the same site?"

She shook her head and looked down. "Well, you can bring in a new fifth grade, but you're going to have to let your seventh graders go back to Jane Long." That was the middle school in Gulfton, an educational sinkhole, in Feinberg's view.

"Hell, no," he said.

"Okay, well then, you are going to have to *not* recruit a new group of fifth graders and just stick with the kids you have now, as a sixth and seventh grade."

"*Hell,* no! I've already been recruiting the new kids. I am not telling them they can't come!"

Patterson looked tired. "Well," she said, "I don't know what else to tell you. There is no other option."

"There's got to be other options."

"Look, I have tried everything," she said. "There is no way. Look at me. I'm a mess. I'm a wreck. I've been crying. I've been yelling at people, crying at people. People are sick of me talking about KIPP. There is nothing I can do."

"There is nothing you can do?"

She said she had tried to take the matter all the way up to the superintendent, Rod Paige, the tall, cerebral former football coach and education-school dean who had made the unusual move from school board member to superintendent. Paige was very focused on raising the achievement of inner-city children. He had visited KIPP and said all the right things about the school. But maybe, some KIPP people thought, that was just his way of playing up to the reporters who had written glowing stories about Feinberg and his kids. Or maybe he really had no options. Paige could not produce new space if none existed. His district was filling so fast with the children of immigrant families that it might explode like an overinflated balloon.

Also, Paige's schedule was controlled by assistants who had grown tired of Patterson's pushing and Feinberg's tantrums. His actions had inspired plenty of anecdotes, passed around school headquarters, that fed their resentment. There were stories about Feinberg's yelling at children. Both he and Levin had done it at the beginning of their teaching careers when nothing else worked. They were young and clumsy and unclear on the alternatives. Gradually they began to see that it frightened more than motivated many children and was really no more effective than well-chosen words spoken in a normal tone. Sometimes the best way to lecture a student was a whisper in the ear.

Levin abandoned the shouting before Feinberg did, although in New York, Levin tried other stunts that he later decided were wrong and dumb. In time, Feinberg also put the yelling aside as counterproductive, but the charge that he was abusive to children had reached so many people that it stuck in their minds.

The anti-Feinberg faction would have been particularly interested in the fact that at the beginning of the KIPP Academy Houston's second year, some parents filed a formal complaint against him for allegedly stealing school funds and physically abusing a child during a scolding. Patterson suspended Feinberg for a week with pay while another administrator investigated. The report came back that there was no evidence of the charges. Feinberg returned to his school. At the time, the incident made him angry. Later he saw it as a warning against being too aggressive, which he eventually heeded. Few of his detractors ever heard of the suspension, which under the rules remained confidential, but they still thought he was unworthy of their assistance. That explained in part why Patterson was not getting more help finding space for his school.

"Look, I have already tried to talk to Paige," Patterson said to him. "He didn't want to talk to me, so why don't you talk to Paige about it?"

She was throwing her frustration back at Feinberg and signaling how annoyed she was at his failure to show much gratitude for her killing herself to help him. The second she uttered the words, she realized she had made a mistake.

"Okay," Feinberg said, his jaw set, "then I will talk to Paige about it."

Uh-oh, Patterson thought. What now? She was too exhausted to say any more. She wanted Feinberg to leave her alone. If a trek to headquarters would get him out of her office, so be it.

The next day, Feinberg called the superintendent's office and asked for an appointment. The receptionist said she would try to get back to him, but he could tell from her tone that she said that to many people without having any hope she would actually do it. Feinberg waited forty-eight hours. Nothing. He drove to the main office, the Taj Mahal. The reception Feinberg got when he arrived at Paige's office was not warm. "If he has time to talk to you," a secretary said, "we will be in touch with you."

Far from ready to give up, Feinberg saw something in the employee parking lot that gave him an idea. He waited two more days, just in case someone connected his name with the superintendent's kind comments about KIPP to the newspapers. When nothing happened, he drove back to the Taj Mahal.

The employee parking lot on the north side of the building covered several acres, all exposed to the hot sun. Feinberg parked his van, grabbed a stack of student work, and headed for a parking space next to the ramp leading up to the building's main door. A maroon Acura sedan was parked there. A wooden sign stuck in the ground near the car's front bumper said SUPERINTENDENT. Feinberg leaned against the rear of the car and settled in for a long wait. He corrected papers to pass the time.

It was early April. The sun was high. There was no shade. Feinberg decided he would last longer if he sat on Paige's rear bumper. He got a few odd looks, but no one said anything to him. He looked harmless, a scholarly young man with glasses. Maybe he was Paige's driver. It was 1997, four years before terrorist attacks made the security of U.S. public buildings a national obsession. After 9/11, Feinberg would have been asked what he was doing sitting on the superintendent's car, but nobody bothered him that afternoon. He waited and thought about what he would say. Paige was obviously in his office and would have to come out sooner or later.

About 6:00 p.m, four hours into his vigil, Feinberg saw the superintendent coming down the ramp. Paige had a briefcase. He looked tired and distracted. But he recognized Feinberg. "Mike?" he said.

"Hi, Dr. Paige, I'm in a pickle," Feinberg said. He gave the older man a look he hoped conveyed his pain and desperation. "You've got to help me. They're trying to take away my babies!"

The superintendent thought about this for a moment. He was amused and impressed by what the teacher had done to get his attention. Thirty years before, when Paige was the football coach at Jackson State University in Mississippi, he had occasionally waited in the headquarters parking lot to corner the university president. It was the kind of persistence that won games and made other good things happen.

"Mike," he said, "what are you talking about?"

Feinberg delivered his story in rapid bursts. "Well, there is no room in Sharpstown for us to stay there, no place for us to move, and they are saying the only option . . ." He paused, realizing he had to get to the point. "I'm being told that I have to give up my going-to-be-seventh graders or give up my fifth graders, and I hope you can help me find a way out of this pickle."

Paige could see Feinberg was upset. "Well," he said, "I'm sure we can do something." He thought some more. "Come around tomorrow morning and we will figure it out."

Feinberg was thrilled. He had finally gotten an appointment with the superintendent. "Thank you, Dr. Paige," he said.

Feinberg arrived at 8:30 a.m. the next day. A secretary ushered him into a small conference room. Patterson was there, looking embarrassed. Feinberg also saw Paige and Paige's chief deputy, Susan K. Sclafani, who had met with Feinberg and Levin in 1994 and approved the original KIPP concept. The small, well-dressed woman looked at Feinberg as if she wanted to boil him in oil. Feinberg was certain that she had developed a dislike for him and his access to powerful people like Barbara Hurwitz and Mayor Lanier. He thought she had convinced herself that he had finally gone completely insane.

Paige tried to keep the meeting friendly. He had Feinberg summarize the situation. Then he spoke to his deputy, his west district superintendent, and the teacher. "Look, I'm sure there's got to be a way we can figure out the space. I love KIPP. KIPP's a great thing, and I want you guys to work it out. I have to go next door because I have to negotiate the food-service contract with Aramark. I am sure you will work out something."

And then, only five minutes into the meeting, he stood and walked out, leaving Feinberg alone with Sclafani and Patterson. The chief deputy did not make any pretense of how she felt. She asked him a series of questions: How was this meeting arranged? What was going on? Sclafani was serving as Paige's tough right hand, protecting him from fools and knaves. She would continue in that capacity for many years, when he became U.S. secretary of education and then when he became a partner in a management firm specializing in education issues.

Whatever Feinberg thought of her, she had always liked the KIPP idea. She was one of Houston's most active supporters of Teach For America and the work of its alumni. But by the time Feinberg stopped her boss in the parking lot, Sclafani acknowledged years later, she had become worried about the KIPP principal, both because of stories about his raising his voice to students and because of the previous year's infamous advocacy lesson. Coaching fifth graders to call headquarters officials in search of information about classroom space had struck her as completely over the line, an unprofessional manipulation of children. She knew that educators with good ideas sometimes had to push hard against stupid rules and insensitive bureaucrats, but she thought other young reformers — she particularly liked Chris Barbic, a former Levin-Feinberg roommate who had started his own charter school group in Houston — pursued their goals more intelligently and appropriately than Feinberg did.

Sclafani was not happy that Paige had welcomed Feinberg into their office. Feinberg recalled her telling him during the meeting that there was no way the district was going to give him any more space. She later said she would never have said such a thing, but she admitted that she was not feeling very charitable toward Feinberg that day.

"What do you mean, there is no way?" Feinberg remembered saying. He was not going to toss away his advantage after four hours of risking skin cancer in the hot sun. "I just heard the superintendent say we are going to get space some way."

He did not tell her precisely how he had arranged the meeting. He said he had run into the superintendent and told him about KIPP's difficulty, and the superintendent had said he thought there wouldn't be a problem working out a solution. It was not that big a deal, Feinberg said, trying to ease the tension. All he needed was space for fifth, sixth, and seventh grades, perhaps 230 or 240 kids, by summer.

Sclafani was determined to waste no more time on the matter. She also realized she had to give Feinberg some hope or he might never leave the building. "Well, I will have to make some calls," she said. "Ms. Patterson and I will talk about this and get back to you."

Feinberg gave her his most electric smile. "That's terrific," he said.

Later in the day, Feinberg visited Patterson's office to see how it was going. Patterson was back in fret mode — elbows on her desk, rubbing her temples. She gave him a wan smile. "So, Mike, did you sit on Dr. Paige's car and wait for him to come out and tell him that we needed more space?"

"Yes, Anne, I did."

"Well, I got reamed out by Dr. Sclafani."

Feinberg looked concerned. "But Anne, you told me to do it."

"But I wasn't being *serious!*"

"You know me better than that," he said. "And three times, Dr. Paige said we can take care of it."

She didn't write him up. In fact, Feinberg saw that Patterson was amused by the stalking incident, mostly because it had worked. Paige soon called a meeting of his staff and said he was thinking of giving KIPP part of the Wesleyan Building, auxiliary space just across their own parking lot that was used for overflow personnel from school district headquarters. Some of the people at the meeting were aghast, Paige recalled, but he stuck with his plan.

Patterson told Feinberg about Wesleyan. "I am going to work on this," she said. "I think we have an option. We might be able to get two floors."

"Well," Feinberg said, "that would be perfect."

34.

Dave and Frank

THE FRIENDSHIP OF Dave Levin and Frank Corcoran often brought comment. They were so different. When they first roomed together in Houston, the quiet Corcoran thought Levin took an interest in him only to get a break from the boisterous Feinberg. But Corcoran had good instincts about children. He was the next-to-youngest of the seven children of a lawyer and a homemaker in Newport, Rhode Island. Nearly everybody liked the slender, blond, sweet-tempered teacher. When Levin and Corcoran started working together in New York, school system officials would often call Levin an obstinate trouble-maker. Those were the same words being used to describe Feinberg back in Houston. They would ask why Levin couldn't be more like Corcoran. "Oh yeah," Levin said wearily. "Everyone loves Frank."

There were priests and nuns in Corcoran's family. For a while he thought he would accept holy orders himself. That was one reason he went to the University of Notre Dame. He embraced many of that campus's cherished traditions. He was a talented musician, rising to first trombone in the Notre Dame marching band his freshman year. He was also an inquisitive student, looking for the deeper meaning of man's place in the universe.

That thoughtful side led him to drop the idea of the priesthood. He saw much need for change in the world. Anger over social injustice gripped his soul. But the church did not seem to be the best place to channel his desire for political and social change. In his junior year he spent a semester abroad in Israel, when the Intifada was at its worst, and learned about the lives of young Palestinians. He persuaded his aunt Anne Corcoran, a nun, to let him work with her for several weeks at her small hospital in Zimbabwe.

By the time he returned to South Bend for his senior year, his mind was racing. He quit the band and added a concentration in peace studies to his history major. He did a research paper on the Reserve Officer's Training Corps, or ROTC. He concluded it had too much influence over the lives of students at Notre Dame.

One night, as a protest, he climbed to the top of the new $6 million ROTC building, still under construction, and wrote " Я A W," with the *R* inscribed in reverse, in nine-foot-high letters with white paint on the steeply slanting roof. He hoped people would see he had written a mirror image of the word *war*, as a sign that the university's priorities were askew. But when he got home, he realized he had accidentally left his keys at the scene of the crime. He would, he was sure, be quickly identified. He saw no point in trying to avoid punishment. He turned himself in. He was suspended for the rest of the year. He would not be able to graduate with his class and had to pay a three-thousand-dollar fine for malicious vandalism and destruction of school property.

His parents were surprised but forgiving. His siblings teased him. "Oh, Frank," one said, "you're no longer the best kid." He worked two jobs for the rest of the year to pay his fine and prove to his parents that he was not a complete loss. He returned to Notre Dame the next year and graduated, adding some depth to his college life by sharing living quarters with a paroled murderer in a program that, as expected, taught him much about the real world.

He signed up for Teach For America in 1991. Adriana Verdin at Garcia made him one of her first recruits. The next year she added Feinberg to her Teach For America collection. Before Corcoran could quite figure out what was happening, he was heading to New York with Feinberg's friend Levin. They rented a yellow Ryder truck, filled it with their furniture and books, and drove it to the Thirty-third Street apartment Betty Levin had found for them. It was twelve hundred dollars a month, twice what they had been paying in Houston. Corcoran considered the higher cost of living part of his New York adventure.

For him the big city was full of surprises, many of them unpleasant. By his count, about 40 percent of the South Bronx families they visited were indifferent or hostile. He and Levin got the impression that the people who had promised them a start in the South Bronx had not believed they would go through with it. They were two nice-looking kids in their twenties. They couldn't really be serious.

At each sticking point, Corcoran heard Levin repeat his mantra to whoever was standing in their way: "We think we have earned this. We have shown what we can do. We have a track record. We have earned the right to this chance." Corcoran let Levin do the talking, but he thought to himself, We haven't really earned anything, at least in the minds of these people. The P.S. 156 principal, Maxine O'Connor, told them, "How can I guarantee that you guys are actually going to come in here and pull this off and not just abandon the kids in the middle of the year?" At least she was honest, Corcoran thought.

Corcoran didn't think he was a great teacher. He could connect with children, but he was not a disciplinarian. He didn't have the toughness he admired in Levin and Feinberg. They were hustling phenoms who had found a way to bring student achievement to new heights. He was nothing like them.

He was amazed that so many of the South Bronx students actually called his and Levin's apartment each night with homework questions. That was what they were required to do, he knew, but school rules usually didn't mean much in that neighborhood. They could have acted like the kids often did in his former classes, ignoring everything he said. Why were so many of them, after a nine-and-a-half-hour day at school, in what some New York KIPP critics were calling the Kids In Prison Program, willing to dial the telephone for more discussion of schoolwork when all their friends and family were sitting around watching television?

Spending every day teaching with Levin, he got a clearer idea of how KIPP might actually make progress, if they could keep it together. Corcoran thought their hard work as teachers motivated their students. Inner-city children were surprised to see outsiders putting in so much time and energy on their behalf. Few of the teachers they had had in regular public schools had done that. Never before had any teachers given them their home phone numbers and insisted they call if they had questions.

In the South Bronx, Levin tried to re-create the conditions of KIPP's successful first year in Houston. One Sunday in Central Park, Levin taught Corcoran all of Harriett Ball's songs and chants. He could have written them down and told his new partner to memorize them, but he thought Corcoran should learn them just as he had, by listening. The Frisbee players and young lovers in Strawberry Fields saw two young men lounging in the grass and singing to each other, partly to the tune of "The Itsy Bitsy Spider," in what sounded like gibberish: "Six, twelve, eighteen, twenty-four, thirty, thirty-six, and the spider said: Forty-two, forty-eight, fifty-four, sixty, forty-two, forty-eight, fifty-four, sixty, sixty-six, seventy-two — how do you do?" The two teachers shook hands. "Sixty-six, seventy-two — how do you do?" They shook hands again.

"Okay," Levin said. "Let's do it again, but snappier."

Levin and Feinberg had taught as a team in one jammed classroom at Garcia, so the first year, Levin removed the dividing screen between his and Corcoran's classroom at P.S. 156 and taught the same way. Corcoran became increasingly convinced that Levin was the best teacher he had ever seen. Corcoran's roommate often seemed laconic in private. He practiced a form of urban cool that was characteristic of young people who had grown up in Manhattan. In the classroom, he kept some of that reserve. He was not as frenetic or effusive as Feinberg. But he was relentless, constantly pushing students to go further and do better.

Levin sought feedback from every child in the room. He had a dozen ways to explain difficult concepts, never quitting until he was sure each student got it. No child was permitted to sit through a lesson without having to answer some questions. "I am missing one person, I am missing one person," Levin would say, as he moved around the classroom. That meant someone was not paying attention. Instead of

going to that one child for a stern lecture, he submitted the problem
to the class as a group, as a team. He would give that child a chance to
correct herself. Often when he said he was missing one person, he was
actually seeing many more ignoring him. He claimed to see just one
so that the slackers would not be tempted to think of themselves as a
large and brave group of rebels. Many students came to hope that the
inattentive one would come around soon so they could keep moving
and see what else Mr. Levin had in mind.

At night, when the two teachers were back in their apartment, Levin
explained to Corcoran the importance of details, things Corcoran had
never considered despite the fact that he had started teaching a year
before Levin had. There was the thinking-skills class, for instance.
They began school each day with a few problems Corcoran xeroxed
at the copy shop near their apartment just before he went to bed. The
quick start set the pace for the whole day. Unlike many regular public
school students, Kippsters were given no time for distracting chats
about what they had seen on TV the night before. Learning started the
minute students entered the school cafeteria to get their free breakfast at 7:30 a.m. They were handed the thinking-skills questions at the
same time they got their milk, cereal, and juice.

Levin told Corcoran he should always look for responses from the
students. Dominating the lesson was bad. He should not be speaking
for two minutes and let students speak for only one minute. It should
be a conversation. Students should be responding regularly to the
teacher, and the teacher to them. Fifth graders, Levin told Corcoran,
could not sit quietly and absorb a lesson for too long at one time. They
had to be kept talking and moving and doing things as a group. That
way, Corcoran would not only keep them interested but monitor how
much they had learned.

To Levin, the best team teaching was like playing basketball. It
ought to be back and forth. The teachers should regularly interrupt
each other. They should keep the lesson lively and lure the students
into giving them the same attention they would give two of their

friends who were arguing. But they had to keep it light. No class would ever learn anything from a death struggle like Levin's five-hour one-on-one hoops marathon with Feinberg.

A well-paced and engaging class could only occur in an orderly classroom, Levin said. On that issue, Corcoran felt inadequate. Levin was strict, jumping on the first small sign of inattention or impoliteness. Corcoran had never been that tough or that quick in his classes. He was convinced this was a major reason why he had not been as effective a teacher as Levin and Feinberg.

He tried to improve. He experimented with thinking of discipline as an acting assignment. He loved the theater. He would become well known at KIPP New York for, among other things, writing and directing the annual Winter Show. In his mind, it wasn't kindly Frank Corcoran who backed a child into a corner, stuck his nose in the boy's face, and asked him if he thought he was such a genius to snicker at a classmate's wrong answer. It was not Frank Corcoran. It was a part he was playing, Fearsome Frank. The thought helped him improve his classroom management — Corcoran would eventually win the same prestigious teaching award that had once gone to Esquith — but he did not think he ever achieved Levin's air of assurance.

Levin and Corcoran agreed, as Levin and Feinberg had, that it was absolutely unacceptable for one student to make fun of or laugh at another student. This was one of Ball's firmest rules. Levin reminded Corcoran repeatedly that he had to get close to the child to make the point clear. He did not have to yell, but he had to be understood: "Oh, so you're that much better than him that you can laugh at him? You're that much better? Let's see you do it. Here's another math problem. Let's see you do it now." The idea, Levin said, was not so much to shame the miscreant, although that was important, but to signal the rest of the class that certain behavior would not be tolerated. As teachers, they tried to draw the lines that could not be crossed. They wanted to build a structure that made learning possible. Their message was that school should be a place where students could feel safe from bullies and wise guys and acts of childish cruelty. For children who already felt the shame and discomfort of poverty, this was key. They strived to make KIPP an island of peace where children could speak their minds and tend to their business without having to defend themselves. It would make them more willing to come to school early and stay late.

Often the problem in the classroom was not defiance but apathy. Some children would not participate. They required an entirely different approach: warm, regular encouragement. Corcoran was better at this. He loved praising the shy and the meek, people like him, and getting them to try to do a little bit more. The message was delivered softly, with little embarrassment to the child: "Look, get up. You're going to sit up here. You are going to participate. Sit up. Come on. Sit up. We're all tired, but we're all doing this."

Levin thought even melodrama sometimes had a place, although he would later admit that some of his performances went too far. One day during his second year in New York, a boy tossed something — it looked like a wadded piece of paper — at another child. It was not the first time that day that Levin had seen the boy throwing things. He was a bully, living proof that Levin and Corcoran's efforts to discourage such behavior had not been entirely successful. Levin was at the boy's desk in a second and escorted him to the front of the class.

"So you like throwing stuff?" he said. He told the boy to sit on a chair, facing the class. He found the classroom wastebasket and placed it in front of the chair. "The rest of you," he said to the class, "you all have wastepaper you need to get rid of. Well, just this once, you can throw it right here, into this basket." The students were delighted. They fired their wadded papers at the wastebasket. As Levin expected, some hit the boy. It didn't hurt him physically, but it shamed him in a way more powerful than Levin had expected. After that, he did not throw any more paper in class. But Levin realized that the lesson had gone too far, and never tried that approach again.

One warm day in spring when the students were unusually lethargic, Levin had another idea. The following day, both he and Corcoran walked into the classroom in full winter garb—coats, hats, scarves, and gloves. They kept them on the whole day, even though it was ninety degrees outside. "You're hot?" they told students. "Well, we're hotter. But we're not going to stop teaching. And so we expect you to keep learning."

They savored the flexibility of their long school day. Their students wrote in their journals every day. They read books each afternoon. During those classes, they sat with their books open, just as Feinberg's students were doing in Houston. They took turns reading aloud. Levin or Corcoran stopped them frequently for questions or comments.

At 3:30 p.m. each day, Corcoran would take the entire class down to the school gym for a snack and their daily dose of dodgeball, the routine Levin and Feinberg had established in Houston. Levin used those forty-five minutes to catch up on administrative work.

Years later, Levin would marvel at the depth of the relationship he and Corcoran developed. Dave and Frank were together nearly every minute of the day. Feinberg, and now Corcoran, had become his brothers. It seemed to all three of them that the depth of friendship and mutual respect was essential to their schools' success. When more KIPP schools began to be born, they urged new school leaders to find teachers with whom they could forge such personal relations and be a family.

For Levin, as for Feinberg, one of the most difficult chores, if his school was to survive, was to find a place to move after the second year. His building principal had no more room for him. If he was going to add a seventh grade, he needed to go elsewhere. He and Feinberg talked about this on the telephone nearly every night, each encouraging the other to break out of the bureaucratic death grip. But it was slow going. When Feinberg secured bigger quarters at Wesleyan, in the aftermath of staking out Paige's car, Levin was even more discouraged. Rod Paige knew Mike Feinberg. Rudy Crew, the chancellor of schools in New York City, had no idea who Dave Levin was. Any attempt to stalk that man would lead to Levin's immediate arrest. He was still without a home for his school the next year.

"I'm Not Going to That School"

IN HIS LARGELY SUCCESSFUL career as a KIPP recruiter, Feinberg had never had a heckler. Some fourth graders might look bored or distracted, but during his spring 1997 visit to Benavidez Elementary School, he did not expect any trouble.

The first class he visited was disorderly, to be sure. It had already run through three teachers that year. Before he even started, a whirligig whizzed past his head. He also noticed a thin boy, shorter than many others in the class, who was wearing a baseball cap sideways, leaning back in his chair, and mumbling to himself, three no-no's at KIPP. But that was typical of nine-year-old tough guys.

"I have some good news, and I have some great news," Feinberg announced. He did his usual teaser: What parts of the country would they like to visit? Chicago? New York? D.C.? Yes, it was true what they had heard. They would be paid once a week in KIPP dollars and go to Wendy's (it had proved to be more convenient than McDonald's) for lunch on Saturdays.

"And you want to hear the better news? You get to come to school at seven thirty—"

"Who'd want to do *that*?" said the boy in the baseball cap, very loudly and distinctly.

Hmm, Feinberg thought. This was new. It wasn't his class. He plowed on. "You get to come to school at seven thirty and stay until five—"

The boy emitted a hiss, a sound of disgust. "Only a bunch of *losers* would do that," he said.

Feinberg gave him a careful look, to remember the face. Then he wrapped up his presentation. A few days later he collected the returned forms and started the home visits. He was in his second year as a Gulfton resident, so he knew each apartment building and could arrange forms quickly in the right order, one block after another. About 7:00 p.m. he reached the door of an apartment on the second floor of the South Oaks complex. He knocked. The door opened. There was that face again, Feinberg's short and slender heckler, looking different. The boy wasn't wearing the baseball cap, and his tone had changed. The child put out his hand very politely and said, "Good evening, sir. How are you doing?"

Feinberg's heart soared. I've got you now, he thought. Whatever this student's behavior at school, the greeting meant he had tough parents, Feinberg's favorite kind. Underlining the point, a woman's voice called out from inside the apartment. "Moo-moo, who's that?"

Feinberg could barely contain his delight. Moo-moo? (An aunt had given the boy the nickname, the same name she called her kitten, shortly after he was born.) Feinberg thought: I really got you.

Feinberg later found out how Kenneth McGregor Jr., one of the least likely KIPP recruits he had ever encountered, got on his call list. The boy had not taken the form home, but the Benavidez principal, Brenda White, called his mother, Sharon Simpson, about this interesting opportunity for her high-spirited son. "Sharon? Where is that paper?"

"What paper?"

"I *knew* that boy didn't give it to you. I'll make sure he has it with him tomorrow. You ask him for it."

The next day she asked: "Kenneth? Do you have a paper for me?"

He looked stubborn. "No, no, no, Momma. I'm not going to that school. That man was mean, and I want to play football."

She told him she still wanted to meet the teacher. Feinberg's chat with Simpson and son went well, Feinberg thought. Kenneth continued to make eye contact with Feinberg. He said all the things he sensed his mother wanted him to say. When it was time for the student to read the Commitment to Excellence form, Kenneth delivered his lines perfectly: "I will always work, think, and behave in the best way I know how, and I will do whatever it takes for me and my fellow students to learn."

"Do you know what that means?" Feinberg inquired.

"Yes, sir."

"Are you going to do that?"

"Absolutely, sir."

"That's interesting, because that is not how you were behaving in class when I saw you the other day."

Kenneth's mother sat up straight. "Excuse me, Mr. Feinberg?"

"Yes, Kenneth was actually talking back to me and kind of making fun of me during the KIPP presentation."

She gave the boy a hard look. "You *know* I don't accept that," she said. "Wait . . . you *know* I don't accept that."

The boy began to cry. With that, Feinberg saw what Kenneth was, a sensitive child not sure what to do with his abundance of God-given energy and wit. Feinberg comforted him. He asked Kenneth some questions. They talked about what had happened in the class and how different his behavior would have to be at KIPP. There would be better days, Feinberg said, if Kenneth remembered to work hard and be nice.

There was no instant transformation. It took a long time for the boy to learn how to control his sense of mischief. He was in many ways like his new mentor, the bright and ambitious but often troublemaking Feinberg. Kenneth tested every KIPP teacher in every way possible. He spent a great deal of time on the Porch. Simpson and Feinberg had many conferences about Kenneth. She always said the same thing: "Mr. Feinberg, you do whatever you want. Kenneth's got more work than he expected, and he knows he needs to listen to you and the teachers. If he doesn't do it, you do whatever you need to do."

Simpson and Kenneth's father, Kenneth Senior, had split up, but they still shared parenting of their two children, Kenneth and Kentasha, who eventually also enrolled at KIPP. There was rarely a field lesson that did not have Kenneth Senior or Simpson as a chaperone.

Over time, Kenneth improved as a student. His bond with Feinberg became particularly strong. He was good at math, and Feinberg was his math teacher. Feinberg coached the school basketball team, and Kenneth was one of his best players, a slashing point guard who loved to unleash on opponents all that pent-up energy. Both coach and player were completely besotted with Michael Jordan. Feinberg talked a lot to Kenneth about the superstar and how he had nurtured his talent with hard work and discipline.

36.

Silencing the Loudspeaker

COLLEEN DIPPEL TOLD herself the summer romance with Mike Feinberg had been just a fling. But when she returned to New York City, she did not go through with her plan to move in with her Manhattan boyfriend. She broke up with him instead. She continued to work at Teach For America headquarters in New York but shelved her law school plans and instead arranged to return to Houston the next summer, this time as a Teach For America corps member beginning her own two-year classroom commitment.

She was assigned a fifth grade at Port Houston Elementary School on the east side. Her class was mostly low-income Hispanic children. Trying to reach them was hard work. She often found herself crying, out of frustration and fatigue, when she drove home from work.

At first she stayed away from Feinberg. Their on-and-off relationship was off at the moment. But she was having such a difficult time with her students that she decided she needed his help. He let her spend many hours at KIPP at Sharpstown, watching him and his teachers in action. He introduced her to Harriett Ball. Soon Dippel's Port Houston students were doing all the chants. Laurie Bieber gave her a social studies unit that had worked at KIPP. Feinberg lent her some of the novels he used in afternoon readings.

By the middle of the year, Dippel was not only a full-time teacher at Port Houston but a part-time teacher at KIPP, tutoring students in computer skills from 5:00 to 7:30 p.m. every evening. She began to create her own KIPP-like program at Port Houston, taking kids on field lessons, making home visits, and ignoring complaints about her independent ways.

She became so annoyed with the announcements on the classroom loudspeaker, which took precious time from her lessons, that she popped open a ceiling tile and cut the speaker wires. When she missed a meeting that had been announced, she said the loudspeaker had mysteriously broken. Port Houston being an overburdened urban school, no one rushed to fix it. She also did not take her students to school assemblies that she considered unnecessary. A visit from Bozo the Clown, she thought, was not going to help their reading.

She told no one at Port Houston about her moonlighting at KIPP or her KIPP swim classes at the Lee High School pool on Saturdays. Her students at Port Houston were doing well. Her principal was more than willing to overlook her idiosyncrasies as long as their math and reading scores were improving.

When her Port Houston classroom blackboards, rotting off the walls, became too hideous to bear, she experimented with a Feinberg-style advocacy lesson. She suggested that her students write to the central maintenance office. The class elected officers to lead the campaign. When nothing happened, Dippel encouraged parents to make phone calls. Shortly after, the principal told her that her class would have to meet in the cafeteria the following week because a maintenance crew was coming to replace her blackboards. She was embarrassed when the other teachers learned they were coming only to Ms. Dippel's room.

She put herself in further jeopardy by worrying over the fact that her students the next year would be assigned to a sixth-grade teacher she thought was verbally abusive and incompetent. There was, she realized, another sixth grade they could go to instead. "Mike," she told Feinberg, "you need to take my kids."

"Well, I don't know," he said. Patterson had warned him not to pick any more fights.

"Mike, I need you to take my kids. I have been working at KIPP. I have been doing the stuff. They are KIPP kids. They got it."

He found it hard to say no to Dippel. He visited her class and did his recruiting routine. A few months later, Dippel's principal greeted her with a frown. "We need to talk," the principal said. "Central office knows you sent eleven kids to KIPP. That amounts to a lot of lost money to them."

Dippel nodded. There was no use in denying it, although she did not see how any money was lost. Her kids were still public school children being supported with public school funds, just at a different school.

"On top of that," the principal said, "it looks like you are going to KIPP a lot yourself."

Dippel nodded again. She liked this principal and accepted her words as a friendly warning.

"I just think you should know," the principal said, "that a lot of people are watching you."

37.

Giving Up

LEVIN AND FEINBERG found their nightly telephone conversations a comfort. It was good to know the other person was also accumulating scars. That meant their battles were the result of shared lofty goals, not bad luck or personality flaws.

Levin loved Feinberg's story of the parking lot meeting with Paige. He could see the look on Sclafani's face. But Feinberg's triumph made his own lack of progress in New York that much more upsetting. He felt trapped. O'Connor had made it clear he was not going to get any more room out of her. He wondered if he deserved any more space. His students were getting better, at least when compared to the kids in the regular Bronx public schools, but their gains seemed to him erratic and underwhelming.

The test scores for his first year's fifth grade had come back. KIPP was higher on average than most other fifth grades in the Bronx but had nothing like the gains the students at Garcia had shown during his year with Feinberg. Twelve of his students had either moved out of the neighborhood or gone back to the regular schools because their parents thought KIPP was too tough or too crazy. He had only found eight new students to replace them. He still had to recruit forty-six more students for a new fifth grade.

Levin looked everywhere for answers. He asked Corcoran to critique his classroom performance. What was he doing wrong? Corcoran tried to be helpful, but he refrained from saying what he really felt: You're running this school. If *you're* doing anything wrong, then jeez, I'm up a creek. Corcoran tried to help Levin by being a better teacher himself, particularly in disciplining students. He did his best to play Fearless Frank, master of the classroom. But he didn't feel he was doing a good job or contributing much to the school. He thought he was dumping the most difficult students on Levin's shoulders.

Every night in their apartment, Levin and Corcoran agonized over what to do. As the second year dragged on, their discussions became more downhearted. Levin thought it was going to be too hard to find space to add a seventh grade the next year. He had no way to root out the languid "whatever happens, happens" attitude that ruled the neighborhood and his students. Apathy was in command. He was making little headway against it. He spoke more and more of returning to Houston. Feinberg, after all, was getting support from his school district. What was he getting in New York?

He wasn't getting paid, for one thing. The checks from the New York City school system were erratic at best, for him and his staff. Despite his objections, the P.S. 156 staff kept pulling some of his students out of his classes for services like special education, which Levin could see was doing them little good. O'Connor had stopped responding to his pleas for information on more space. The district superintendent appeared to have taken a dislike to him and left the same message Feinberg had gotten in Houston: Forget about adding any more students next year. A woman he had been dating for eight months had just told him she had been engaged all that time to someone else and would not be seeing Levin anymore.

He had no safety net and no track record in New York. Feinberg told Levin that although he had his new space, he could use Levin's help. It would take both of them to rescue the original Kippsters from their mediocre middle schools. As the year dragged on, Levin decided Feinberg was right. He told Corcoran he had had it. This would be the last year of KIPP in New York. He called Feinberg and told him to make room. He was coming back.

Feinberg was ecstatic. He told his staff. He told his students. He told his friends. He contacted many of the original Kippsters and told them. Mr. Levin was coming back! KIPP would have space for all of them at its new quarters near the Taj Mahal. They could all return like POWs released from Vietnam.

Meanwhile, Corcoran listened to the outburst of defeatism from Levin, his roommate, friend, and boss, with mounting confusion, then resignation. Corcoran had decided he was not going to leave New York, no matter what Levin did. He and Levin had promised their students that they were going to be there for them. He had taught these Bronx children for two years. He could not bear the idea of abandoning them. He and Levin agreed that when KIPP New York closed, it would be monstrous to dump its students back into the regular New York system. They knew what the other middle schools in the Bronx were like. They looked for schools that could give the KIPP refugees something extra. They visited private schools like Fordham Prep, some Catholic schools, and some public magnet schools.

Corcoran heard about a school in Manhattan called De La Salle. It was a middle school designed mainly for gifted students. His inquiries brought hints that the school might have places for well-prepared students from the Bronx. One day, when Corcoran's class schedule left him a long midday lunch break, he took the subway to De La Salle to see if it was as good as he had heard.

The school seemed wonderful. It was a serious place where his students could pursue the higher goals that KIPP had aimed for. He added it to the list he was compiling. Maybe he could get a job there too. On the subway back to the Bronx that afternoon, a train broke down in the tunnel ahead of him. He sat in the cramped, fetid subway car for more than an hour. He grew increasingly irritated with himself for not allowing more time to get back to school. When he finally arrived at KIPP, panting from his run from the subway station, he was an hour late for his afternoon class. He dashed up the stairs. In the hallway he saw Jason Levy, one of the new KIPP teachers. "Did somebody watch my class?" Corcoran asked, hoping he had been spared the embarrassment of explaining his tardiness to his students, and to Levin.

Levy looked puzzled. "I didn't know you weren't there," he said.

Corcoran walked quickly to his classroom, ashamed of himself. He was no better at being tough with himself than he was with his kids. Just before he entered the room, he noticed something odd. It was very quiet in there. Had they all gone home? If conditions were as chaotic as he assumed, he should be hearing some noise. The only sound was the voice of one student, speaking in clear and forceful tones. It sounded as if she was running the class.

He stood with his back against the wall just outside the open classroom door. He did not want the students to see him until he had figured out what was going on. He took a deep breath and listened carefully. He was hearing two students, not one. They were Dominique Young and Alexis Rosado. They were teaching, going over the thinking-skills work that had been done that morning. No one was speaking out of turn. Everyone was paying attention, although at one point Dominique saw something she didn't like. "You wouldn't do that if Mr. Corcoran were here," she said, "so don't do it now."

Corcoran leaned against the wall a few more seconds, soaking it in. This whole thing, he thought, the school they were about to abandon — it was working. It was actually working.

Some days later, on his twenty-seventh birthday, March 16, 1997, Levin sat on a stool at the far right end of the long bar at Patrick Kavanagh's, an Irish pub a half block from his apartment. He was feeling sorry for himself. He was going back to Houston. He was never going to respect himself again. He had been preaching to his students that they shouldn't quit, no matter what, no matter how hard it gets. He had been telling them they had to believe and have faith. Why hadn't he told himself that?

The more he wallowed in the feeling, sipping his beer, the more he realized he couldn't do it. He could not walk away. He had lost sight of what was really important. It wasn't about the way the District 7 people were treating him. It wasn't about the stronger support Feinberg was getting in Houston. What was important was to fight the fight regardless of what happened, to keep going until they shut the school down. At least it would not be him giving up, walking away from his kids. They couldn't walk away from the difficulties in their lives.

So it was settled. Mike would kill him, but he had changed his mind. He was going to stay and raise all types of hell and see what happened. He felt the same way he had felt the day he dropped Quincy into his seat. Levin had been frightened that day, but he kept going.

Levin went back to the apartment to tell Corcoran what he had decided. "Frank, I am not quitting," he said. They were both near tears. Corcoran's reaction was relief, and then anger. They had almost blown it. They had something with great potential, and they had almost let it die. Corcoran was not prone to loud outbursts, but he could not let the moment pass without telling Levin how he felt.

Mild-mannered Frank grabbed his friend Dave around the neck and shook him and then yelled at him, trying to get some of that raspy, ugly District 7 administrator tone into the words so that Levin would not forget them.

"Okay, if you are going to do this, then *you're going to stick with it. No pussying around! Don't be a pussy!* And if you *ever* do this to me again, *I'm going to kick your ass!*"

38.

Moving Fast

AFTER A DIFFICULT CONVERSATION with Feinberg about not return-ing to Houston after all, Levin got back to work. He needed more space for his third year in the Bronx. Feinberg's advocacy lesson would not work for him. But he could make the phone calls himself. He called Chancellor Crew's office several times. He called the borough presi-dent. He called the school board representative for the borough. He called a member of the city board of regents.

And then at the last minute he found his own Anne Patterson, a counselor-protector-friend. Her name was Susan Winston. She was dark haired and direct and, at forty-eight, about the same age as Patterson. She had fought similar battles to raise achievement for low-income minority children. Like Patterson, Winston knew where all the levers were in her school district's complex administrative structure. She knew exactly what to look for in a classroom. She was as quick to see the worth of what Levin and Corcoran were doing as Patterson had been when she encountered the Feinberg-Levin team.

Winston first visited KIPP New York in May 1997. Her initial im-pression when she showed up to inspect Levin's little school-within-a-school was that it was going nowhere unless it got some help. There was no sign in front of P.S. 156 or in front of his classrooms saying anything about KIPP. A casual visitor, Winston thought, would have noticed little difference between what Levin and his teachers were do-ing and all the other things going on in the fortresslike school. Levin had only five years of teaching experience and was much too young, many people in the district thought, to be taken seriously as a school leader.

But Winston had run a 180-student program in Newark, New Jersey, when she was twenty-eight. She was less interested in his age than in what his kids were doing. In the second-floor KIPP classrooms, she saw students alert and engaged in their lessons. They responded quickly to frequent and friendly teacher questions. The classes were almost completely devoid of the chatter, inattention, and mischief that characterized many of the schools Winston visited.

She began a series of conversations with Levin to see what was motivating him. She wanted to know if he had the stamina and intelligence that he would need to survive in New York. "How much of what you do is genuine, and how much of it is Thursday school?" she asked him.

"What do you mean?"

"Thursday schools are schools that do everything they say they do just on Thursday, and that's the day they have all their visitors. How genuine are you, on a scale of one to ten?" she said.

"Have you ever seen a ten?" Levin asked.

"No."

"Then we're a nine."

She was the director of middle schools and building operations for District 7, a post only slightly less powerful than Patterson's superintendency of Houston's west district. Levin told Winston he was still hoping for space in Intermediate School 151, just down the street from P.S. 156. The building was so underutilized that five hundred students from a neighboring district had classes there, yet there were still many empty rooms. Winston went to see some people. She secured promises of six classrooms at I.S. 151.

Such promises, she warned him, did not necessarily mean he was going to get the space. Levin was given a target date in August to move all of his books and equipment down the block to his new rooms on the fourth floor of the intermediate school. Just one day before moving day, with everything ready, he heard that an elementary school, P.S. 31, had had its building declared structurally unsound and was going to override his claim to I.S. 151. P.S. 31 had a strong-willed, experienced principal, Carol Russo, who was not going to be outmaneuvered by some kid.

The deputy superintendent for District 7 telephoned Levin to let him know what was happening. "We should probably wait on your move until the superintendent comes back," she said, "because we don't know if we will have space for you anymore."

"Well, is that the direct order of the superintendent?" he asked.

"No, it's just what I'm thinking."

"Well, where is the superintendent?"

"She's on vacation."

"Well, our direct orders were to move today, so I am going to follow those orders."

He hastily assembled his small staff, found twenty students happy to be part of the action, and got them moving boxes, books, pencils, everything, from P.S. 156 to I.S. 151. Winston had explained to him the importance of squatter's rights in the New York school system. Once he moved in, it would be hard to move him out.

Two days later, the superintendent returned from vacation. She was briefed on P.S. 31's need for space in I.S. 151. "Well," she said, "let's not have KIPP move, then." But it was done. Inertia was king in the Big Apple. Levin was allowed to stay.

He would pay for his victory. Russo took other space in I.S. 151 and did not appear, at least to Levin, to like sharing her building with KIPP. She controlled the timing of events like fire drills. Levin thought she called them whenever she pleased, without asking if they interfered with his schedule. When he wanted the building open for Saturday classes, she said that would be a problem. When he tried to bring snacks to his classrooms from the kitchen, she said that violated the rules.

But Levin had finally managed to hire, on a full-time basis, the dangerous but talented music teacher Charlie Randall and his friend Jerry

Myers, an experienced teacher and administrator who knew how to win over the most troubled students. KIPP New York was bigger now and had room to grow. Levin's and Corcoran's moods improved. Their new teachers, both old and young, added a bolt of energy. Classes began to hum. Another veteran teacher Levin hired, Fred Shannon, had a system for making all the parts work together.

Levin spent a great deal of time with Randall, a genius in raising student morale. His orchestra was to Levin a miracle. He could not have imagined having every student in the school engaged in the same complex activity, but Randall made it happen. Randall brought on board one of his former students, Jesus Concepción, to succeed him in making the orchestra the public face of KIPP Academy New York for many years.

Jerry Myers was much quieter and less noticeable than Randall, but his touch with the most emotionally disturbed students was unerring, another gift. The two men knew more about the mysteries of straightening out urban students than anyone Levin had ever met, with the exception of Ball. The fact that they had such a deft touch with boys was particularly welcome.

Test results went up. Its third year in New York, Levin's school had the highest scores in District 7, just as Feinberg's school was achieving the highest scores in its part of Houston.

Levin, Corcoran, Randall, and Myers became a posse, often inseparable. They talked about students before school, after school, and on weekends. On Friday afternoons the four men would invite one class — the fifth graders one Friday, the seventh graders another Friday — to join them in the music room for ninety minutes of talk about everything: what was happening at school, what was happening on the street, what was happening at home. The presence of Randall and Myers made the sessions work. The two older teachers knew the families. They knew the culture. They knew the language.

About once a month, after school closed on Friday, Corcoran, Levin, Myers, and Randall would climb into Levin's car and head for Atlantic City. There they would indulge in two of Randall's and Myers's favorite recreations, gambling and eating. Randall and Myers preferred the slot machines. Levin and Corcoran sampled the blackjack and craps tables. Much of the time, they would just eat, talk, and drink — Randall, a recovering alcoholic, would sip a club soda. The conversation was always about kids.

About 2:00 a.m. they would get back in the car and return to New York, just in time for a couple hours of sleep and a shower before they appeared at school at 8:00 a.m. for Saturday classes — music, art, decorum, all the things their students needed in order to have rich and full adult lives.

Those were the classes that appealed to Dominique Young, who joined Levin's original class in its second year when she was a sixth grader. She was one of the two students who took over Corcoran's class when the subway breakdown made him late. Her start in life had been inauspicious. Her parents were so young at her birth that if the KIPP Academy had then existed, they could have enrolled. Her father, Derrick Young, was fourteen when she was born. Her mother, Monique Jones, was thirteen. They did not marry, nor did they ever graduate from high school. But they passed on a quick intelligence and a talent for music to their short, round-faced daughter. When Levin arrived in the Bronx ten years later, both sides of Dominique's family thought his school would be good for her. She was getting top grades at a local fifth grade, despite doing little work. She was bored and often in trouble for talking.

Randall knew she could sing. He remembered her parents' talents. He had her perform with the school orchestra. He also let her play the drums. She was a natural. If she misbehaved, he could pull her back in line with a few words: "Dominique, I heard what you did in math class today. I know you don't want me to get on the phone with Linda." It was chilling to have a teacher who referred to her grandmother by her first name.

Years later, when KIPP New York was on its feet and both Randall and Myers had retired, Levin hired them as consultants to work on problems in the string of other KIPP schools he was starting in New

York. Winston also retired and became the official KIPP Foundation adviser to the four new principals Levin had hired. Levin was grateful to Ball and Esquith for what they had given him, ideas that had changed his life. But he was certain that he would never have gotten past the breaking point, to where he could ignore harassment by building principals and clumsy interventions from the district, if he had not had Randall, Myers, and Winston to calm him down and tell him how to survive in the Bronx.

Winston had found the challenge irresistible. Randall and Myers had been much more difficult to persuade and had only been lured to KIPP by Levin's enticing suggestion of a legacy. He realized after just a year of working with them that as their beneficiary, he would be getting much more out of the deal than they would.

A Chair Takes Flight

FEINBERG DID NOT GET as much space in the Wesleyan Building as he had thought he was going to get. There were a few offices that he converted to classrooms, as well as a small auditorium in the back that provided makeshift learning space, with student lockers as dividers. Still, it was enough to invite back as many of the original KIPP students as wished to come. Reintroducing them to KIPP, though, was not as easy or as pleasant as he had hoped.

Feinberg had broached his plan in the cafeteria of Burbank Middle School, where several of the original Kippsters were having lunch. Vanessa Ramirez, Lupita Montes, Melissa Ortega, and Jaime Espinoza were in the Vanguard magnet program at Burbank. The minute Feinberg made the offer, Vanessa knew she was going back to KIPP. Her father had left the family a few years before. Sara Ramirez considered Feinberg a surrogate parent for Vanessa and her two sisters. Whatever he wanted them to do, they were going to do.

Feinberg enlisted Vanessa, Lupita, Melissa, and Jaime, as well as former KIPP students Joe Alvarez, Javier Romero, and Zaira Melissa Johnson. The parents of a few Vanguard students who had never been in KIPP also signed up, having heard glowing accounts from former KIPP parents like Vanessa's mother. Several of the KIPP returnees' Burbank friends scoffed at their decision to transfer. "It's prison over there. We heard about it," one said. "You're going back to jail."

Feinberg's third year running a school without Levin turned out to be, at least in his eyes, his worst at KIPP. The spirit of teamwork and cooperation that he had tried to nourish was continually under threat.

Rules were ignored. Study habits slumped. Every day he seemed to be fighting some outbreak of whiny adolescence, or reteaching practices and habits that he thought had been deeply ingrained.

Much of this, he realized, was his fault. He had taken on too many obligations. He had let himself get too excited about Levin's ultimately aborted decision to come back to Houston. He had 225 fifth, sixth, and seventh graders, plus 25 eighth graders from the original KIPP class. He soon realized that the older students had been so neglected, even in their magnet programs, that they were not performing any better than the KIPP seventh graders from Gulfton. He continued to refer to them as eighth graders — the psychological effect of doing otherwise would have been disastrous — but he put them in the same classes with the seventh graders, and it was not always a good mix.

His seventh grade was down to fifty students from the seventy-two he had started with. Some families had moved. Some students had tired of the KIPP workload and transferred back to regular schools. This would become a common occurrence in KIPP schools as the network expanded. Principals who followed Feinberg and Levin looked for ways to reduce enrollment losses caused by the greater demands placed on students. Critics would call these students dropouts even though they were not leaving school but moving back to neighborhood classrooms. The critics would call this a serious weakness in the program, a sign that KIPP could not fulfill its promises to many children. KIPP advocates noted that many of these students were moving out of the area, and KIPP principals had found ways to significantly reduce the number of students dropping out because of the workload by giving more attention to students who arrived more than two years below grade level, warning them in advance that they might need to stay in KIPP an extra year.

Feinberg told new generations of KIPP principals never to repeat his mistake of bringing in so many seventh and eighth graders so late in the KIPP process. His eighth graders more or less remembered what KIPP had been like in fifth grade. But he had added fifteen seventh graders who had never been in KIPP before. They were recommended to him by teachers and parents, but their adjustment to the long days and heavy homework proved to be difficult.

Feinberg also struggled with the fact that he had a larger staff than ever before — a dozen people. His management style had been to lead by example. He thought that if he was a good teacher, if he kept the standards high in his own classroom and in meetings with his faculty, all would be well. As the year deteriorated, he realized he was not nearly as good a manager of adults as he had thought. Although Feinberg and Levin appreciated kind words as much as anyone, they had grown weary of big smiles and gushing praise from visitors. Few of them understood how hard it had been to get this far and how much further their students needed to go. Their results were so good, compared to what other schools in their neighborhoods were doing, that many people seemed to think they had some magic touch. They knew that was nonsense. They could not throw a KIPP shirt on a kid, wave a wand, and transform the child's character, habits, and academic performance overnight. The change came slowly. They had to establish a relationship with each child. In their third year of running their separate schools in Houston and the Bronx, that was much more difficult to do because they had so many more students than before.

Patterson knew Feinberg was teetering on the brink of something. She had seen what could happen if he pushed himself too hard. She decided he needed someone on his staff who was experienced in dealing with parents and with school district rules. That person could warn him if he was getting too frantic. Patterson found a kind and patient administrator, Sylvia Doyle, who was willing to take the job. She relieved Feinberg of much of his paperwork so he would have more time to manage his growing staff.

Nonetheless, Mount St. Mike finally exploded, overcome by fatigue and despair at having too much to do, without Levin to help.

The episode began the day the seventh and eighth graders, his most troublesome students, were watching a video of *West Side Story* on the small stage at the end of the auditorium section of the school. They were preparing to see the musical when it opened in Houston. They had read the book and libretto of the Broadway show. Now they were watching the Academy Award–winning film.

When Feinberg looked in on the class, few of the students were paying attention. It was 3:30 in the afternoon, and some were asleep. Others were whispering or giggling. The teachers seemed to be snoozing too. At the film's dramatic conclusion, after the star-crossed lovers, Maria and Tony, had sung a few last measures, Tony died in Maria's arms, and Maria kissed him. "Ewww," a student said, "she's kissing a dead guy!" Several students laughed.

That was it for Feinberg. "Turn it off," he said. "I want all faculty and all seventh- and eighth-grade students to assemble here tomorrow at 3:30 p.m. I will have some things to say about what I have seen here."

The next afternoon, at the appointed time, the students filed into the auditorium and saw Feinberg was sitting in a chair on the stage by himself. He was leaning forward and looking at the floor. "I was standing at the back of the room yesterday," he said, "and I watched all of you watch the end of *West Side Story* like typical seventh and eighth graders. Today we are going to watch the last twenty minutes *again,* this time as Kippsters."

He pushed the play button on the VCR. The students and teachers watched the end of the film in silence. When it was over, Feinberg, still in his chair on the stage, began to talk about time and place and the mission of the school. It appeared that he was talking to the students, but the message was meant for the teachers. "Tonight your assignment is, I want you to reflect on this," he said. "You are going to go home, and I want you to think about — compare and contrast — what it meant to watch *West Side Story* like a typical seventh or eighth grader versus watching it as a Kippster. I am not telling you how long the assignment should be. That's going to be part of the life test. You determine how long it should be."

Everyone turned in the assignment the next day. Feinberg was mostly pleased with the results. Several students wrote essays about the need to be more mature than other kids. They said they had to make sacrifices. Many referred to a regular KIPP theme, the exertion needed to climb the mountain to college. But two students, both seventh graders new to KIPP, turned in only a few sentences. That upset their principal.

He had asked the class to meet with him again the next day, same place, same time — 3:30 p.m. He began by saying he was mostly pleased by what he had read. Then he began to talk about the two new students who had not understood what he wanted. His words to them contained a message for the entire seventh and eighth grades. "What were you saying?" he said. "How can this be an adequate response? Action is louder than words, and what do these actions say? After everything that went down, you still don't get it — you don't appreciate why you are here."

The students watched him silently, not certain what would happen next. Feinberg went with his feeling of intense disappointment. "You've failed the test," he said. "I didn't say what you had to write, but you didn't even try. This is not your best. This is not putting your heart and soul into it. So now I'm telling you, your two or three sentences will have to become twenty or thirty pages. We are going to talk about how much more you are going to write."

The rest, he thought, was just detail. He would work it out in a personal chat with the two students. He was beginning to calm down and consider the angles. What he needed was a dramatic exit, the coach raging out of the locker room after a big loss. He jumped off the stage and pounded down the makeshift corridor on the left side of the large room.

There was a folding chair in his way. He put his hand on it and shoved it to the left. He wanted to show that nothing would stand in his way. But he got his hand underneath it, and somehow it was aloft. As Feinberg glanced back, astonished, it sailed into the air and smashed into one of the six-by-four-foot windows that lined both sides of the auditorium. There were no students near it, he was glad to see, but the window shattered into hundreds of small pieces, ruining much of the student work that had been pasted on it.

Feinberg kept moving. He walked directly to the office of his new administrative director, Sylvia Doyle, assigned to tell him when he was going too far. He told her what had happened. He gave her a signed check for the damage, leaving the amount blank. He was not sure what it would cost him beyond the mere dollars she would fill in on that check.

40.

Letting Go

DIPPEL'S EFFORT TO MOVE her students from Port Houston Elementary to KIPP Houston was not a complete success. A child named Serena, one of Dippel's stars, quit KIPP after two weeks of summer school. She thought the work was harder than even what Dippel had assigned at Port Houston, and it was a long drive from her home to the Wesleyan Building.

But there were also pleasant surprises, such as Marcos Maldonado. Feinberg had visited the Maldonado home to recruit Marcos's sister, Laura, who had been in Dippel's class. As usual, Feinberg went after every potential student in the house. That included Marcos, sitting quietly listening to the big stranger talk to his sister.

"Well, what grade are you in?" he asked the boy.

"Fourth."

"Well, you'll be a fifth grader next year. Do you want to come to KIPP?"

Soon he had both sister and brother, and their parents, signing the Commitment to Excellence contract. Laura would prove to be a fine student, but Marcos would be even better, rising to rare heights, becoming an award-winning exemplar whom KIPP teachers would talk about for years afterward.

With her second year at Port Houston nearly over, and her commitment to Teach For America fulfilled, Dippel wanted to be a full-time KIPP teacher. Her decision, she told herself, had nothing to do with her personal relationship with Feinberg. She admired his teaching and felt an obligation to the Port Houston students she had sent to KIPP.

Feinberg had no hesitation about hiring her. It was the beginning of the fourth year of KIPP Houston. For the first time, he was going to be in charge of a full-size fifth-to-eighth-grade middle school. He no longer had time to teach fifth-grade math. Dippel was the obvious choice as his successor in that job. No one else at the school had spent as much time with Ball or Feinberg as she had. She had taught fifth-grade math the KIPP way for two years at Port Houston. It occurred to Feinberg that there was actually no one else in the country, other than him, Levin, and Ball, who had as much experience as Dippel teaching math to ten-year-olds the Ball way.

Feinberg was drowning in the details of setting up his new campus. The year before, he and his friend Chris Barbic, founder of the YES charter school, had started writing an application for a state charter that would free them from having to deal with the Houston Independent School District. They realized that if they cut that cord, they would have to get their own modular classrooms and find some land to put them on.

This was, Feinberg realized, way beyond his competence. Once again he had swum too far out into the middle of the lake. But this time he had a rescuer, Shawn Hurwitz, the local businessman who was the son of Barbara Hurwitz, one of the first KIPP board members. Shawn was now the KIPP board chairman. Feinberg told him how scared he was of not being able to get to the next level. Hurwitz, a big man like Feinberg and about his age, listened quietly and gave Feinberg a pep talk that contained a warning. They could get this done, Hurwitz said, but Feinberg would have to grow up a bit. Hurwitz spoke seriously and respectfully, as he always did, but what Feinberg heard was that being young and cute and an inspiration to teachers and students wasn't enough now that they were talking about ground leases and million-dollar loans.

Hurwitz insisted that Feinberg come to his office every week from late 1997 to the summer of 1998 to confer and report on the progress in getting the state charter. Hurwitz secured a loan for the lease purchase cost of the modular classrooms for both KIPP and YES, about

$2.1 million. Hurwitz arranged the ground lease for KIPP at a vacant field on the Houston Baptist University property.

After that, Feinberg never made a move without Hurwitz at his side. He told friends that his school had been two months away from being homeless, and Shawn had saved him. They became close friends, going to heavy metal concerts and having the occasional golf outing. When KIPP began to expand, Feinberg made sure Hurwitz was on the national board. He told everyone who ever asked him how to start a school that they had to talk to Shawn.

But Hurwitz could not help Feinberg adjust to giving up his fifth-grade math babies to Dippel. Feinberg had visited each of their homes. He had watched each of them read the Commitment to Excellence form. The quality of the teaching they would receive their first KIPP year was vital. The fact that he was handing them over to a woman who was, whatever lies he told himself, more than just another staff member made the transition that much more complicated.

As Dippel predicted, Feinberg proved incapable of making a clean break with his responsibilities for the new class. He asked Dippel if he could be the one to teach the Ball chants to the new kids, using some of the time in his thinking-skills class. Sure, she said. She wanted to emphasize conceptual math anyway. As a math tag team, she told herself, she and Mike could give their students the best of both teachers.

Dippel felt she could separate her feelings about Feinberg as a colleague from her feelings about him as a man. She loved his teaching style. He was very good at motivating kids. He was inspiring to work with. But when she found out he was checking up on her teaching, like an overbearing father sneaking peeks at his daughter's homework, she did not like that at all.

Feinberg did not try very hard to hide what he was doing. "Alejandro doesn't know how to multiply," he said to Dippel one day after school.

"What are you talking about?"

"Well, he can't say his nines." Alejandro had not mastered the Ball chant that helped students remember nine, eighteen, twenty-seven, and so on.

"Okay," Dippel said, burying her resentment. She explained that the boy couldn't say his nines to Feinberg because the big teacher made him nervous and he would stutter, but he did know his nines. She tried to handle Feinberg's nit-picking as professionally as possible. But she felt the pressure, and the widespread parent doubts about her did not help.

Kenneth McGregor's parents were a prime example. They were infatuated with Feinberg. He was in total sync with their view on how their son should be raised. But their daughter, Kentasha, had just enrolled in KIPP, and their hopes for her getting the fantastic Mr. Feinberg for fifth-grade math had been dashed. They had to settle instead for this inexperienced young woman, Ms. Dippel. The parents of several other students felt the same. Why, they wondered, sometimes out loud, were their children not getting Mr. Feinberg, as they had expected? Kenneth, extremely astute about voice tones and body language, informed his mother with great certainty that his sister's math teacher was Mr. Feinberg's girlfriend, but Simpson laughed that off as a little boy's fantasy.

On Dippel's first back-to-school night, just one month into the new job, she could see several parents sitting in the back of her classroom, their arms folded and their faces skeptical that this skinny girl could carry the load. Yet the fifth graders grabbed everything she gave them and surged ahead. They went home and told their parents they loved their new math teacher. Dippel gained enough confidence to joke about the change, telling some parents, "I know you all want Mr. Feinberg, but I am a prettier version."

The pressure was still there, all the time, all year. By 1998, KIPP was well known in Houston. There had been several articles in the newspapers, and frequent reports on local TV. It was presented as a bright exception to the dreary reality of inner-city education. Feinberg used that to motivate his staff. He set goals for each teacher each year.

He made them sound like predictions rather than orders, akin to his frequently expressed hope that Michael Jordan would take his beloved Chicago Bulls to the NBA championship. But his teachers got the message. He told Dippel he thought at least 89 percent of her fifth graders would pass the state math tests. That was a very high number. Dippel could not stop thinking about it.

Near the end of the school year, a few weeks after her students had taken the Texas tests, Feinberg pulled her out of the classroom. "We got the test results," he said. "How do you think you did?"

She took several breaths, hyperventilating. "I don't know, maybe eighty-nine, maybe ninety?"

"One hundred percent," he said with a big smile.

"Really?"

"That's what it says here."

The feeling of relief hit her like a shock wave. She began to sob, taking great gulps of breath. So I'm not a failure, she thought. She was so proud of her kids, but she realized her reaction was way out of proportion. She had not realized until that moment how much of a strain she had been under. It was as if she had been smothering, and now her airway was free and clear. She gasped for more oxygen.

Feinberg was startled. "Why are you crying?" he asked.

Between gulps of air, she tried to explain: "I just didn't . . . know how . . . the kids were going to do."

Her fear of failure had been so high, her expectations so great. Oh my God, she thought, I need a valium or something.

41

Kenneth and the Golden Ticket

KENNETH MCGREGOR, AT his previous school, had been like many bright children. He had been considered a problem, not an asset. He sensed the fear and hostility and reacted negatively, exacerbating the cycle of bad behavior. Teachers at his old school had not given him anything very difficult to do, for fear of inciting a bad mood. He got by on little work, which led him to lose respect for the routine of going to school each day, which made him misbehave even more.

It took Kenneth some time to grow accustomed to his change of circumstances at KIPP. Eventually he realized that the hard work he was getting at KIPP was not another annoying school chore but a sign of respect. These people, as irksome as they were with their demands and tough talk, cared about him, just as his mother did when she tied him up with all her rules.

He still got into trouble. For instance, he was denied the trip to Utah at the end of sixth grade.

Feinberg and the other teachers, inspired by the Roald Dahl book *Charlie and the Chocolate Factory,* introduced the concept of the Golden Ticket. Each April they announced who was going to go on the trip to D.C., or Utah, or New York, whatever the field lesson destination was for that class. Feinberg presented each lucky student a Golden Ticket, just like the children in the book who got to visit the chocolate factory. At KIPP Houston, the ticket was a yellow sheet of paper with the trip details and a permission slip printed on it.

At the ceremony, Feinberg enumerated the responsibilities that came with a Golden Ticket. There was, for instance, the rule named after a student in the first year of KIPP at Askew: Luis had received his Golden Ticket but lost his chance to go to Washington, D.C., when he stole candy from the backpack of one of his classmates. He was barred from the trip only twelve hours before the plane took off. Acts had consequences, Feinberg said, different consequences depending on the circumstances. If you did something bad in September, you would probably go on the Porch, and your parents would be called to the school. But after a few weeks, you could earn back the lost trust and return to the team. Life would again be full of possibilities.

"But remember Luis," Feinberg said, raising his voice. "He got a Golden Ticket and he decided to do a crazy screwup. No one is perfect, but there is no time to make up for it and re-earn our trust if you do something like that this close to the trip. So I am not saying you have to be a perfect human being, but I am saying that for the next month before the trip, on the majority of things, you do have to be perfect. And if you're not perfect, you could still lose this Golden Ticket. Capisce?"

Nonetheless, the Luis rule did in Kenneth McGregor. In 1998, he was among ten members of the sixth grade who met unsupervised in one of the back rooms at Wesleyan and played a kissing game. It was G-rated, but it was still a gross violation of the rules. Feinberg met with the group in a classroom and delivered the bad news. He was depressed that he had to say this to children he loved, especially Kenneth. "You are not going to be able to re-earn our trust by May sixteenth to go to Utah, so you have lost the Utah trip. It is not necessarily because of the kissing game, but because of when you did it. There is just no time left to re-earn our trust."

Kenneth bounced back. He made both the seventh- and eighth-grade trips. He continued to excel as a student and a person. His seventh-grade basketball team won nearly every game. He received a full scholarship to Strake Jesuit College Preparatory in Houston.

At graduation, Feinberg made him and his mother a promise. Feinberg still remembered how he'd felt when Kenneth missed the Utah trip. He said he would make sure, given the record that Kenneth compiled at KIPP, that he would get a free trip to Utah someday. "Don't worry," Feinberg said. "Sometime in high school or college you are going to come back and you are going to chaperone a group with me and go to Utah."

42.

"You Can't Say That to Me"

DIPPEL AND FEINBERG agreed on how to teach math to fifth graders, but there was no such consistency in their feelings about each other. Their romantic instincts were rarely in sync. They were busy people. They did not know if they had any spare time or energy for love. From the first night they squeezed past his Xerox machine to get into his apartment, there was an obvious attraction. The thing just never quite jelled.

Once, when Dippel was still teaching at Port Houston, she summoned the courage to ask him the question. "I feel like I know you, you're a great teacher, we like each other," she said. "But please tell me there is going to be a time and place where this thing can get serious. Tell me you want to commit."

He shook his head. "No, I don't want to commit," he said.

Well, she thought, that's that. It was time to cut this off for good. "Don't talk to me anymore, except about school," she said. "Don't look at me anymore. Whatever you do, definitely don't smile at me anymore."

He tried to comply, but it was difficult. On October 20, 1998, Feinberg's thirtieth birthday, after Dippel had been working full-time at KIPP for a few months, they had a huge fight. She had gone into his thinking-skills class late in the day and found him reteaching fractions to her fifth graders. She had taught the same lesson just days before. It was, she thought, typical Mike, just so annoying.

As they walked to their cars in the parking lot, she ripped into him.

She told him what she thought of him and his sneaky way of dealing with his teachers. He defended himself, somewhat feebly, only making her angrier. Then, as often happened, she calmed down. "Sorry," she said. "Don't worry about it."

She got to her car and pulled out a wrapped birthday present. "I got you this," she said. Feinberg felt numb, then happy. "Thank you," he said, and gave her a hug. The hug lasted longer than he had intended. He found he could not let go. He was teetering on the edge of confessing his feelings. But he stepped back and said nothing more.

She had told him she had a new boyfriend. She said that she was serious about the guy and that Feinberg might see this person on the basketball court, since he was friends with Farabaugh. She told Feinberg she wanted him to know so that there would be no awkward moments.

Feinberg thought about it that day, and the next day, and every day after. He could not get her out of his head. He was seeing a great deal of her. There were so many reasons to go by her room. He still felt what he had felt during the hug. He decided he would have to do something about it.

They were having dinner at the Black Labrador, an English pub on Montrose Boulevard. Dippel had ordered the Guinness cheddar soup, which was delicious. It was a fun evening, a relief after a hard day of teaching.

Then Feinberg spoiled it by telling her he loved her. "I guess my timing is bad, but I just wanted you to know how I felt," he said.

She put down her spoon and gave him a look of intense exasperation. "You know what?" she said. "You can't say that to me at this point." She was silent for a moment, getting herself together. "You know, that's ridiculous! I have a boyfriend — who I am really serious about!"

Feinberg admitted he was out of line. He said he was sad, and he looked it. "I know I'm a little late," he said. "I am really a little late, but I am really in love with you."

The rest of the dinner passed quietly. But over the next few days, Dippel learned the consequences of saying no to Mike Feinberg. The man launched a full-scale campaign for her heart. He was not going to fade into the background just because the woman he loved had another suitor. He sent five dozen roses to her classroom. It really annoyed her. It was so very Mike — big, public, loud, out of control. She told him to stop it. He didn't. The note that came with that first gift of roses said each dozen was for each of the four years they had known each other, plus an extra dozen for their future years together. There were more notes and flowers. She told him it was not going to work. He was her boss. His actions were grossly unprofessional. And anyway, he didn't really love her. There wasn't room in his life for anything but KIPP.

He didn't listen. He kept telling her how he felt, and then telling her some more. And as both of them knew would happen, it worked. In February she broke up with her boyfriend. At the end of February she told Feinberg she was in love with him too. They were a couple again, this time committed, but would it last?

Dippel had been helping Feinberg test a computerized classroom-assessment system designed by Stacey Boyd, a young San Francisco-based educational entrepreneur whom Dippel considered a kindred spirit. When Boyd offered Dippel a job helping set up the system in Chicago, Dippel said yes. She saw it as both a professional opportunity for her and a test for Feinberg. He was focused on her at the moment, but who knew what that meant? If he was not full of crap, she told herself, moving to Chicago that summer would prove it. "I am moving to Chicago and I am not coming to Houston every weekend," she told him.

That was fine with him, he said. Her ambition was one of the things he loved about her. This was a good move for her. He went to Chicago to see her almost every other weekend. He talked about moving to Chicago himself.

KIPP Houston was about to graduate its first eighth-grade class. It was humming along at cruising speed. It was a state charter, free of school district red tape. He was in a typical Feinberg mood, a bit bored, looking for something new. With his closest confidants, Dippel and Levin, he would sometimes joke that what he really wanted to do was become a FedEx driver. Then he would have no one to manage but himself. He could enjoy the satisfaction of making measurable progress every day. There were FedEx jobs in Chicago. Why not?

"That's Where It Starts"

BECOMING A CHARTER SCHOOL was liberating, but it came at a cost. Rod Paige was unhappy that Feinberg had chosen a state charter when the city schools would have been happy to give him one. Feinberg's guide and protector, Anne Patterson, had stopped talking to him after he said things at a parents' meeting that she felt did not defend her in the way she expected from someone for whom she had done so much. Years later, they would reconcile and she would go to work for KIPP, but for the moment some of his best friends were not thinking well of him.

Still, he had escaped the Wesleyan Building and found an empty lot on the campus of Houston Baptist University. It was a close call, getting the drainage work done and the plumbing installed before opening day. He had rented an apartment across the street from the school site. He persuaded some of the workers to stay late and help make his deadline, as he held up a flashlight to illuminate their work.

Levin's situation had also improved. His all-school orchestra, organized by Randall, was beginning to perform in front of large audiences. KIPP parents had become very well organized, particularly after the staff of P.S. 31, the regular public school that shared the building with KIPP, made an attempt to persuade the District 7 school board to move Levin and his school elsewhere. The P.S. 31 advocates made the tactical mistake of handing out flyers at the school, some of which fell into KIPP parents' hands.

At the school board meeting, Levin counted more than two hundred KIPP parents and only a handful of people from P.S. 31. When the agenda item was announced, many in the crowd began to chant, "KIPP, KIPP, KIPP, KIPP, KIPP, KIPP . . ." The district superintendent pleaded for quiet, but the chanting continued until Levin was given the microphone. He thanked everyone for coming out. He said he thought the school board had a good idea of how the community felt about moving KIPP. The minute he handed the microphone back to the superintendent, the chanting resumed. The meeting was adjourned. No one raised the issue again.

Then Levin and Feinberg got calls from Paul C. Gallagher, a young producer for *60 Minutes*. He wanted to bring correspondent Mike Wallace to both the South Bronx and Houston. Wallace's report, broadcast in September 1999 and rebroadcast the following summer, was a triumph for KIPP and for Gallagher, who was making his debut as a segment producer. The broadcast inspired a widening circle of interest in what KIPP was doing.

The *60 Minutes* story also caused ill will inside Feinberg and Levin's schools and among their friends. There was no reference in the broadcast to either Ball or Esquith. Randall and Myers were not shown. Neither was Fred Shannon.

What most viewers probably remembered were the two young men and a few remarkable students. Dominique Young glowed on the screen as she mentioned her scholarship to Saint Mark's. "The teachers show us so much love and they want us to be successful and they care about us," she said. "It starts somewhere and that's where it starts." Kenneth McGregor and his mother were the stars of the Houston segments. Wallace seemed as taken with them as Feinberg had been.

> Kenneth: First year, I thought I was still in my old school, so I had my old ways.
> Wallace: Like for instance?
> Kenneth: I threw temper tantrums every time the teacher told me to do something I don't want to do.
> Wallace: That must have been nice for you and for the fellow students and for the teachers.

Kenneth: It's all right. At the end of the year fifth grade, I started kicking in and maturing, coming up on KIPP's level, obeying the teachers, following the rules.

Wallace (*turning to Simpson*): Has KIPP changed Kenneth?

Simpson: Oh yes, yes.

Wallace: How?

Simpson: They brought him out. They let him know it's not a shame to be a nerd, be a nerd in the right way.

Wallace: How are his grades?

Simpson (*with a big smile*): He is an honor-roll student.

Wallace (*mimicking the smile*): *No* pride at all in that.

Within a year, Levin and Feinberg would have another national television appearance, both more controversial and less noticed. Feinberg had gotten to know Mark McKinnon, a Texas campaign-advertising expert who started his career helping Democrats but became friends with Governor George W. Bush. McKinnon was so taken with Feinberg's program that he began seeking political and financial support for it, even planning a documentary. He contacted the governor, whose father had been a strong supporter of one of Feinberg and Levin's heroes, the Los Angeles math teacher Jaime Escalante. When McKinnon staged the 2000 Republican National Convention in Philadelphia, he conceived the idea of putting Feinberg, Levin, and their students on the stage. They would introduce Laura Bush, who would be speaking about education, with a KIPP class conducted right on the convention rostrum.

Feinberg and Levin said fine. It would make an exciting field lesson for their students. They weren't going to wave any GOP flags. But many of the people closest to them deeply distrusted Bush and were apoplectic when they heard about Dave and Mike's latest adventure. Feinberg's mother asked him about it and was satisfied when he said the focus would be on their students, and not on Levin and him. Levin heard a much sharper reaction from his sister Jessica, an education policy expert. She reached him on his cell phone as he was driving to Philadelphia. "*Why* would you want to help Bush get elected?" she said. "He *doesn't* care about those kids. The whole convention is a charade. They've tried to portray themselves as great educational reformers, but they're not."

"We will handle it," Levin said. He and Feinberg saw no reason to miss a chance to take their message to several million television viewers. They had to raise money for their schools. There was talk of expansion. They had support from Democratic politicians too. They would have been happy to appear at the Democratic National Convention in Los Angeles if they had been asked.

Whether it was the unusual pressure on them from people they loved, the live format, or just fatigue and little chance to rehearse, they looked and sounded awkward when it came their turn at the convention. The cavernous hall and echoing sound system robbed them of the warm intimacy of their classrooms. Feinberg had brought KIPP Houston eighth graders — students who had earned the privilege — to perform some crisp chants, but they found it hard to project the exuberance they had had when they were fifth graders shouting out the Ball words for the first time.

Feinberg and Levin made a point of mentioning Ball and Esquith in very short speeches. They also praised Randall, Myers, Shannon, and other staffers who had been left out of the *60 Minutes* broadcast. They did not endorse Governor Bush, but they thanked him for his support. Given the context, it came strangely close to a political statement.

They rarely mentioned their convention appearance again. The measured television audience for that part of the evening was only 6.1 million, low enough to get canceled if it had been a regular prime-time show. Whatever embarrassment KIPP might have suffered from its founders' nervous brush with party politics, it faded as they moved on to more celebrated television appearances, such as on *The Oprah Winfrey Show* in April 2006.

Shortly after their GOP convention appearance, Levin told the *New York Times* that "there are no Democratic or Republican kids — just kids." Several years later, at different times and in different places,

Levin and Feinberg were each asked if he was a Democrat or a Republican. They gave precisely the same answer: "I am a teacher."

There was little chance, according to voter research, that two Jewish Ivy League graduates in their thirties who chose careers in inner-city public education were Republicans, but Feinberg and Levin continued to decline to discuss their politics. Well-known members of the GOP, particularly conservatives like Newt Gingrich, cite KIPP as an example of what can happen when good management, high standards, and character education reach urban schools. Feinberg and Levin note that many liberal Democrats, including House Speaker Nancy Pelosi and Representatives John Lewis and Charles Rangel, have also praised their schools. They are teachers, they say, and they plan to stay that way.

KIPP Today: Jaquan Improves

As the school year at the KIPP DC: KEY Academy moved into the spring of 2007, Jaquan Hall continued to learn. It was nothing spectacular, but Mekia Love and her fifth-grade team kept their expectations for him high. He became less likely to rush through his work. He got off the Bench and stayed off.

Both Love and Jaquan's mother, Sharron Hall, looked for ways to motivate the restless child. Sports was one option. To reward him for a string of completed homework assignments, Love took him to a basketball game. He began to play tackle football in a recreation league. He was a running back, small but quick. He loved it. Once, when he turned in sloppy homework, his mother made him skip practice and spend more time on his next assignment.

He remained a poor reader and a poor test taker. His comprehension of what he read improved, but only slowly. Love spent extra time with him, practicing ways to grab meaning from a page in a book. She emphasized prediction, asking questions, inferring, connecting, and finding the idea. She wanted Jaquan to ask himself, What was this story really about? He struggled with inferences and conclusions, particularly if he had to come up with them on his own. In a small group of other children, he seemed more comfortable and more likely to contribute something.

Over the course of his fifth-grade year, he was benched five times, mostly for failing to finish homework but in one case for snorting juice out his noise at a hilarious moment with his friends in the lunchroom. He took the isolation gamely. He worked at doing better. He was a child who needed to be with his friends, so benching was something he did not want to happen too often.

As the D.C. Comprehensive Assessment System tests, the DCCAS, loomed in April, Jaquan's teachers were sure he would do better than he had the previous year, for no other reason than that he had learned the importance of focus and taking his time.

The team had lost Foote, the social studies teacher, during the Thanksgiving holiday. She had been transferred to the seventh-grade team to teach reading because two seventh-grade teachers were struggling and Hayes, the principal, needed her help. By Christmas, both of the new seventh-grade teachers were gone. Hayes concluded that they had not improved even after weeks of expert help from colleagues. She scolded herself for bad judgment in having hired them. Foote stayed on the seventh-grade team. A replacement, Michelle de Simon, filled her place in fifth-grade social studies.

They had to be careful of what was on the walls of their rooms when the tests began. KIPP classrooms, like those in many schools, displayed math formulas, vocabulary, rules of grammar, and other items that could be declared violations of the rules by the proctors sent by D.C. school district headquarters. The teachers at KEY were under particular pressure, they felt, because of jealousies created by their school's good test results in previous years.

The team discussed the deadline to select which fifth graders would go on the year-end trip to Florida and Disney World. They were also going to recommend that five or six students repeat fifth grade the next year. Jaquan, Love said, was in no danger of being held back. He was moving forward. But by May it was clear that he was not going to make the trip to Florida. His mother could see he was disappointed. She sat him down for a talk. "I know you didn't make it this year," she said, "but I have no doubt that you can make it next year." Her older sons at KIPP, Shareem in the seventh grade and Cyheme in the sixth grade, did not make their trips either. But they came closer than Jaquan did, and they seemed to be making progress.

Jaquan's Stanford Achievement Test 10 results, based on the standardized test given by KIPP teachers at the beginning and end of each year, showed that his math skills had gone from the 4th percentile in September to the 24th percentile in the spring. On the D.C. math test, proctored by D.C. officials, he was still scoring Below Basic, the lowest of four levels, in the spring of fifth grade.

His reading results were harder to explain. His overall reading result on the Stanford 10 had not changed at all. He was still near the bottom, at the 4th percentile. His reading-comprehension subscore had gone up slightly, from the 2nd to the 4th percentile. Holtzman, the fifth-grade science teacher who later became the operations director for KIPP DC headquarters, said this was an indication of a child so deep in a hole at the beginning of fifth grade that although he had made progress, he was still far behind the rest of his class. He was like a long-distance runner who had been two miles behind the pack and was now only a mile behind. Compared to the other students, he was still in last place, or close to it.

One sign that he had made some progress was his results on the DCCAS test. In reading, he was not in the bottom category, Below Basic, but in the next highest category, Basic. In the regular D.C. public schools, 24 percent of all students had scored Below Basic and 42 percent had scored Basic in reading. Holtzman noted that the D.C. test, unlike the Stanford 10, had some questions that required students to write out answers. KIPP's focus on writing might have helped Jaquan there. He was ahead of many other children in the city, but KIPP had a higher standard. His sixth-grade reading teacher would put him on her list of children who needed special attention.

Jaquan's class of 2014 at KEY began the year at the 27th percentile on average in reading and finished the year at the 46th percentile on the Stanford 10 test. In math they advanced on average from the 30th to the 80th percentile in just that one year. In 2007, Mekia Love, Jaquan's favorite teacher, was the D.C. winner of the U.S. Education Department's American Stars of Teaching Award for 2007.

The same day Love won her award, the federal department also named the KIPP DC: KEY Academy a Blue Ribbon School. KEY was again one of a handful of D.C. public schools to meet all federal learning targets under the No Child Left Behind Act. It had the highest middle school math scores in the city, with an 84 percent proficiency rate. It placed third among D.C. middle schools in reading, but the two schools ahead of it were in northwest Washington and had mostly middle-class students.

Just before the regular school year at KEY began in August, Jaquan discovered he had lost one of the instruction sheets from summer school that he was supposed to keep in his binder. He sat down, without prompting, and wrote a letter to his sixth-grade homeroom teacher, explaining that he had lost it and that he would make up for it. He was still a playful child, but his mother noticed he was making choices he had not made before. He thought that this year he had a shot at making the spring trip, camping in West Virginia.

"He's taking responsibility for himself," Sharron Hall said to a visitor. She smiled at her son and congratulated him for his letter, in which he capitalized the first word in each sentence and made sure each predicate agreed with each subject. That week, she told him, he would definitely be going to football practice.

Starting Many Schools

Six People in a Room

IN JANUARY 1992, as Levin and Feinberg were writing up their applications for Teach For America, a tall, dark-haired former U.S. Education Department policy aide named Scott Hamilton was showing up for his first day at a new job. He had been hired by the Washington office of the Edison Project, an effort to improve inner-city schools and make a profit. The only person Hamilton found there was a talkative, red-haired twenty-three-year-old researcher named Stacey Boyd, in whom he took an immediate interest.

In the annals of the charter school movement, the meeting of Hamilton and Boyd would take on considerable significance, particularly in the history of KIPP. By the time they married in 1997, as Feinberg and Levin were completing the second year of their new schools, Hamilton was the chief charter school official for the commonwealth of Massachusetts, and Boyd was establishing what would be a successful Boston charter school as she completed her MBA at Harvard. By 1999, the couple was in San Francisco, where Boyd had started a new company, Project Achieve, developing a way to assess the progress of every child in a classroom. She was also working with schools in Chicago and had hired Colleen Dippel to help there. Hamilton was working in San Francisco for two of the richest people in the country, Doris and Don Fisher, cofounders of the Gap Inc. clothing stores. They wanted him to find education projects where money from their new foundation could make a difference.

Boyd, Hamilton, and the Fishers were too busy to watch much television. None of them had seen the *60 Minutes* report on KIPP in September 1999. But several city mayors and state governors had and were enthralled. Some called Feinberg and Levin, asking if they could open another fifteen or twenty KIPP schools right away. Such calls were naive, but they intrigued Feinberg. He urged Levin to join him in the effort to take KIPP national. Levin agreed that something had to be done. He liked the idea of teaching successful inner-city teachers how they might start their own schools. Feinberg looked for people who, unlike them, knew something about building large organizations. One of his first calls was to Boyd. She was an entrepreneur. She was very familiar with how his school worked and what it could do. She was thrilled with the idea and called Hamilton right away.

Hamilton promised to check it out. In the back of his mind, though, was the memory of the Fishers' cautionary note when they hired him. They said they did not want to start anything new. They were too old to launch another Gap. They wanted Hamilton to find worthwhile projects to support and help grow, but no start-ups. Hamilton visited KIPP Houston, observed Feinberg at full speed, and saw what Boyd was talking about. He visited KIPP New York and got a dose of Levin's wily charm. Hamilton hadn't discussed KIPP in any detail with the Fishers. At the end of 1999, Hamilton popped a tape of the *60 Minutes* report into the VCR in Don Fisher's office. When the segment ended, Fisher's comment was: "What the hell am I supposed to do with that?"

"I don't know yet, but something," Hamilton said. "This is worth something."

Dining at their favorite San Francisco restaurant, PlumpJack, Hamilton asked Boyd what she thought of an idea forming in his mind: business training for charter school founders, focused on what made KIPP work. Boyd liked it. Hamilton got moving, still not telling the Fishers what he was up to. They did not want to do anything new. What he was thinking was very new, and very big. He invited Feinberg and Levin to meet him in Chicago in late January 2000 to conceive a

KIPP master plan. Each of them could bring one other person. Hamilton asked Boyd to come. Levin selected his sister Jessica. Feinberg brought one of his most innovative reading teachers, Elliott Witney, who would eventually become principal of the original KIPP school in Houston.

The conversation in a suite on the thirty-seventh floor of the Fairmont Hotel lasted eight hours. Hamilton began with a PowerPoint presentation. He predicted that by the third or fourth year, they could be training 150 school leaders. What would the KIPP schools have in common? Hamilton brought in a large easel, flipping over each page as it filled with ideas. The big points seemed obvious: high expectations for all students, a longer school day, a principal totally in charge, an emphasis on finding the best teachers, rewards for student success, close contact with parents, a focus on results, and a commitment to preparing every child for a great high school and, most important, college. They decided to call the main principles the Six Pillars, later whittled down to five. Some people said it sounded too Islamic, too T. E. Lawrence. But the Five Pillars stuck: (1) high expectations, (2) choice and commitment, (3) more time, (4) power to lead, and (5) focus on results.

Boyd thought the meeting was going too well. New organizations were breeding grounds for dissent. They had to talk about that. By afternoon she was at the easel, picking at scabs in the Levin-Feinberg relationship, looking for unresolved issues in what had been their surprising and exciting but largely unexamined success.

She saw the three big men at the table. (At six foot four, her husband was taller than even the KIPP founders. Witney, aware he was the least prominent person present, was five foot four.) They had plenty of youth and energy and ideas, but how were they going to make decisions together? If two of them thought an applicant for the leadership program should be accepted, and the other disagreed, how would they resolve that? If one of them thought that corporate human-relations training should have two full days in the leadership course, and the others thought it only needed a couple of hours, how would they work that out?

They nodded patiently and said they could handle that. The idea was to give each school leader the same freedom to innovate that Levin and Feinberg had enjoyed, just as long as they showed good results. They had the confidence of youth. Two of the six people in the room, Levin and Witney, had not yet reached their thirtieth birthdays. The oldest person was Jessica Levin, about to turn thirty-five.

Hamilton still had to persuade two members of a very different generation, Don Fisher, seventy-one, and Doris Fisher, sixty-eight, to give a large chunk of their money to these kids. He took the Fishers to see Levin's school, starting the tour in the P.S. 31 portion of the building so they could contrast the noise and disorder with the quiet intensity of KIPP's fourth-floor sanctum. (Doris Fisher was pleased to discover that one of Levin's grandmothers was the daughter of her father's law partner.)

Hamilton spent several weeks writing and rewriting a business plan. It was going to cost at least $15 million. He did not think the Fishers were going to react very well. It was a start-up, and it wasn't going to be a certain success. He confessed to Boyd a sense of doom, and a pugnacious willingness, if the Fishers said no, to quit and find some other backer for the KIPP expansion. He sent one copy of the business plan to each of the Fishers. Despite his apprehensions, they loved the idea.

Don said he had never thought of running schools in the same way he ran a company. But as he considered the KIPP plan, it dawned on him that schools were a business and that charter schools in particular were a business. They needed principals who were trained in management fundamentals and could make their own decisions. He might have sounded gruff after he saw the *60 Minutes* video, but he had actually been moved by it. He wanted to get going right away. He welcomed Feinberg and Levin to a meeting at his office overlooking San Francisco Bay.

"So, Mike and Dave, you're really thinking you can pull this off, huh?"

"Well, Mr. Fisher, I don't know," Levin said, "but we'd be more than happy to use your money to find out."

It was eventually decided that Feinberg, with Dippel, would move to San Francisco to be the chief executive officer of the new KIPP Foundation. No one was surprised. Feinberg told friends, including Levin, that if Levin could raise enough money to fully endow his school, sign an agreement that would guarantee KIPP New York enough space for the next hundred years, and keep teaching fifth-grade math, he would be as happy as a pig in a barnyard. For a while they amused themselves by pretending the decision was up in the air. If they were in a bar with a dartboard, Levin would declare that the first to hit the bull's-eye would go to San Francisco.

Feinberg moved west and discovered that Don Fisher was even more impatient than he and Hamilton were. Laura D'Andrea Tyson, the former chief economic adviser to President Clinton and the dean of the Haas School of Business at the University of California at Berkeley, quickly said yes when Fisher, chair of her school's board, asked if she could provide space and faculty experts for the business-training part of what they were going to call the Fisher Fellowship leadership course. Feinberg, Hamilton, and Levin were pleased that Tyson, unlike other business-school deans they contacted, did not suggest they involve education-school faculty in the project. All three of them distrusted education schools. Feinberg and Levin planned to do most of their recruiting among Teach For America veterans like them. They thought such people would have the most drive and imagination and the most experience improvising in difficult circumstances.

But it seemed to Hamilton they were rushing it. The original plan was to start that summer. The principals-in-training would take classes at Haas for two months, while they completed the paperwork that would launch their schools. In the fall they would work at one or both of the KIPP schools. By the New Year they would be in the cities they had chosen for their schools, recruiting teachers and students and finding a space for seventy to eighty fifth graders in the summer of 2001. Like Levin and Feinberg, they would add a new grade every year until they had fifth-through-eighth-grade middle schools of about three hundred students.

It was already May. Hamilton felt they did not have enough time. They had selected four Fisher Fellows. One dropped out, and the other three looked good, although headstrong. Schaeffler, who would start the KEY Academy in D.C., and Caleb Dolan, a North Carolina teacher, had rejected Feinberg and Levin's request that they start schools in Atlanta, where Governor Roy Barnes was drooling over the KIPP results. The third fellow, a teacher at KIPP Houston named Dan Caesar, was happy to start a second school in Houston, as he was asked to do.

Hamilton went to see Don Fisher. "We've got to pull the plug," he said. "We've got to take a breath and then do all this next year so we have time to plan it and do it well. I think we are just throwing stuff together here too fast."

Fisher smiled. Feinberg, Hamilton, and Levin had no business training. He figured they would make mistakes. He explained to Hamilton, based on a half century of experience, that it was much better to get started and address problems as they came up rather than sit at a desk and try to plan for everything that could go wrong. "Let's keep throwing stuff together," he said. "You are going to learn more by just getting started than you are going to learn over the next year studying this. Even if it is imperfect, I promise you it will be better this way."

45.

Too Big a Heart

By 1998, Vanessa Ramirez had finished eighth grade and was part of the first KIPP class to enter high school. In a few years, KIPP would begin opening high schools to keep such students in the family. But at the beginning they lacked the resources for that. They depended instead on finding the most challenging public high schools and private schools willing to take a chance on kids from inner-city Houston and the South Bronx.

Vanessa did her best to be a good student at Episcopal High School of Houston. But she wondered if she could adjust to such an alien environment. She had not wanted to go to Episcopal, a private school. She had been terrified when Feinberg drove her, Lupita Montes, and a few other KIPP students to the school for their admission interviews. When, to her surprise, she received a letter of acceptance, she burst into tears. But Feinberg urged her to go, and that was all her mother needed to hear. Some mornings, Sara Rodriguez dropped Vanessa and Lupita off at Episcopal, usually an hour and a half early because her housecleaning job started at 7:30 a.m. Some days, Lupita's mother had the morning car-pool duty and Vanessa's mother picked them up in the afternoon. Whether they could play soccer or go to a dance depended on the work schedules of their mothers.

They were, they said to themselves, the only real Latinas at the school. The other Hispanic girls never spoke Spanish to one another and had parents with good jobs and nice houses. Lupita didn't care. She could make friends with anybody. But Vanessa did not wish to abandon what she considered her true friends back in her north side neighborhood. She went out of her way to look for signs that the rich girls at Episcopal were making fun of her.

THE NEXT YEAR, 1999, Dominique Young was in the eighth grade at KIPP New York, thinking about high school for herself. She was clever. She was popular. She was one of Mr. Levin's and Mr. Corcoran's favorites. She had her heart set on the trip to California, the sort of place where musicians like her belonged. Then, without thinking about the consequences, she talked back to a teacher who had asked her to quiet down in class. The teacher scolded her. She talked back again. Levin heard about it and dropped the bomb: no California trip.

Dominique was enraged. She could not believe he would do such a thing. She would eventually admit he was right, but that would be years later. She got back down to business, motivated to show she was still the smart girl, under control. A private program that prepared inner-city children to apply to top private schools accepted her. She worked hard for a year. Levin gave her permission to miss both Saturday class and summer school at KIPP, since the prep school preparation classes conflicted. She won admission to Saint Mark's School in Southborough, Massachusetts, an astonishing thing for a girl from her neighborhood, but she did not like the school much. She was stuck on campus each weekend because her mother could not afford to come get her. One weekend she was caught drinking and briefly suspended.

Her home life began to disintegrate. Her grandmother and mother fought for her affection and loyalty and then fought with her. When she visited New York, she sometimes had no place to stay. In her senior year, she became friends with a Saint Mark's girl who had no money problems but still liked to shoplift. In November 2002, they were arrested after taking clothing from the Filene's in Marlborough. Dominique called Levin, asking for help. He got in his car and was there in Massachusetts, looking stern and worried, the next morning.

She expected one of his forty-five-minute lectures, at least. Levin coldly told her they first had to fix the situation. He found a lawyer, who arranged for her to withdraw from Saint Mark's so there would not be an expulsion on her record and arranged a guilty plea that brought a sentence of eighty hours of community service and the prospect of having a clean record in a year if she did not break the law again.

It sounded as if everything was fixed, but it seemed to Dominique that her life was over. After her drinking suspension, her mother had said that if Dominique messed up again, she would not sign permission for any more private schooling, even if Mr. Levin found a way to pay for it.

Helping her pack up her room, Levin began to tell her exactly what he thought about what she had done. It took him a long time. "If you ever needed something, you could have called me," he said. "Why did you steal?"

ONE EVENING IN SEPTEMBER 2001, Feinberg was on Highway 101, driving home from his office at KIPP headquarters in San Francisco. He was weary after another day struggling with being chief executive officer, a job that did not suit him. He took a call on his cell phone from Sam Lopez, the teacher who had become interim principal of KIPP Academy in Houston.

"Mike, have you heard the news?"

"No, what?"

"Kenneth died."

"*What?*"

"Kenneth collapsed on a basketball court and died."

Feinberg fought to control himself and keep his car on the highway. There was no need to ask which Kenneth. For Lopez and him, there was only one person who deserved the honor of being known simply by that name. Feinberg could not believe it. He asked for details.

Kenneth McGregor had done well at Strake Jesuit. He had grown tall. He had been in his junior year, keeping up with his studies and playing basketball. It happened during an all-season basketball league game at Bellaire High School. He complained that his chest hurt, and then he collapsed. They rushed him to the hospital, but he did not regain consciousness. His mother's family tried to get her to the hospital without telling her how serious it was. When she saw him, she fell to the floor, weeping. The doctors said it was an undiagnosed congenital heart defect. Feinberg, who cried often in the next few days, thought this was poetic: Kenneth died because his heart was too big.

Feinberg needed to get to Houston to be with Sharon and Kenneth Senior and Kentasha. They were his family too. He called Levin in New York. They had had trouble communicating lately, with the stress of creating so many new schools and dealing with the growing KIPP bureaucracy.

As usual, Feinberg got Levin's voice mail. He used their code from *Lonesome Dove.* "Dave, I need you," he said. "I need to get Gus off the porch." Levin went to Houston and helped make the arrangements while Feinberg stuck close to the McGregor family, talking about Kenneth, celebrating Kenneth, being happy that Kenneth had turned out to be the wonderful person they all knew he could be.

The funeral was at the family's church. Feinberg and Levin spoke. Later there was a memorial service at KIPP Houston's new building in the southwest warehouse district, on a new street named, thanks to Feinberg's political friends, KIPP Way. After Kenneth's death, the KIPP Houston board decided to name the school's field house after him. At the memorial service, T-shirts with a photograph of Kenneth were given to everyone. Feinberg rose to speak about his student.

He had put on an old Chicago Bulls jersey, with Michael Jordan's number, 23. He paused for a moment. It was going to be hard to get through this. "There is one thing that KIPP teaches, that it teaches all of us. It is if you do the right thing, good things will happen," he told the crowd of mourners. "If you do the wrong thing, bad things happen.

"However, life doesn't always work out that way. That's the way it works out most of the time, but there are occasions when you do the right thing, and bad things still happen."

He paused. "We know there must be a God because there must be a higher purpose for Kenneth that we just don't know about. And we will keep his memory. His legacy is going to live on. We are going to establish the Kenneth McGregor Jr. Scholarship every year for a rising junior in high school. The winner is going to get the scholarship for the remaining two years of high school and all four years of college.

"So when the scholarship winners walk across the stage to get their diplomas, Kenneth will too."

46.

Skeptical of KIPP

CAROLINE GRANNAN, A JOURNALIST and blogger in California, and Peter Campbell, a college educator and skilled Internet user in Oregon, were both parents and public school advocates. They were interested in charter schools and in 2005 began to look for more information on KIPP.

By that year, the schools begun by Levin and Feinberg were still largely unknown to anyone not immersed in education issues. Grannan and Campbell were among the few people regularly discussing KIPP on the Internet. Bloggers on education topics spent far more time debating No Child Left Behind, the federal school-rating act. Few newspaper reporters wrote frequently about KIPP. Broadcast and cable television networks had little time for stories about disadvantaged schoolchildren, the *60 Minutes* story on KIPP being a rare exception.

Grannan and Campbell admired much of what Levin and Feinberg's schools did for children. What they did not like was the bashing of traditional public schools based on comparisons with what they considered inflated claims about KIPP. The California Department of Education kept good data on public school enrollment. Grannan discovered that those records showed some KIPP schools were losing kids at a high rate. In the 2005–6 school year, six of the nine KIPP schools in California saw decreases in entering fifth-grade cohorts from 20 to 59 percent. The worst case was KIPP Bridge College Preparatory in Oakland, whose original fifth grade of 87 students was down to just 36 students by the time they reached eighth grade. Grannan and Campbell were particularly disturbed that the number of African American boys in some KIPP schools dropped as their class moved from fifth grade to sixth grade. The number of African American boys decreased from 35 to 23 at the KIPP Academy of Opportunity in Los Angeles, from 19 to 10 at the KIPP Academy Fresno, from 24 to 12 at Bayview, and from 35 to 8 at KIPP Bridge.

These declines, Grannan and Campbell concluded, made KIPP's results look better than they ought to be. The students who left were most likely low-performing students. KIPP's average eighth-grade scores at those schools looked terrific compared to their average fifth-grade scores, but that might be because the lowest-scoring fifth graders had transferred to other schools, leaving only the higher scorers.

Campbell and Grannan were distressed with the way the media, and some education commentators and policy makers, interpreted the rising KIPP achievement statistics. Some media reports left the impression that KIPP was the answer to the problems of inner-city education. It was silly and deceptive, Grannan and Campbell thought, to suggest that saving a few kids made the pernicious cycle of poverty and misery go away. They said those commentators were sugarcoating reality, making it more palatable. Guilt-ridden policy makers could blame all of those inner-city children for not pulling themselves out of the ghetto through their own efforts. Policy makers and educational reformers would have an excuse for abandoning efforts to eradicate systemic poverty and inequality. They could instead point to KIPP and say, "If they can do it, why can't you?"

Reporters writing about KIPP rarely sought the views of Grannan or Campbell. They were among the most articulate critics of KIPP on the Internet, but they did not represent any major institutions. They had never spent any time inside KIPP classrooms. They had no background as educational researchers. There was one widely published independent expert on KIPP, though, who did have a solid scholarly reputation. His name was Richard Rothstein, and he began to take an important role in the small but growing debate about Levin and Feinberg's schools.

Rothstein was a research associate at the Economic Policy Institute in Washington and a visiting lecturer at Columbia University's Teachers College. He was also a former education columnist for the *New York Times*. He insisted that he was not a KIPP critic. He simply wished to correct what he thought was the false impression that KIPP students were just as disadvantaged as the non-KIPP students in their low-income neighborhoods. Rothstein shared Campbell's and Grannan's concern about the way KIPP was being portrayed by scholars who emphasized the need for better teaching in the inner city rather than the social reforms that Rothstein thought were at least as important. Rothstein's 2004 book, *Class and Schools: Using Social, Economic, and Educational Reform to Close the Black-White Achievement Gap*, argued for a balanced approach. Improving schools was important, he said, but could have only a limited impact because of the effect poverty had on children's lives outside the classroom. More government spending, particularly on health care, was also necessary to close the gap in academic achievement between poor and middle-class children.

In *Class and Schools*, Rothstein mentioned Levin and Esquith as good teachers who deserved recognition but whose impact on urban children had been exaggerated and exploited by others. Rothstein found a lapse in the KIPP Foundation's policy of avoiding broad claims. He quoted a sentence in the KIPP 2004 annual report that said that KIPP's success would trigger "the widespread expectation that public schools everywhere can help students overcome disadvantages to succeed academically and in life."

Rothstein interviewed Levin for his book and said the KIPP co-founder was more circumspect about his schools' success. Rothstein paraphrased Levin as saying, "KIPP narrows the achievement gap but can never eliminate it, even for its specially selected students, because the gap is fixed by differences in home literacy years before students enter school." Asked about that paraphrase three years later, Levin said it was not entirely accurate. "While I do believe that we can't close the achievement gap completely, I would never describe it in that way," he said, "nor do I think we have specially selected students."

When the Economic Policy Institute decided to publish a book

analyzing the growing debate over charter schools, Rothstein and researcher Rebecca Jacobsen volunteered to do a chapter on KIPP. They
wanted to compare the academic backgrounds of KIPP students to
non-KIPP students in the same neighborhoods. It was only part of the
book *The Charter School Dust-Up: Examining the Evidence on Enrollment and Achievement,* which they coauthored with Martin Carnoy
and Lawrence Mishel. But it was the longest and most detailed published work by recognized scholars that in any way challenged the
positive impression of KIPP among the few people who had heard of
the schools.

In their chapter, Rothstein and Jacobsen acknowledged that most
KIPP students were from black or Hispanic families under the poverty line. But their examination of four KIPP schools, they said, indicated that KIPP students starting the program in fifth grade had
more motivated parents and better test scores than their community
averages. The difference between charter school and regular school
students was important to the theme of the book. It reported federal
data that showed that charter schools on average did not have higher
achievement than regular schools, and in some cases had achievement
that was lower. Some charter school advocates had responded to this
argument by saying that charter students had more serious economic
and academic disadvantages than students in regular schools and thus
could not be expected to do as well.

Rothstein and Jacobsen, using data from KIPP and local school districts, said the fifth graders, all of them black, who entered the KIPP
Ujima Village Academy in Baltimore in 2002 ranked on average in the
42nd percentile in reading and the 48th in math, whereas graduating
black fourth graders for all of Baltimore ranked 36th in reading and
34th in math. Of the students entering Levin's school in the Bronx in
2002, 42 percent had passed New York's fourth-grade reading test,
compared to only 28 percent of the fourth graders in the thirty-one
regular public schools in that area.

Jacobsen, who had previously taught in Harlem for Teach For America, interviewed twelve teachers who had referred students to KIPP

schools around the country. Many said they encouraged their best students to transfer to KIPP, a sign to her and Rothstein that among those disadvantaged children, the ones going to KIPP were ahead of the game. The book said one Houston teacher confessed great frustration with some parents' unwillingness to consider KIPP even though the change of schools would not have placed many demands on them. "When I talked to parents [of] the kids I thought most needed it," the teacher said, "parents said stuff like 'sounds too serious and he needs another year to grow up' . . . [One] parent said it was too hard to get her [child] to the bus stop to get her to the school. This was ridiculous, though, because the bus stops at [the regular public school where I taught] so it isn't hard to get her there. Those were two of the lowest-ability kids and they both signed up but then decided not to go. A lot of the kids who aren't doing so well, the parents didn't want to sign them up and send them."

KIPP Foundation spokesman Steve Mancini released statistics that contradicted the data gathered by Rothstein and Jacobsen. Mancini focused on the KIPP DC: KEY Academy in Washington, D.C.; KIPP Gaston College Preparatory in rural Gaston, North Carolina; and the KIPP 3D Academy, the second KIPP school to open in Houston. These three schools, all in their fourth year of operation, were the first established after Levin and Feinberg's original schools in Houston and the Bronx. KIPP statisticians compared them to regular public schools in their neighborhoods. The KIPP students were somewhat less economically disadvantaged, being 80 percent low-income versus 89 percent for the local schools, and somewhat more likely to be black or Hispanic, 98 percent at KIPP compared to 86 percent in the regular schools.

The KIPP data showed test scores of incoming KIPP fifth graders in 2004 at those three schools were close to those of regular school students. The new students at KEY in Washington were at about the 34th percentile in reading, compared to about the 46th percentile for graduating fourth graders in neighboring schools. The KIPP officials acknowledged that it was hard to be certain about the D.C. comparisons because the KIPP students' fourth-grade files from the D.C. school system were incomplete, and their data was based on standardized tests administered by KIPP teachers at the beginning of fifth grade.

At Gaston, 80.9 percent of the new KIPP students were at or above grade level in reading, compared to 74.6 percent of graduating fourth graders in neighboring schools. At 3D in Houston, 80.5 percent of incoming KIPP fifth graders had passed the state reading test, compared to 79.4 percent of the students in neighboring schools. To KIPP teachers, these high percentages reflected state tests that set the passing mark very low, but they did show that students coming into KIPP were at about the same place as their neighbors.

The *Charter School Dust-Up* authors wrote that their conclusions were "not meant as a criticism of KIPP Schools . . . We do not suggest that its apparent effectiveness is solely attributable to its more favorable parental involvement, prior student achievement, or gender imbalance. KIPP supporters claim, and we have no evidence that disputes this, that KIPP provides children with the motivation and opportunity to excel that they might not have in their regular public schools. Our evidence is also not inconsistent with the notion that regular public schools might have a great deal to learn from KIPP's philosophy and strategy."

Levin and Feinberg said that they often wished they had the time and resources for more extensive and authoritative research on their results. The KIPP Foundation commissioned or cooperated with several independent analyses, including a 2005 report by the Educational Policy Institute that said KIPP schools had made "large and significant gains" in math and reading compared to traditional urban public schools, and a 2006 report by SRI International that said students in the five Bay Area KIPP schools scored significantly higher on standardized tests than students at comparable neighborhood public schools.

Both of those studies recommended that the foundation support a multiyear longitudinal study that would show how much KIPP students throughout the country had improved compared to similar students in regular schools. By 2008, KIPP had received a grant from the Atlantic Philanthropies for such a study and awarded the contract to Mathematica Policy Research Inc. That research project — comparing KIPP students to similar non-KIPP students — would eventually add a great deal more data to the ongoing discussion, stimulated by interested outsiders like Grannan, Campbell, Rothstein, and Jacobsen, over what impact KIPP was having. In the meantime, KIPP still grew, gaining more notice and inspiring more debate over the size and importance of its success.

Little Laboratories

OVER TIME, THE DEBATE about KIPP among educators has grown, full of misinformation and misimpressions because few of the people talking about KIPP schools have actually seen them in action. Some teachers think it is unfair that KIPP has extra money to spend, when in truth most KIPP schools, like most other charters, receive fewer tax dollars per pupil than regular schools. Some critics have the impression that KIPP is expelling every student that presents any problem, when the KIPP expulsion rates appear in most cases to be far lower than in regular public schools. In a few KIPP schools, such as those in the San Francisco area, significant numbers of students were at one time being withdrawn by their parents, mostly because they considered the standards too high for their children, even though similar children were thriving at the schools. But the number of dropouts has diminished as school leaders have found ways to assure those parents that their children will be well cared for.

Few of the KIPP schools are unionized, another sore point for some teachers. But KIPP teachers are paid more than union teachers because they work longer hours. Many KIPP critics are angry about the growth of charter schools in general, not just KIPP, because they think this drains resources from regular public schools. Some critics also feel, as Rothstein and Jacobsen explored in their research, that KIPP students have a family advantage over their non-KIPP neighbors. Many KIPP parents and grandparents are committed to their children's and grandchildren's academic advancement and choose KIPP for that reason, but there is yet little data to prove they are different in any significant way from parents and grandparents whose children attend regular schools. Many KIPP teachers who have worked in regular schools say they see no difference in the parents they encounter in KIPP. Some are cooperative and supportive. Some are not. What is important, they say, is the attention the teachers pay to their students, and the parental loyalty that grows out of each school's success.

There are some indications that KIPP students may have no real family advantage when they start the program. The KIPP system puts less, not more, responsibility on parents than regular public schools do. KIPP parents get what is in essence free child care for the two hours each afternoon from 3:00 to 5:00 p.m. when their children would have been home if they attended a regular school. The same goes for KIPP's every-other-Saturday sessions and three-week summer school. There is also significantly less pressure on KIPP parents to help their children during homework time — for many American parents the most stressful part of the day — because KIPP requires students to call their teachers with any questions.

Whatever the quality of KIPP parents, it is unlikely they have much to do with the rise in their children's achievement when they enroll at a KIPP school. From prekindergarten to fourth grade, most future KIPP students score below average on nationally scaled tests. From fifth grade through eighth grade, after they have started at KIPP, most of them score above average. In most cases they have the same parents and the same home situations that they had before they got to KIPP. And yet it was only during the KIPP years that their scores rose so significantly. It is hard to accept the argument that the parents, not KIPP, make the difference.

Even if research eventually shows that KIPP is serving a somewhat more prepared and somewhat less impoverished segment of the inner city, their students' gains will still be a major, and unexpected, accomplishment. That would indicate that a significant number of low-income families are willing and able to benefit from more challenging schools but were denied those opportunities until KIPP and schools like it came along. KIPP will not save all of the inner city, but it can help those families who seek better schools, and that is a significant improvement.

Simply watching KIPP teachers teach makes the best case for what Levin and Feinberg have created. Many older visitors say the KIPP atmosphere reminds them of the inner-city Catholic schools they once attended, with warm but strict teachers whose commitment to their students is motivated by far more than a weekly paycheck.

For people who do not have an opportunity to see KIPP in action, the test-score results are the most important indicator of how much impact those teachers are having. The most recent KIPP figures show that the scores of the fourteen hundred students at twenty-eight schools in twenty-two cities who have so far completed three years of KIPP improved on average from the 34th percentile at the beginning of fifth grade to the 58th percentile at the end of seventh grade in reading and from the 44th percentile at the beginning of fifth grade to the 83rd percentile at the end of seventh grade in mathematics. A sample of somewhat more than one thousand eighth graders who had been at KIPP for four years went from the 32nd to the 60th percentile in reading and from the 40th to the 82nd in math.

Those are extraordinary numbers. Ordinarily, most low-income children remain stuck in the lower percentiles. About 80 percent of KIPP students have family incomes low enough to qualify for federal lunch subsidies. Most of the rest of the KIPP students are close to that poverty line. Yet KIPP students are reaching academic levels comparable to what suburban children achieve. Caution and clarity are necessary when judging those results. They are statistical snapshots, which can be distorted by circumstances. Both the Stanford Achievement Tests administered to KIPP students twice a year by their teachers, and the state tests they take once a year have safeguards to prevent cheating and scoring mistakes, but they are not infallible. Also, the students who remain in KIPP through eighth grade are going to be those who did not reject the program and thus may be more motivated than those who leave. Still, the fact that KIPP schools have been show-ing very positive test results over several years in dozens of schools reduces considerably any doubt that the achievement gains are real.

A further proof of the authenticity of KIPP teachers' work is the existence of several other schools that take similar approaches and achieve similar results. These school networks do not have as many students as KIPP, but they are growing. Such programs include Achievement First, YES, Aspire, Green Dot, Edison, Noble Street, Un-common Schools, IDEA, and several others that share a commitment to placing low-income children in small, intense learning environ-ments. They are alike enough to share a label, although no one has produced one that has stuck yet. Leo Linbeck III, a KIPP adviser who is a management expert at Rice and Stanford, has dubbed them the public, high-impact, low-income, open-enrollment group, or PHILO schools.

The leaders of these schools are mostly in their thirties and early forties. Their teachers are mostly in their twenties and thirties. Some observers of KIPP and similar schools have wondered if their reliance on young educators could backfire, since they are likely to seek less time-consuming work when they start to raise families. Recogniz-ing that, many KIPP schools have devised work schedules that reduce the daily hours for teachers in that situation. They have also recruited some teachers and school leaders in their fifties, like Charlie Randall and Jerry Myers in the south Bronx.

Almost all KIPP schools are independent public charters, which is why their teachers do not have to belong to labor unions. The unions have mostly refrained from criticizing KIPP. One national union leader served on a national KIPP advisory board. But KIPP's relation-ships with organized labor could become more difficult as KIPP grows larger.

The close ties between KIPP and similar schools and the Teach For America program has also been a source of controversy. Teach For America is unpopular with many education-school professors, who say it throws untrained people into low-income schools that already suffer from bad teaching. A 2005 study by Stanford researchers, including the TFA critic Linda Darling-Hammond, said uncertified Teach For America corps members in Houston were less effective than credentialed teachers. A 2004 study by Mathematica Policy Research showed the TFA teachers were doing slightly better teaching math than other teachers with similar experience. The contradictory research has not kept Teach For America from becoming one of the most popular postgraduate programs in the country, but its future is likely to have a significant impact on KIPP.

Some analysts say KIPP schools cost too much to run, given the higher salaries for the longer school day and the expensive trips. KIPP estimates the extra cost averages about $1,100 to $1,500 per student. So far, they have been able to find the money in their per-pupil charter school grants or from fund-raising. Feinberg argues that the extra costs evaporate when KIPP schools reach full size and when states pass laws that give charter schools the same per-pupil payments that regular public schools receive. Levin notes that his schools in New York spend less per student than regular public schools in the city.

The most important characteristic of KIPP schools, it seems to me, is not their size or their cost or the age of the teachers or the motivation of the parents. It is their willingness to change, and quickly, when students don't improve. This was apparent to me at the KIPP School Summit in Scottsdale, Arizona, the first week of August 2007, which I attended to get a sense of what KIPP schools looked like when their staffs were all gathered in the same place.

The food was cheap, simple, and abundant — potato chips, popcorn, corn chips, juice bars, hamburgers, and fajitas on tables outside the many meeting rooms. About twelve hundred teachers were decked out in every imaginable color and variety of KIPP T-shirt and polo shirt. Their pride was evident. They knew that KIPP had the highest achievement gains for low-income children of any public school organization. What struck me was that they didn't appear to think they were doing all that good a job. All the speeches, all the panels, all the training sessions, were about getting better.

The dropout problem that Grannan and Campbell had identified in the California schools was a hot topic. The KIPP Foundation released a detailed accounting of the Bay Area schools most affected by the loss of students after the fifth-grade year. At KIPP Bridge in Oakland, for instance, of the eighty-seven students who enrolled in 2003, thirty-two later moved out of the area and thirty had parents who decided to remove them from KIPP for other reasons. Twenty-two went back to their regular public schools: because of a last-minute change just before the school opened, they had found themselves in a KIPP location much farther from their homes than they had expected. Nine left because they did not like the long school day, and thirteen left because KIPP had wanted them to spend another year in fifth grade.

KIPP Bridge principal David Ling said that when he told parents that repeating the grade would help get their children up to grade level, they often said they thought their children were already excellent students and would be stars back at their regular schools. It was an *American Idol* moment, reminiscent of the weak singers who insisted they would win because their relatives and friends had been telling them for years that they had wonderful voices. Other KIPP schools were trying new approaches to the problem. The Baltimore schools instituted a Rapid Readers program to serve all fifth graders who tested below the second-grade level in reading. Their parents were told from the beginning that it might take them five years to get to the eighth-grade level. There were no surprises. If they didn't like that idea, they were free to withdraw, but most didn't. During their first fifth-grade year, they spent three hours a day on reading. KIPP Baltimore executive director Jason Botel said that by the end of their second year in fifth grade, the children were ready for sixth grade. At most, only one or two of those dozen families each year transferred their children back to the regular public school system.

New ideas from KIPP school leaders drew big crowds at the summit. It was standing room only at a day-long presentation by the World Class Writing Project, funded by the KIPP Foundation and led by the English language arts specialists Caleb Dolan, of the KIPP middle school in Gaston, North Carolina; Elliott Witney, of the original KIPP middle school in Houston; and Beth Napleton, of a new KIPP middle school in Gary, Indiana. Witney had been the only KIPP teacher, other than Feinberg and Levin, to attend the meeting at the Fairmont in Chicago that launched KIPP's expansion. Dolan was one of the first three principals trained with the Fishers' money.

They were unhappy with KIPP writing instruction. They gave a sample from a seventh-grade KIPP student's essay on the Elie Wiesel book *Night:* "In the novel, his father protects Elie by not telling him what's going on so he won't be scared. And when his father is saying he's being hit, Elie moves in with him to try and protect us [*sic*]. This proves he is protecting." They compared this to a sample they had found on the Internet of a private school ninth-grader's essay on the Robert Frost poem "Design": "The speaker's focus on the role of outside forces in shaping the natural world leads the reader to consider the alternative possibility that humans themselves impose meaning and form on nature, an interpretation that is underscored by Frost's very deliberate imposition of meaning and form on this poem."

They asked the assembled KIPP teachers if the KIPP student was really just two years away from reaching the level of the private school student. "If I am going to teach him, yes!" said one teacher, full of can-do spirit. But most of the audience agreed that if that was going to happen, they had to do a much better job of teaching critical thinking, sophisticated syntax, and vocabulary.

To these teachers, KIPP schools were little laboratories to test the most promising ideas for raising achievement. They felt as Feinberg and Levin had from the beginning. There was nothing better than trying out something that might help kids learn. And if it didn't work, they would try something else.

Mentors

By 2008, Harriett Ball Enterprises Inc., the corporate identity of the gravelly-voiced educator who saved Levin and Feinberg from classroom disaster, had trained teachers in Georgia, New York, Indiana, Illinois, Nevada, Arizona, Louisiana, Mississippi, Ohio, Oregon, Kentucky, California, South Carolina, Florida, Missouri, Kansas, Michigan, and of course Texas.

Ball's clients often asked her to come back. What she called her "total body participation" approach to teaching elementary school students captivated principals and gave teachers a good physical workout while they learned the rhythms. Her Web site, harriettball.com, translated her chants and games and workbooks into the technical language that educational consultants like her needed to be taken seriously. The Web site discussed "multi-sensory teaching" and cited the work of the Harvard educational psychologist Howard Gardner, particularly his view of the importance of tactile-kinesthetic intelligence. Ball's mnemonic technique, her Web site said, "builds long-term memory and boosts the ability to easily transfer to higher level thinking." The Web site said, "Our Mission: Leave NO teacher OR child behind. Now the Ball is in your court. What are you going to do with it?"

Ball reminded Web site visitors that "her teaching style is divinely designed for those who are not mathematically inclined and/or learning challenged in any basic subject area." Ball explained to her trainees: "Math is abstract, full of rules. And the rules have rules, the kids don't know what they mean. So the kids become frustrated, and they give up. I will take what they are already familiar with, something concrete. I notice the radio plays songs over and over. You might hate the words to them, but you still remember them."

Academic experts confirmed she was on the right track. Patricia Campbell, an associate professor of mathematics education at the University of Maryland, said students needed to understand multiplication and know when to use it to be proficient in math. But if students didn't remember their facts, it was harder to be proficient. A 2007 study by Accurate Learning Systems Corp. suggested that less than one in five American fifth graders knew their multiplication tables. Campbell said one of the keys to methods like Ball's was that "the children like it, and therefore they do it, and they practice it."

Ball had an impressive home in an affluent suburb north of Houston. She had many friends and a strong connection to her former apprentices, Levin and Feinberg. She was a regular presence at KIPP training sessions and the summer summit. Despite that success, she missed her students. In 2007 she cut back on travel and drew up plans for her own charter school. She picked out a low-income neighborhood of north Houston called Acres Homes. The school she envisioned would cover grades two to five and have a teacher-training institute so that she could invite other educators to see how it ought to be done.

She planned to start with thirty students per grade and take it from there. She had a pinched nerve in her right leg. If she had to walk long distances, she used a wheelchair. But that, she said, was fine. "Just get me in the building," she told a friend. "They want what's in my head, and I can teach without my legs."

By 2008, RAFE ESQUITH was the most interesting and influential public school classroom teacher in the country. He had become a best-selling author. His first book, *There Are No Shortcuts,* a short autobiography, had done well. His second book, *Teach Like Your Hair's On Fire: The Methods and Madness inside Room 56,* was a sensation. He was on several best-selling lists, was being translated into foreign languages, and was speaking constantly. Yet he still arrived at Hobart each morning at 6:30 a.m. He often found several students waiting for him and his early morning thinking-skills class. He remained until dinnertime and was often in room 56 on weekends, vacations, and holidays, helping former students study for the SAT and prepare their college applications.

During one ordinary day in early 2006, there were forty students in room 56, including several alumni who had come to visit. Esquith's fifth graders rehearsed Shakespeare, practiced music, read and discussed parts of *To Kill a Mockingbird,* and played a game called buzz. The class counted to one hundred, with Esquith pointing to students in turn. If the next number was a prime number, the student had to say "buzz" instead.

As in previous years, he taught his class how to play baseball, with step-by-step precision and practice as if he were teaching them how to defuse a bomb. He ran the Young Authors project, in which each student over the course of a year wrote a book. He continued to have his students learn the surprising rules of finance by running an entire economic system in the class, with paychecks, rents, and many other real-world complications.

His relationships with Levin and Feinberg had had their ups and downs. He saw imperfections in KIPP. But he also welcomed KIPP classes and teachers who wanted to see the Hobart Shakespeareans. He seemed proud that his two disciples had gone so far.

His wife, Barbara, set him straight on his more outlandish decisions. Her four children did the same. One of them, a physician named Caryn, told him that a class he had just proudly demonstrated for her "may be the worst science lesson I have ever seen." So he found a way to get lab equipment suitable for ten-year-olds and brought the science class up to her standards. He always looked for ways to improve. He frequently puzzled people who found it hard to relate to such overwhelming dedication, but it worked for him and for his students.

Alumni

IN HER FRESHMAN YEAR at Episcopal High School, Vanessa Ramirez was surprised to discover that the headmaster, Edward C. Becker, knew who she was and often came to see her and her friend Lupita. The two girls were struggling with the homework, adjusting to a system where they no longer had their teachers' home numbers and permission to call at night. But Becker told them they were doing great. "I've talked to your teachers," he said, "and they say they can't believe how mature you are, how much more mature you are than these other kids, how respectful you are."

It occurred to them that the old KIPP values had a place, even in a very un-KIPP-like school. By habit, courtesy of having had Feinberg and Levin as teachers at an impressionable age, they automatically paid attention, sat up, and asked questions. If nobody else was participating — even in a fancy private school, ninth graders were not that keen on showing off in class — Vanessa and Lupita were always among the few students who would try.

Gema Porras, one of Vanessa's non-KIPP friends at Burbank who had joined her when she returned to KIPP, was at another private school and called to say she had discovered an exciting junior-year-abroad program. It was in Zaragoza, Spain. They would live with host families and improve their Spanish. Vanessa got tentative approval from her mother, who was confident that such an exclusive program would not accept her daughter. When it did, and Becker said her Episcopal scholarship would cover the cost, Sara Ramirez panicked. "You mean you actually sent in the application?" she said to her daughter.

"Yes, Mom, and I'm going."

Vanessa's mother, as Vanessa had expected, called Feinberg. Vanessa was prepared for that. She told him this was something she wanted to do. She was firm with him, as he had often been with her. He was learning, despite his lack of any firsthand experience as a father, that children grew up and you had to start listening to what they were saying.

"Do you think it is okay that she go on this?" her mother asked her old teacher.

"Well," Feinberg said, "I am kind of nervous about it, but I am sure this will help her grow. And it seems like a great program, so yeah, let her go."

She and Gema were the only Latinas in Zaragoza. The rest of the group were non-Hispanic middle-class Americans. They had a wonderful year. Levin visited, amazed at how mature they had become. When Vanessa returned for her senior year, she had an entirely different attitude about Episcopal. Her soccer friends were happy to see their swift-footed wing back on the team. She no longer looked for ethnic slights. She got into several colleges and decided to go to Occidental in Los Angeles, another step in her campaign to get out of Texas and see the world.

Occidental, a beautifully landscaped, very selective school, had its drawbacks. Most of the other Hispanic students were well off, with little understanding of her upbringing in the barrio. She started as an economics for business and management major, but when she developed an interest in education courses, her adviser suggested sociology instead. Every other Latino he knew was a sociology major. Wouldn't that suit her too? She said no.

She graduated in 2006 and realized that her fascination with how children learned might qualify her for a job in the growing KIPP empire. She spent a year working at the KEY Academy in D.C. on the KIPP to College program, an effort to keep in touch with KIPP middle school graduates and help them navigate the college admissions process while they were in high school. She moved back to Houston to be the KIPP to College feeder-pattern manager. She became an officer in the KIPP Alumni Association, which helped uncertain KIPP alumni, people like her, apply the values they had learned in their very odd middle school — and in the new KIPP elementary and high schools — to a wider and scarier world.

She owed KIPP a great deal, she thought, but KIPP also owed her something. Back in middle school, she had been such a frugal girl, never cashing in the steadily mounting earnings on her weekly paycheck. It wasn't real money, but she still rebelled against the funny-money prices at the KIPP store, such as three hundred dollars for a T-shirt. She was saving her earnings to buy something big. Like many KIPP students, she never did. Although paycheck points helped determine who was going to go on trips, the teachers never charged the bank accounts of those who went.

Vanessa, now a young woman with a college degree and firm views on personal finance, figured she had $1,087 KIPP dollars in her KIPP account. It was out there somewhere. Working at Mr. Feinberg's new headquarters building in southwest Houston, out among the warehouses near Beltway 8, she would have time to roam around the offices. She would find it.

DOMINIQUE YOUNG, IN HER MIND if not in fact, was a convicted felon as she prepared to leave Saint Mark's. She listened quietly to Levin's long, anguished, rambling rant about how disappointed he was with her. She began to cry. Her life was over. She told him she did not see any way to go forward. "You aren't going to worry about that," he said. "What you are going to worry about now is what I am talking to you about."

He left her at her mother's new home in Temple Hills, Maryland, outside Washington, D.C., and went to work getting her back on track. He found a place for her at Oldfields, a private girls' school north of Baltimore. It was January 2003. They would not allow her to graduate that year. She would have to repeat the second semester of her junior year. He secured financial support for that tuition, persuading her mother to sign the papers.

When Dominique expressed some concern about attending a girls' school, she found he was still very angry and spoke exactly as she imagined a father would. "I don't care," he said. "You got in. You're going." Soon, however, she realized she loved Oldfields. There was no more preening for boys, no more gender power games. Her grades went up. She scored a 1220 on the SAT and got into the University of Maryland at College Park.

Her mother, happy to have her oldest child nearby and in college, found herself reconnecting with some old family ambitions. She told Dominique about auditions for the third season of the network reality show, *Making the Band*, with P. Diddy, aka Sean Combs, as host and judge. Dominique passed the audition and became a star during the ten episodes, showing off the best singing voice and sharpest wit. She presented herself as a tough Bronx homegirl. Asked about a marathon all the contestants had to run in Central Park, Dominique's televised comment was, "I don't run anywhere, unless I'm being chased." She survived until the show's finale, when her poor dance skills led Combs to rule her out. But she had won considerable notoriety. She found an agent and began to sing rhythm and blues in clubs all over the Washington area, while still working toward her degree in communications.

When she told Levin of her musical ambitions, he surprised her. "You're young," he said. "Give yourself three years. Work on the music." He had started teaching the same way. Teaching had intrigued him, but he had not known if he could make it work for him. His first three years in the classroom had made the difference.

"You've got room," he told her. "Don't be depressed about not making it or depressed about being broke. You're still a kid. You still have room to do those things."

"Tall Teacher, Sweet Face"

AT AGE THIRTY-THREE, Nikki Chase was taking a long break from work. Her career as a marketing and public relations executive had soared since she graduated from Michigan State. As the only child of two public school educators, having grown up in Muskegon, Michigan, and attended a small Christian school, she was surprised to find herself so well off that she could spend a year traveling to Latin America and Ireland and visiting the Guggenheim Museum, not far from her apartment on Manhattan's East Side. That year, on a night in early May 2005, she showed up for a speed-dating event at an East Village restaurant, the People's Lounge.

It was her first speed-dating experience. She told her friend Adrian, who had also signed up with cupid.com, "I am going to find a good Christian brother." She met twelve men in slightly more than an hour during the African American part of the evening, then stayed for the multicultural session — all ethnicities welcome — when the event coordinator said she had some vacancies.

It was a fun night. She laughed off the African American man who said, when he learned her age, "When you finally meet that person, would you feel you have to get married and have kids right away? Because I don't know if I'm into that." She had the same reaction to the young Asian who confessed that "my mom would die if I brought a black girl home."

About 9:00 p.m., four or five dates into the multicultural session, a tall white man with dark, curly hair sat down across from her. She liked the way he looked. He had the sweetest face, boyish and lively.

They talked about her travels. It was good, she thought, that she was not working. It freed her from dreary first-date exchanges about offices and career status, with the six-minute clock ticking. It took a while before she learned the tall guy, with the name Dave Levin on his badge, was a teacher.

"Oh, that's so great," Chase said. "My mom's a teacher. My dad is in education. I have cousins who are principals. I come from a family of educators."

Levin gave her another sweet grin. His puzzle-loving mind, typical of an adept math teacher, noticed something about Chase's full name: Chanda Nichole Chase.

"You have a *ch* in each of your names," he said. "Did your mom mean to do that?"

Chase had never thought about that before. She liked a man with an inquisitive outlook. The bell rang. Their six minutes were up. She was surprised the time had gone so fast. On her sheet, she wrote down Levin's name and badge number, and a note to herself to remember him: "Tall teacher, sweet face."

It was also Levin's first experience with speed dating. Days before, he had been talking on the phone to an older woman he knew in Boston, someone he thought should be getting out more. To motivate her, he had proposed they both try speed dating and then report back to each other on how they had done. The woman lost her nerve, but as usual Levin followed through.

He wondered, as he went online to find a speed-dating venue, if he ought to make more of an effort to meet Jewish women. His dating preferences up to then had been famously diverse, a topic of conversation among his friends. His college girlfriend had been of Chinese descent. He had had a series of relationships, including some with black women. During one of them, Levin had told Feinberg his latest love was perfect in every way but one.

"What is that, Dave?"

"She hates white people."

So he thought it might be time to introduce himself to Jewish women, but he did not want to rush it. He signed up for the multicultural session at cupid.com as a way of easing himself in. Jewish people were multicultural too.

Despite her announced intention of finding a man who shared her religion and ethnicity, Chase was pleased to get the e-mail confirming that Levin was among the five men who had picked her. A traditionalist in these matters, she waited for them to contact her. Several days passed with no message from Sweet Face. She was disappointed, but she too had had a series of relationships and knew the score. Days later, far longer than she considered appropriate, an e-mail from Levin arrived. She might have been irritated, except the wording was so clever that she eventually accepted his vehement insistence that he had responded right away and that his first message must have been misrouted.

The e-mail said: "If I didn't get the hint and you're deliberately ignoring my first e mail, then please forget I ever sent this one. However, if my first e-mail was misplaced or ended up in spam, please give me a shout. I would love to get together."

They had dinner the next Monday night, then a Friday night date, then a nine-hour marathon date on Memorial Day. He usually wore dress pants, an untucked dress shirt with no tie, and a blazer. She wore blue Levi's with a variety of tops. She loved to tease him. When he confessed under questioning where he had gone to college, she was in his face. "A Yalie, huh?" she said. "Well, please remember I went to a land grant college, so take it slow, okay? You know, go easy." Learning he had grown up at Eighty-first Street and Park Avenue, she was on him again. "Remember," she said, "I'm from Muskegon, Michigan. Go easy."

He liked being treated that way. Her smile, he thought, was pure joy. She thought he had a really strong spirit. He was so down to earth, she told herself. He mentioned that, like Chase, a high school sprinter, long jumper, and cheerleader, he also had some athletic skill. But when much later she finally saw him play basketball, she was surprised that he was so good. She told friends it was "one of those white-boy-can-jump moments."

He managed a kiss on their second date by taking advantage of a moment when, as they were walking along and teasing each other, he was standing in the street and the five-foot-seven-inch Chase was up on the curb. Having achieved height parity, he went for it. She did not resist.

Chase liked Levin so much that she was uncharacteristically slow with her security precautions. It was not until their third date, on Memorial Day, that she asked if he had ever been arrested. He said no. It was not until their fourth date that she googled him, and that was only because of some strange answers he was giving to her questions about his job. He had told her he was a teacher in the Bronx. When Chase probed for more, she learned the school was called KIPP. "I'm kind of a teacher and a superintendent," he said. The woman from a family full of educators was not buying that. "I know enough about the public school system to know that's not possible," she said. "You can't be a teacher and a superintendent."

"Well, actually I founded this school, called KIPP, and there are now four KIPP schools in the city. They're charter schools, like I told you."

"That's cool. Charter schools are good."

"I still teach, but I am the superintendent of these four schools because these schools need a superintendent."

They changed the subject, but as soon as Chase got home, she went to her computer and did a search for KIPP and Dave Levin. The first item was an interview Levin gave to C-SPAN's Brian Lamb. Whoa, thought Chase, a public relations professional. This little school must be a big deal. She began reading the interview. Hmmm. She checked out the KIPP Web site. The tall teacher with the sweet face had co-founded forty schools in thirteen states.

She called him. "So you're a teacher, huh? Give me a break." Her father was impressed. Her mother began playing a video of the C-SPAN interview in the teacher's lounge of her elementary school in Little Rock, Arkansas. "Look, this is my daughter's boyfriend," she said. This was going further than Chase had planned. This was supposed to be just a fun time. She was not looking for the love of her life. But gradually she found herself failing to return phone calls from other men and spending more time with Levin. They were both very busy people. She was taking bigger consulting jobs, getting back into the rhythm of her working life. He was still running four schools, taking a leading role in training the new KIPP principals, and setting up a new teacher-training institute.

But they grew closer. They had both come far enough in their work to know that they had a good grip on their futures. They could breathe a little and pay more attention to the other parts of their lives. Chase met Levin's family, who were always interested in the young women in the life of David, the only Levin sibling not yet married. Levin met Chase's family, including a visit to her uncle Timmy's home in Maryland. Levin had had time for only one sip of his beer when Uncle Timmy popped the question: "So, I understand you're Jewish." Levin took another sip and leaned back in his chair. "I am, but let's just think of it as another denomination." His girlfriend smiled. "And we're all in agreement on Book One," she said.

They talked about raising their children in the Judeo-Christian tradition. She knew Levin also felt responsible for many children in difficult circumstances at his school. It was one of the things she loved most about him. In September 2005 she accompanied him to a benefit for victims of Hurricane Katrina. The KIPP orchestra played. Levin spoke, the first time she had heard him do so publicly. She listened as his words embraced the audience. He made everyone in the room feel that they were loved. It was awesome. She was done. This was it.

She could tolerate the chaotic character of his life as a teacher, superintendent, mentor, and friend to many students struggling with getting into and through college. He was in his car, a black Acura, several hours each day, visiting his schools, calling on families, seeing financial donors, attending meetings. Beside him in the car were always his cell phone and his PDA. On the car stereo was a tape, softly playing something urban, a taste he shared with his students. A typical Dave Levin moment was his pulling into a fast-food drive-in window, maybe the McDonald's near his Bronx school, his cell phone in one ear and his eye on the PDA, and ordering and then eating, while still driving, a burger and a large helping of fries.

He explained to Chase his two-call rule. He did not have to take every call on his cell phone. That would be insane. The thing seemed to play its ragtime ring tone every two or three minutes. But if a call came in twice from the same number, one call right after the other, then he would have to excuse himself and answer. Someone close enough to him to know about the two-call rule needed him.

His habit of doing several things at once may explain in part what happened to him after their memorable Memorial Day date, when he said he had never been arrested. He dropped Chase off at about 11:30 p.m. and was headed south on Second Avenue to meet a KIPP graduate who was about to go to college. Levin had some money with him to help the boy get started. At Sixty-seventh Street a police car pulled him over. One of his headlights was out. They asked for his license and registration and then came back and told him to get out of the car. "You're under arrest," one of the officers said.

"For traveling with a broken headlight?"

"No, your license is suspended."

"No, it's not."

"That's what the computer says."

"The computer is wrong."

Nonetheless, he soon found himself in the back of their squad car, his wrists handcuffed behind his back. This was not good. As they drove to the Nineteenth Precinct, he realized, as a native Manhattanite, that he was destined for Central Booking. On a holiday weekend, it was going to be crowded. He would have to spend the night there, at least.

His friend Feinberg had been arrested when only eighteen, at a drunken hotel party that was barely worth mentioning. Levin was thirty-five, and he knew he was going to be hearing about this from his friends for the rest of his life. At the precinct, he pleaded with a sergeant not to send him into the system. "I'm a teacher," he said. The sergeant was skeptical. What kind of teacher would be driving around near midnight with $750 in cash and his cell phone ringing every minute?

But he let Levin make some calls to see if he could find someone to bail him out before the shuttle bus left for Central Booking. He called his brother Henry and then Susan Winston, who hitherto had only had to rescue him from angry building principals. They both arrived in time to spring him. He got some sleep at Henry's apartment, then called Chase the next day.

"I just wanted you to know I had a great time yesterday," he said.

"Me too," Chase said. "Did you get some sleep?"

"Sort of. You actually asked me something yesterday and at the time I told you the answer was no. Remember?"

"Uh, yeah."

"Well, I got arrested last night."

She listened to the story with mounting astonishment, relief, and amusement. She knew Dave Levin well enough by then to know it was a very funny story. She felt even closer to this man, a nice addition to her family of educators.

"I jinxed you!" she said.

"Never," he said.

Master Class

By October 2005, Levin's personal life was in fine shape, but a crisis had developed at one of his new schools, the KIPP STAR College Prep Charter School in Harlem. The sixth-grade math class was not going well. The new teacher was not performing up to the school's standard. At almost any other public school, the problem would have been considered minor, and the solution long-term. But Levin and the KIPP STAR principal, Maggie Runyan-Shefa, were considering getting rid of the teacher right away, only three months into the school year.

The soft-spoken young man had come well recommended. He appeared to know his subject. He loved children. But he was a poor classroom manager and motivator. The aisles of his classroom were cluttered. His students were inattentive. A look at their work showed they were falling behind where KIPP wanted them to be.

In most urban schools, such failings would have been difficult to detect because the standards were so low, a result of the widespread feeling that not much could be expected from such disadvantaged children. If a teacher's flaws were enough to catch the attention of a principal, she would talk to him and ask that he observe some of the school's veteran instructors. She would encourage him to borrow their techniques. She would never consider firing him in the middle of the term. Anyone she might be able to replace him with would almost certainly be worse.

In the normal course of events, the teacher's disappointing performance might earn him a bad mark on his end-of-the-year evaluation and a request that he take more courses and try harder. At the end of his probationary period, if he made no significant improvement, he might be let go. But by that point he would have been in the classroom for three years. The several dozen students he taught during that time would have had to settle for less-than-adequate instruction. Their chances of success in math in seventh grade and beyond would have been sacrificed to administrative inertia and no ready alternatives to bad hiring decisions.

KIPP schools were different. The longer school day made class schedules more flexible. The intense recruiting of the best available educators meant that the administrators, including principals like Levin, Feinberg, and Runyan-Shefa, often had exceptional classroom skills and could take over a class if needed. If the sixth-grade teacher at KIPP STAR did not improve, Levin and Runyan-Shefa planned to turn the class over to the school's vice principal, who had a master's degree from Columbia University's Teachers College. Runyan-Shefa, as well as Levin's troubleshooter Jerry Myers, had been working with the math teacher. Levin had stepped in one day, toward the end of the teacher's lesson, to show him some techniques. He showed up the next morning to teach a complete class.

In the little world of KIPP math instructors, Levin was a legendary figure, the best math teacher many of them had ever seen. Runyan-Shefa hoped his reputation would help the young teacher see how much better he could be. Levin had observed the sixth-grade class. He had talked to the teacher and to Runyan-Shefa. He knew that one of the teacher's stumbling blocks was a disruptive student—a slender child whose wit and talent for mischief were reminiscent of Kenneth McGregor's. Levin had this in mind as he walked up the stairs of the five-story brick school on a residential Harlem street and approached room 433, where the young teacher taught three classes of sixth-grade math every day.

The teacher had his twenty-eight students lined up in the hallway, as he had been asked to do. Levin went to the front of the line and stood outside the closed classroom door. "Everyone face me, please," he said. "Let's go. I'm missing one person's eyes." He waited a moment.

"Thank you. I wanted the joy of getting back with you today to finish up what we started yesterday. We need one minute in the room to finish setting up."

Levin reached out to the eleven-year-old chief troublemaker, who had been asked to stand near the front of the line. He escorted the child, just him, inside the classroom. He shut the door, leaving the other members of the class, and their teacher, out in the hall while he had a private chat with the boy. He shook the sixth grader's hand. "Hi. I'm Mr. Levin. You remember me from yesterday. You don't know me very well, but I think you will find it a bad idea not to listen today. You will enjoy being my friend. Any other options are off the table."

He asked the student about himself. He had the boy help him rearrange the desks and chairs, making the aisles wider and the rows straighter. He opened the classroom door and welcomed everyone in to start on their introductory problems. "Thank you. Go to your desks. We will do the first five problems. Don't worry about putting stuff into your binders. We will all put it into our binders at the end. Directions are on the board. They are also on the sheet, to be done by yourselves. Any questions? Okay. I am missing one person's eyes."

He waited. It was time for the formal opening of the class. "Hi, Kippsters!" Levin said with a smile.

Just two voices said, somewhat uncertainly: "Hi, Mr. Levin."

"How many remember when I spoke to you last? How many of you actually remember what my name is? Veronica?"

"Mr. Levins?"

"Mr. Levin. There is no *s*. It is like the number *eleven* without the *e* in the front."

He tried again: "Hi, KIPP STAR!"

"Hi, Mr. Levin," came a somewhat louder response. He asked them to try again.

"I would like everybody's attention, and do me a favor: When you bump into someone on the street, you don't whine their name, do you? You don't say" — he adopted a very languid tone — "'Yo . . . wha'ssss

up?' You've got to deal with someone. So we are going to learn to inter-
act normally."

"Hi, KIPP STAR."

"Hi, Mr. Levin!"

"Hi, KIPP STAR."

"Hi, MR. *Levin!*"

"Good," he said. "Not any whining, not that long-drawn-out
thing."

The students were sitting straighter than they had been when they
sat down. This teacher was annoying, but he had energy. "All right!
You smile, right? So we are going to go about thirty, thirty-five minutes together. In that thirty to thirty-five minutes I do really want to
hear from everyone, all different groups and individuals. If I know
your name, I will call on you by name, but if I don't know your name,
tell me your name before you start speaking so I can kind of learn
your names. With all these beautiful and handsome ladies and gentle-
men in the room, I should at least know your names."

To Levin, a class was a conversation that involved every child. He
had to stay positive and pass that feeling on to them. "This is going to
be good, going to be good," he said, pacing in front of the class. "I love
this stuff. All smile. Did you all know that smiling keeps your brain
awake? You didn't know that? When you sit up, you smile. Your brain
gets oxygen, and when your brain gets oxygen, you are smarter and it
makes you better looking, and some of you really need to smile a lot
more. All *right!*"

The problems on the board involved long division. "Shamira, how
does twenty-one go into forty-two? Two. Anyone confused by that? I am
missing one person. Does the two pop up? What is two times twenty?"

"Forty!" several voices said.

"What did I do wrong, man? What did I do wrong on purpose?"
he said. The intentional error on the board was an old trick for keeping everyone engaged. Tricky teachers needed close watching. Eleven-
year-olds loved correcting their elders.

"I can't hear you," he said. A few voices identified the mistake. "Exactly, right under here. Two minus zero?"

"Two!" they said.

"Perfect. Check this out. Raise your hand if you can count by twenties. Okay, now raise your hand if you can count by sixty-twos. Not so easy, right? But the steps are exactly the same. We are going to take a look at this one, we are going to take some notes, and you are going to be able to do it on your own." He employed a standard motivator, the reach for a challenge. Each class was a team. They were drawn to the excitement of fighting and beating a tough opponent. Smart teachers would often say they were offering a problem that was beyond what kids in other schools were getting.

"How many of you like chicken wings?" Levin asked. "You order them mild, medium, and spicy, right? Mild, medium, and spicy." He chose metaphors for which he had a genuine passion. His students seemed to enjoy the vibe. "Raise your hands if you want a mild problem to start. How many want medium? Spicy?"

He started with medium. He called on several different children. He needed to be reminded of some of their names, but as the minutes passed, he recognized more of them. No one could avoid participating. He kept moving around the room. "Raise your hand if I lost you. Raise your hand if this is seeming easier to you. Raise your hand if you are almost ready to do it by yourself."

Every child had to get the concept. He was not going to pull too far ahead. "Raise your hand if you got it," he said. "Everyone check me for a second. Everyone track me for a second. This is an important number. You have to pay attention here. This number cannot be bigger than what? This number cannot be bigger than what? Fatima?"

She gave an incorrect answer. He tried a few other students who did not get it. "One step too far," he said. "Eyes up, please. Eyes up. We will give you the next one on your own again. Watch this. We said we were going to be done by nine, and we are pushing up on the time. You guys are pretty close, though. So watch this."

The period was over. Twenty-eight children had watched intently and responded to questions for more than forty-five minutes. They seemed to be holding their own. The class bad boy, Levin's special project, had been a model student. The young teacher had taken many notes. There would be several more weeks of extra work for him. Then, still unsatisfied, Runyan-Shefa would, with Levin's approval, find him another job in the school, not as demanding or as important as sixth-grade math.

The New York State assessment tests were given to the KIPP STAR sixth graders the following spring. Seventy-three percent of the seventy-eight sixth graders scored at the proficient level or above, compared with 45 percent of all sixth graders in the same Harlem district and 60 percent of sixth graders in New York State.

Ninety-two percent of those KIPP STAR sixth graders were from low-income homes. Ninety-seven percent were black or Hispanic. They had been taught to listen, think, and respond. For most of them, it had worked. Their teacher had struggled, but for them the standards had remained high. They would be ready for seventh-grade math, which at KIPP schools was beginning algebra, begun two years earlier than at most American schools.

Remembering Room 220

IN MID-APRIL 2005, eight new KIPP school leaders gathered in the playground of Houston's Garcia Elementary School. They were Fisher Fellows, being trained with Don and Doris Fisher's contributions, which would eventually pass the $50 million mark. They had studied business management the previous summer, then interned at KIPP schools in the fall. In the winter and spring they recruited students and teachers for their new schools, which would open in three months.

Their schedule gave them a week in April to compare notes with one another and with Feinberg, who was happy to be back in the city of KIPP's birth, having handed the job of running the KIPP Foundation to Scott Hamilton. Feinberg was a good person to advise new principals on how to open and how not to open KIPP schools. He held the record for last-minute near disasters.

Feinberg thought their week together should be a rite of passage. He wanted to mark the end of the school leaders' year of preparation. Why not have a ceremony? Feinberg loved the rituals that KIPP schools had created: opening day's Awarding of Trust, the reformed miscreant's Return from the Porch, the top students' Winning of the Golden Ticket. He had in mind a perfect spot for the blessing of the Fisher Fellows: room 220 at Garcia Elementary School. It would be the tenth anniversary of the completion of his and Levin's first year of KIPP. He picked up a phone to start the planning.

Unfortunately, Feinberg still had an image problem in the Houston Independent School District. When he asked permission to have a brief ceremony after school in his old classroom at Garcia, he was told no. How about the hallway outside? No. The main lobby? No. The playground? No. A KIPP staffer familiar with Houston Parks and Recreation Department regulations pointed out to Feinberg that during after-school hours, the public had free access to all public playgrounds, including the Garcia Elementary jungle gym and rubberized play surface. That was where Frank Corcoran had once painted a map of the world. It was still there.

Feinberg arranged for two school vans to take thirteen folding chairs, eight fellows, and five KIPP Foundation officials, including him, to the north side Houston school. He enjoyed remembering that year, a golden time for Levin and for him. They had been so young. They had taught together with a passion and a joy that they could never duplicate now that they were weighted down with big expectations and responsibility for scores of other people.

In his mind, the Fisher Fellows now were like he and Levin had been then. They were starting something new, schools they could take in their own directions. As he stood to speak, he glanced up at the windows of room 220, thinking about Levin and the children who were with them then. "It's fitting that we are here talking about this," he said, "because I am so proud of each and every one of you. Frankly, you guys are my heroes. You are my heroes because you are doing something that is incredible.

"I like to joke all the time that knowledge is power, but ignorance is bliss. I am very proud of what Dave and I accomplished, but every day was a brand-new day. We were building the plane as we flew it, and we didn't really know what was in store for us.

"If we knew back then what we know today, when we were up there, up there in the corner — and I can point to the window — and when we were out here with the kids on the playground, I don't know if we would have been able to be as successful, and it would have been a very scary thing to decide. Would we still go through with it, knowing all the crazy things that were going to be in store for us on this road? I would like to think so, but we never had to make that decision."

He was feeling it. He took a breath and tried to maintain his composure. "It is no longer just a one-classroom thing. It is no longer even just a one-school thing. What you are going to do with your kids is going to be phenomenal. And you will be plugging that into what each and every one of us is doing in each of our schools.

"So congratulations. I am glad we could all be here to visit where we started and think about where we are going."

Five of the Fisher Fellows were men. Three were women. Four were black. Four were white. They were all in their twenties and thirties. Like Levin and Feinberg, they would find that the drag of poverty and hopelessness and poorly staffed inner-city schools and dysfunctional families had left their new fifth graders in the bottom third of the country in reading and math. And like Levin and Feinberg, after a year of loving and intense teaching, giving each child the extra time and encouragement he or she needed, they would find that reading and math achievement among their first class of fifth graders had climbed substantially. Every one of the eight principals would record a gain of at least 10 percentile points in the first year in each category. In many cases the gain would be greater, in one case 60 percentile points.

At each school they would worry about the students who had decided not to return for the next year. They would fret about students who had failed to keep up with the class and would have to do another year in fifth grade. They would meet with their teachers. They would discuss different approaches for the coming year, trying to do better, not listening to people who told them they were so great, remembering the children in their classes who had not made much progress.

And like Feinberg and Levin, they would look forward to the next school year, and the next. They had had their own scary, exhausting, thrilling first year, their own room 220 experience, what Feinberg had tried to explain at the Garcia playground. They could learn from that.

COMMENCEMENT

Mike Feinberg and Colleen Dippel married in 2001. She was not happy moving back to what she referred to as "that hot hellhole," Houston, Texas. But that was where he thought he would be happiest and most valuable to KIPP. They wanted a family, and it was difficult to arrange that when he was traveling all the time, so she relented. In 2005, Feinberg set to work on a master plan, conceived with his two business-executive friends Shawn Hurwitz and Leo Linbeck, to have forty-two KIPP schools in Houston by 2017. By 2008 they had raised $65 million, a charter school record.

After Scott Hamilton took over as KIPP Foundation CEO, the number of KIPP schools nationally continued to expand. To the surprise of many education reporters, accustomed to such franchises petering out, the achievement results at nearly all the schools were as good as they had been at Feinberg and Levin's first two schools, and sometimes better. It was another blow to the assumption that low-income children couldn't learn very much, no matter how hard they tried.

One morning in October 2005, as Hamilton headed toward his office near the San Francisco–Oakland Bay Bridge on the Vespa he had started riding to work, his front tire caught on a streetcar rail on Market Street. He went flying into the air. He cracked his helmet when he landed, and was unconscious for several days. Boyd, told to expect the worst, stayed with him and saw him gradually recover. She used her management skills to organize a rehabilitation program that by the spring of 2006 had him sounding and moving as if nothing had happened. They decided to try living with their young daughter in a scenic part of Wyoming. Boyd started an online preschool-finding service, the Savvy Source. Hamilton left KIPP to work for the Thomas B. Fordham Foundation, an education reform group run by Chester E. Finn Jr., the former Edison official who had first encouraged the Hamilton-Boyd romance.

LEVIN, ACKNOWLEDGING IT was his turn to be the boss, ran the foundation temporarily from New York when Hamilton had his accident. Much of Levin's administrative chores were done on his cell phone while he drove his car around the city. The number of schools continued to grow. Eventually, Levin and Feinberg and the Fishers persuaded Richard Barth, an executive at Edison, to take over the leadership of the KIPP Foundation.

Barth was known to both Feinberg and Levin because he was married to Wendy Kopp, the founder of Teach For America. Barth ran KIPP from New York. By the summer of 2008, the school network had sixteen thousand students in sixty-six schools located in nineteen states and the District of Columbia.

IN LATE APRIL OF 2005, Dippel, eight months pregnant, was in Connecticut visiting an old friend whose mother had died. Feinberg was in Houston, planning the annual KIPP fund-raising gala. In the middle of the night, he got a call from his wife saying she was bleeding a bit and getting a quick check at a hospital in Poughkeepsie, New York, close to where her father and stepmother lived. She put Feinberg on standby. The next day she called and told him to catch the next plane.

He was there for the labor, which lasted several hours. At one point she asked him to give her a back rub. When he did not press down hard enough to suit her, she upbraided him for a lack of manliness with the exact words Corcoran had used when Levin almost gave up his effort to establish KIPP in New York.

At 11:00 a.m. the next day, April 30, a large, healthy baby boy was born. The couple had to drive him back to Houston in a rented blue

Toyota SUV because the airlines would not take Dippel so soon after childbirth. They stopped every three hours for Dippel to nurse the infant. The trip took three days. It was a stressful journey. Feinberg later claimed they decided to get divorced in Georgia but reconciled in Mississippi.

They named the boy August Phillip Feinberg. Phillip was for Phillip Dippel, Colleen's father. August was for Augustus McCrae — the character in *Lonesome Dove* that Feinberg thought was so like his friend Dave. Just like Captain McCrae, ex-Texas Ranger, the boy would grow up being called Gus.

AT 6:00 P.M. ON August 11, 2007, David John Levin married Chanda Nichole Chase in a ceremony presided over by a minister and a rabbi at the Ohio Street Beach on Chicago's Lake Michigan shore. Marrying on the beach was against city rules. But Levin, remembering Feinberg's persistence with Rod Paige, staked out the office of the Chicago Parks Department official in charge and worked out a deal. A local bride's magazine was so taken with the novelty of the occasion that they sent a photographer.

There were sixty guests in attendance, including Feinberg, Dippel, Ball, Corcoran, Winston, Barth, and Kopp. Ball's pinched nerve forced her to use a wheelchair for the short walk from the hotel to the beach. The ceremony had a mix of Christian and Jewish rituals. The bride wore a silky off-white dress, no poufs. The groom was in a tan suit.

After a two-week honeymoon in Hawaii, the first nonworking vacation Levin had had in fifteen years, they returned to New York. Chase resumed her consulting in the marketing industry. Levin continued to oversee plans to expand to nine KIPP schools in New York, adding KIPP high schools and elementary schools as Feinberg had done in Houston. Levin also announced the establishment of a new state-certified teacher-training institute at Hunter College.

The idea was to raise the classroom skills of a new generation of teachers to the level Dave Levin and Mike Feinberg had attained by listening to Harriett Ball, Rafe Esquith, Charlie Randall, Jerry Myers,

Anne Patterson, Susan Winston, and Shawn Hurwitz and by working as hard as they could to help each of their students climb the mountain to and through college.

Feinberg and Levin began their teaching lives in some of the worst possible circumstances and found they were unprepared. But if they had never been faced with such embarrassing failure, they would never have mustered the energy to try to overcome their own inadequacies and their students' disadvantages.

Most American schools in the poorest cities and towns continue to fail in the same way Levin and Feinberg did at the beginning. Their decision to build more schools grew from their hope that their story of revival could be repeated. They were just two educators, and they were going to need many more who were willing to believe that good teaching can make a big difference and that all children will learn if they receive the time and encouragement and love they deserve.

HONOR ROLL

I have a tendency to persuade fine educators to let me write about them and their schools and then, without seeking their permission, apply the troublesome adjective *best* to what they have done. In my experience, applying the "best" label to anything inspires arguments, but I don't apologize for it. I decided when I became an education reporter twenty-seven years ago that I could help readers best — uh-oh, there's that word again — if I identified and wrote about the most successful educators. It has been my mission since then to find the schools and teachers who have done the most to overcome poverty, apathy, and racial and class bias and raise their students to new heights of achievement. The KIPP schools created by Dave Levin and Mike Feinberg are the most promising and the best I have found in the United States, judged on those terms. That is why I wrote this book. But it is important to note that it is I, not they, who have decided to describe their schools in this way.

I welcome any evidence of schools better than theirs. That is how I learn as a reporter. The more people we have looking for and talking about our best schools, the more likely we are to give all of our children the challenging educations they deserve.

So I thank this book's two young subjects, who have done so much to further my quest, and the hundreds of people who shared with me their memories and views of how Feinberg and Levin created KIPP. I am particularly grateful to Levin and Feinberg's principal mentors, Harriett Ball and Rafe Esquith, spectacular teachers in their own right, who were generous with their time in explaining to me how and what they taught their eager students Mike and Dave. Esquith and Ball also blessed KIPP with many attention-getting slogans. "Work hard. Be nice" came from Esquith and has been so widely adopted by KIPP teachers across the country that we made it this book's title.

All the names and people in this book are real. Every person mentioned whom I could locate has been given relevant portions of the manuscript to check for errors, but any mistakes remain my responsibility. Conversations and events that I did not hear or see have been reported as the participants remembered them, with emphasis on those elements found in more than one account.

I want to thank my editor, Amy Gash, for her great questions, deft pencil, and remarkable patience with my frequent revisions, and my agent, Heide Lange, for being so enthusiastic and so brilliant at finding publishers for books, like this one, that I would be miserable if I were not allowed to write. Joe Mathews, Don Graham, Nick Anderson, Jonathan Schorr, and Steve Mancini read the manuscript and made helpful suggestions. My editors at the *Washington Post* and washingtonpost.com, Nick Anderson, Monica Norton, R. B. Brenner, Phyllis Jordan, Paul Bernstein, Tracy Grant, Lexie Verdon, Liz Heron, Scott Vance, Mike Semel, Jo-Ann Armao, Bob McCartney, Steve Coll, Phil Bennett, and Len Downie were, as usual, understanding and supportive.

My wife, Linda; my children, Joe, Peter, and Katie; and my daughter-in-law, Anna, tolerated my often overabundant excitement about what I was discovering in my research, and asked good questions. My mother, Frances Mathews, the professional educator closest to me, was also willing to listen and offer sound advice.

I would also like to thank in advance the many KIPP teachers, principals, and students in dozens of cities who are likely to be hearing from me in the coming years as I research a second book about the surprising growth of KIPP. There are now sixty-six KIPP schools, most of them performing as well as the first ones. That is not supposed to happen. Smart and experienced analysts have often pointed out that initially successful schools or school ideas almost always lose potency when the next generation of leaders tries to produce the same results on many more campuses in new and different circumstances.

KIPP seems to be defying that expectation. In this book, I have presented the best evidence we have so far on why that is happening, but there is a good deal more to learn. I have to find out what is going on, not only at the many new KIPP schools but at the several other schools that use similar methods and whose results are approaching KIPP's. In the search for the best schools, I still have a lot of work to do.

INDEX

HILARY SCHWAB

Jay Mathews covers education for the *Washington Post* and has created *Newsweek*'s annual Best High Schools rankings. He has won the Benjamin Fine Award for Outstanding Education Reporting for both features and column writing and is the author of six previous books, including *Escalante: The Best Teacher in America*, about the teacher who was featured in the movie *Stand and Deliver.*